Beyond the Triple Bottom Line

Beyond the Triple Bottom Line

Eight Steps toward a Sustainable Business Model

Francisco Szekely and Zahir Dossa
foreword by Jeffrey Hollender

The MIT Press
Cambridge, Massachusetts
London, England

This book was set in Palatino Lt Std by Toppan Best-set Premedia Limited.

Library of Congress Cataloging-in-Publication Data

Names: Szekely, Francisco, author. | Dossa, Zahir, author.
Title: Beyond the triple bottom line : eight steps toward a sustainable business model / Francisco Szekely and Zahir Dossa ; foreword by Jeffrey Hollender.
Description: Cambridge, MA : MIT Press, [2017] | Includes bibliographical references and index.
Identifiers: LCCN 2016031915 | ISBN 9780262035996 (hardcover : alk. paper) ISBN 9780262552806 (paperback)
Subjects: LCSH: Business enterprises--Environmental aspects. | Sustainable development. | Social responsibility of business.
Classification: LCC HD30.255 .S973 2017 | DDC 658.4/083--dc23 LC record available at https://lccn.loc.gov/2016031915

To my lovely wife Sally and my dearest son Ariel Szekely, who have given me inspiration and unconditional support throughout the years and who have always been there for me with their everlasting love.

To the memory of my professors Barry Commoner and Dan Kohl, who taught me about the importance of protecting our life supporting systems and who unleashed my passion for the environment and for creating a better and more just society.

To Samira, Natasha, Rozy, Mike, and Miriam for their infinite love.

To Phil Thompson, Otto Scharmer, Karen Polenske, Alice Amsden, Katrin Kaeufer, and Dayna Cunningham for their incredible guidance.

To all those who have raised their voice to protect our planet, and are committed to creating a better and more sustainable society.

Contents

9   **Sustainability Innovation: What Makes Sustainability Innovations Unique?   165**

10   **Making It Happen   177**

Foreword

In business, there is fundamental confusion between the notion of "less bad" and what it means to be truly "good." In fact, I would argue that most businesses no longer know what "good" even means. A "good" future is essentially one where we settle on trying to minimize and mitigate the problems businesses had a primary role in creating in the first place: climate change, poverty, waste, inefficiency, injustice, and inequality. Though most businesses would describe themselves as sustainable, sustainability can be equally perplexing, even if we define it as meeting our present needs without compromising the needs of those who come after us.

Fundamental confusion aside, it is increasingly recognizable that something drastic needs to be done—the world we live in has reached a point where "business as usual" requires radical change. In response, you may find yourself leading this change by building a business case for sustainability: a transaction that outlines how an investment in a new way of doing something can create value for business, minimize your risk, and continue economic growth for your organization.

But let us imagine instead that you meet the call for change with a more transformational approach. This new paradigm for doing business will require that you create a vision and a mission for both your personal and organizational leadership—a vision driven by what is *wanted* rather than what should be *avoided* and a mission of what to *aspire to* rather than what you want to *prevent*. You will need to base your decisions on what will be best for tomorrow, not just for today, and what will bring greater prosperity to all, not only to a select few.

One certainly sounds easier than the other at face value, doesn't it? Yet something tells me that you inherently know which direction forward is the one that needs to be taken. Perhaps this is because you understand that when it comes to sustainability, it is futile to reduce the change that needs to occur in the current paradigm to a simple transaction—what is at stake is not something to be sold. Perhaps you already know that sustainability is not a definitive destination, but a journey we need to take to get to *any* kind of future. Or perhaps, as a leader, you inherently understand that to create the future we are truly capable of, you cannot limit yourself to anything less than the highest of aspirations.

What Francisco Szekely and Zahir Dossa understand is that for today's leaders in a world full of wicked problems, the existing business paradigm is not enough. In their words, "In order to go on the sustainability journey, business leaders and organizations must change the existing mental models that they have been following for many years." With the new framework they propose, including the beliefs that can guide sustainable leaders' thoughts and actions on their journeys, they essentially define the future of moral imperatives for business. Sustainable business ethics provide a framework for decision making that guides leaders toward choosing mutually advantageous ways to practice commerce, as well as embracing beneficence—the moral obligation to do good (not just less harm).

With an ethical business compass in hand, *Beyond the Triple Bottom Line* prepares today's organizations to embark on transformation, poignantly highlighting the organizations that are venturing into this new territory and providing a solemn reminder of what can be at stake if one ventures too far afield.

The book also tries to prepare you for the bumps you will encounter along the way, and I can assure you there will be bumps as well as potholes. The road between capitalism and sustainable commerce is a rough one. Can a sustainable business model survive in a market that attempts to maximize economic growth through increasing consumption and production of goods and services? Not if economic growth continues to be the highest value of society, and the expected way to "make it" in the business world remains concentrated on individualistic, materialistic, and competitive means.

Undoubtedly, there will come a point of compromise when an ethical decision will need to be made carefully. If not everyone can benefit, then who should, and how? Compromise is not necessarily a bad thing, provided your fundamental moral principles are not sacrificed in the process.

It does not take much to get off track. In fact, expect it to happen almost every day. You might end up somewhere only to realize that you failed to institutionalize your mission, vision, and values into your corporate structure or failed to build in the capacity for constant innovation within your organization, or to realize that at some point, you made the wrong compromise.

You will likely do harm. All businesses do. From my perspective, I have always questioned the extent to which both Seventh Generation and Sustain Natural are truly sustainable brands because of the compromises they must make as they pursue their journeys to becoming "all good." Both companies must balance the conflicting objectives of financial success, consumer preferences shaped by a society that gorges itself on disposable products, and an economy that reinforces the externalization of costs.

Finally, and most importantly, you will do good—sometimes it may only impact one customer and sometimes it will transform entire communities. Even just the possibility of this can be a limitless resource to you and those you work with; it will serve as a beacon and an aspiration for all that you do.

Whatever path you may choose, I hope you embrace the lessons from this book and join many others who see the opportunity business has to create a future where we are not just sustained but thriving when we lead the way on the journey to "good."

Jeffrey Hollender

Preface

Industrialization has brought benefits to many people in many countries. Yet we have created social and ecological deficits by the way we have been exploiting the planet's natural resources along with its inhabitants to such an extent and speed that we are destroying the health of our life-supporting systems. We need to find a different way to satisfy our accelerated demand for food, labor, and energy. This is the task of many societal stakeholders, and business has a central role to play in advancing the sustainability agenda. This book is written for those business leaders who will develop the sustainable organizations that will promote a healthier, sustainable society.

Writing a book as coauthors on the subject of sustainability has been a rather fascinating experience. Although it was clear from the start that we were both passionate about sustainability, the issue that brought us together to write this book was our dissatisfaction with the present way business has been responding to societies' sustainability demands. In examining why business was not fully engaging in sustainability, we asked ourselves if it was due mainly to a lack of commitment on the part of the organizations, or if there was something more fundamental that prevented business leaders from achieving better sustainability results. We concluded that more commitment is definitely necessary, but after deep soul-searching and inner thinking, endless productive debates, thorough literature reviews, extensive exploration with many experts, and numerous interviews with sustainability practitioners, we felt that there was something more basic missing. The economic model in which business operates today—the same model that has been in existence since the Industrial Revolution—was never meant to be sustainable, and the sustainability approaches that attempted to make that economic model sustainable have failed. Why? Mainly because the traditional business model is based on the assumption that profit maximization should occur even at the expense of silent or weak stakeholders. In fact, the central focus of the current business model is precisely that—profitability. But what about a model that revolves around value creation and addressing social needs? Thus, we recognized the need to develop a new business model that would respond to the sustainability call.

Most organizations and academics have been attempting to patch their existing business models to make them sustainable. In their pursuit of sustainability, they have been using an environmental approach developed more than twenty-five years ago that is based on the concept of the *triple bottom line*. This approach essentially concentrates on minimizing harm while maximizing profits for the organization. The model in fact accommodates business because it assumes that the organization will only follow the sustainability path as long as its short-term profits are not jeopardized. We felt that there was something fundamentally wrong with this approach. Our view was that the focus of the organization should not be on minimizing harm but rather on maximizing good. As Jeffrey Hollander—former founder and CEO of Seven Generations—put it so simply and clearly, "Less harm does not equal good."[1] This statement became revealing and inspiring for us. It prompted us to ask the question, So, what is good?

We put our minds, passion, and souls together to write a book that had not been written—a book that would address the business dilemmas that organizations and leaders face when attempting to walk the sustainability path. We broke away from the thinking that there has to be a business case for sustainability; instead, we moved toward a new way of thinking whereby the purpose—or raison d'être—of the organization that wants to go on the sustainability journey must, from the start, focus on how to address a societal need. We clearly understand that profitability is absolutely necessary, but rather than an end, we see it as a means to support the sustainable organization.

Another important topic we explored was how to measure sustainability performance. We found that sustainability is not a *zero-sum* game. In other words, a good deed that an organization undertakes or supports does not count as a credit that can be applied to an environmental harm or social conflict that it generates.

An aspect that distinguishes our book is the emphasis we have placed on leadership. We are convinced that sustainability is still a new paradigm for business—and society—and it is necessary to have leaders who think and act sustainably. Leaders are defined as those people who are not happy with the status quo and are brave enough to question the system. They inspire and mobilize others, and take risks when necessary. Hence, we identified leadership as the sine qua non for the new sustainability model we have developed. This realization triggered us to search for *sustainability heroes*—those people who have made a difference and been able to move the sustainability debate forward.

For Francisco, a natural hero was his former mentor, Professor Barry Commoner, who clearly indicated that the *impact* of a person on the environment is a function not only of *population* growth but also *affluence* and *technology*. Commoner was the first to indicate in the 1970s that the negative impacts of business on society were largely ignored. He realized that regulations were generally nonexistent and the only implications for the impact businesses had on sustainability were at the industry level. At the industry level, businesses were viewed as important actors that should take responsibility for internalizing all of their unwanted externalities.

Zahir, a member of the upcoming generation of leaders, identified Elon Musk as a sustainability hero mainly because Musk had the courage to address the challenges that nobody else had tackled with regard to developing the electric car. Most business leaders—notably Roger Smith, the former CEO of General Motors—had rejected the idea of the electric car because it was too slow, had a low range, and was too costly. Musk proved otherwise, and today he runs Tesla Motors, a company that sells in one year what General Motors—the former industry leader—sells in one day, but Tesla Motors is worth just over 60 percent of the US giant in terms of market cap.

Another driving force for our work is our values. We felt that the sustainability debate in business lacked transparency. Our research indicated that the vast majority of companies today rely on corporate social responsibility reports to identify various issues, develop key performance indicators to measure them, and then track performance. In fact, most of the companies that were affiliated with the Dhaka factory tragedy in Bangladesh that killed over a thousand people were guilty of this. This is a mistake, however, and evidently a deadly one. Corporate social responsibility reports only serve as a one-way communication vehicle. Instead, companies need to get closer to stakeholders and actually listen to what they have to say. Before attempting to measure performance, companies need to listen to stakeholders to understand what they should be measuring.

In our discussions, we challenged each other's thinking frequently and found that we were bringing two worlds to this project. On the one hand, the experience of an academic and practitioner who has been researching, teaching, and publishing for over thirty years, and who has had the opportunity to work as the deputy minister of the environment and natural resources in Mexico, the thirteenth-largest economy in the world. On the other hand, we had the thinking of a member of the younger generation with a PhD in sustainability, and one who demanded the creation of a better world. He had access to the best skills at one of the most prestigious academic institutions in the world—MIT—and founded the Argan Tree, a sixty-woman beauty cooperative in Morocco that returns 100 percent of its profits to its members. It was a mutual dissatisfaction that brought the past and future to the table. The endless debates that ensued resulted in this book, which aims to provide a pragmatic, realistic, and new way for leaders to promote what society has been seeking for a long time—sustainable enterprises.

Francisco Szekely, Lausanne, Switzerland
Zahir Dossa, Dallas, Texas

Executive Summary

Many books have been written in recent years that advocate the pressing need for organizations to become more sustainable. Few, however, explain specifically how organizations can become sustainable or examine the role of the leader in promoting sustainability.

This book provides a pragmatic new business model for sustainability that includes eight steps and forty-eight actions that will help business leaders who want to transform their organizations into sustainable enterprises. While the different dilemmas and frameworks proposed have been approached with academic rigor and reviewed by peers, we have adopted a case-based approach to highlight dilemmas and present the best practices in the field.

Although we recognize that many global organizations have made important steps toward sustainability, we find their contributions still fall short of addressing the sustainability challenges society faces now and in the near future. We argue that the way forward requires a higher level of leadership in organizations and new way of thinking about sustainability.

The sustainability journey starts by exploring the notion of a sustainability mission, which extends beyond the traditional corporate mission in that it forces an organization to define its purpose for being: How is it contributing to society? The book also stresses the need for a long-term vision and addresses a crucial business dilemma: How, in a world where they are pressured to provide short-term results, can business leaders focus on the long term?

We concentrate on how to develop a business strategy that aims to have a positive impact on all those social actors who—willingly or unwillingly—have a stake in the company. We discuss how an organization can engage its stakeholders to support and participate in the company's sustainability strategy, and the important issue of measuring sustainable performance to provide leaders and organizations with a yardstick for assessing their sustainability progress.

We also look at a new element in the debate about business sustainability: the relevance of values in the sustainable performance of the organization. In particular, we examine the significance of transparency and scaling. Finally, our new business model develops a template to promote sustainability innovation.

The strategic frameworks presented are not meant to be quick, easy fixes; instead, they will take many years of strong leadership, commitment, and resources to implement. In many cases, a sustainable version of one's organization will bear little resemblance to its present state. Corporate sustainability is a continuously evolving process that should never cease from steering the core of an organization.

Acknowledgments

We are grateful to a number of people and institutions that have contributed to our research and made this book possible. A special recognition goes out to Mr. Pierre Landolt, who provided the financial support for IMD's Sandoz Chair of Sustainable Leadership. This support allowed me to create the IMD Global Center for Sustainability Leadership (CSL), under which we conducted various research projects on sustainability leadership and developed a number of case studies that served as the basis for this book.

Thanks also to Dominique Turpin, president of IMD, for his trust and support of IMD's sustainability agenda. IMD's Anand Narasimhan, the Shell Professor of Global Leadership responsible for thought leadership as well as research and development, Marco Mancesti, research and development director, and Cédric Vaucher, research resources manager, assisted us with the research activities of the CSL. Virginie Boillat-Carrard, as coordinator of the CSL, was a constant support in making this project possible. I am also indebted to my colleagues Carlos Cordon, the LEGO Professor of Strategy and Supply Chain Management, for our discussions on supply chain, and Bala Chakravarthy, professor of strategy and international management, IMD Southeast Asia and Oceania, for his comments on business and sustainability. Also, special thanks to Jane Macdonald, acquisitions editor at the MIT Press, for her support in bringing this project to fruition.

The rich case studies we were able to incorporate into this book are due in large part to the help we received from individuals closely connected to the sources. We collaborated in great depth with Katrin Kauefer, who has studied the sustainable banking sector extensively, and the individuals within Triodos Bank's stakeholder network offered us with an insightful look at one of the leading sustainability pioneers in the present day—in particular, Dirco te Voortwis of Lindenhoff Farms. Jeffrey Hollender was extremely helpful in sharing how he developed a sustainability agenda firsthand at Seventh Generation. Similarly, members of the Mondragon Group provided keen insights into the Mondragon network.

Finally we want to express our deepest gratitude to Beverley Lennox, who worked with us with great enthusiasm in the development of this book and invested herself in this project to make it more attractive to the reader. She has been a great source of support and collegiality for us.

1   Introduction

What does it mean to be a sustainable business? How do you transform your organization into one? And what kind of leadership will it take to create sustainable organizations? Over time, the relationship between business and society has evolved. Business has had a significant impact on society in a variety of ways, including the way we travel, homes we inhabit, foods we eat, and conveniences we enjoy. Every product and service we enjoy is a testament to the positive differences businesses have made in our everyday lives. But has this improved quality of life come at a price?

Industrialization has brought many benefits to society. Business has played an important role in developing products and services that have improved the quality of life, health, and economic situations for many people and nations. Yet we have been interacting with our natural environment to produce goods and services in a way that is focused on achieving short-term gains at the expense of the long-term health of our planet. Some facts clearly indicate that the world faces significant sustainability challenges—serious challenges that require urgent attention—today and in the foreseeable future. Humanity presently uses the equivalent of 1.6 planets to provide the resources we use and to absorb the waste we produce. Furthermore, if each living person on the planet adopted the consumption standards of the average US citizen, we would need 5 planets.[1] This consumption is in stark contrast to today's 1 billion people who live in conditions of extreme poverty (less than US$2 per day), 783 million people who do not have access to clean water, almost 2.5 billion who do not have access to adequate sanitation, and 85 percent of the world's population that lives in the driest half of the planet.[2] In December 2015, government representatives of 195 nations signed an agreement aimed at limiting the increase of global warming to 1.5°C, since this would significantly reduce the risks and impacts of climate change. Scientists have warned that if no action is taken to successfully curb climate change, our planet will experience an increase in temperature of 4.5°C by the end of the century, creating damage that will be serious and often irreversible.[3] These trends are not sustainable. We have created an ecological deficit by the way we have being using natural resources and consequently are destroying the health of our life-supporting systems. We need to find a different way to satisfy our accelerated demand for food, water, and energy use as well as eliminate poverty. This is the task of many societal stakeholders, and business has a central role to play in advancing the sustainability agenda. This book is written for business leaders who will develop the sustainable organizations to promote a healthier, sustainable society.

Beyond the Triple Bottom Line is different from every other book on sustainability. Most discuss best-case scenarios, and explore how businesses are moving beyond compliance in order to reduce their harm to the environment and society.[4] Many of the organizations cited, in fact, have been able to reduce their negative impacts (or *externalities*) while increasing profitability. As a result, the books and articles informing managers on the *business case for sustainability* are superfluous. To argue that sustainability pays off, their authors and champions highlight cases such as General Electric's *ecoimagination* initiative, which has reduced greenhouse emissions at General Electric by 32 percent, or the 50 percent reduction of plastics in Aquafina's water bottles.[5]

But what happens when there is not a business case for sustainability? While certain cases demonstrate that sustainability is indeed profitable, many sustainability leaders acknowledge that these are the *low-hanging fruit*. So what happens when leaders need to reach a little higher for their sustainability initiatives? Many of the sustainability innovations, like those described above, are particular to only a certain segment of a company's portfolio. Some companies often attempt to offset the negative impacts from one division of their operations with improvements in another. Others set aside profits, frequently obtained from damaging activities to the environment, to provide donations to nonprofit organizations that aim to improve society or the environment. Is that enough? We argue that it is not. There are certain resources that are finite, and certain damaging impacts to society that last generations or are irreversible. If we kill the last West African black rhino, we kill the last West African black rhino.[6] In addition, supplying *real* value to certain stakeholders, such as higher wages to producers, costs money that cannot always be recuperated. The truth of the matter is that *real* sustainability does not always pay off, at least not according to traditional business models. Often a more profitable alternative is slightly less sustainable.

Are business leaders properly equipped with the right competencies to embrace the sustainability approach and new paradigm? While we commend the progress certain companies have made, there is still a long, tough road for companies to traverse. The purpose of this book is not to convince companies that such a road exists, or that they should be on it, but rather to offer a template that can help them shape how they think about sustainability. There are some elite thinkers, both academics and practitioners, who can serve as anchors for enlightenment.[7] There is also an abundance of rich literature on sustainable enterprises, which we stress all organizations should become. If the history of the relationship between business and society is any indicator, we know that organizations will need to do more than merely minimize harm or eliminate negative externalities. Jeffrey Hollender, while serving as the CEO of Seventh Generation, a responsible business he founded that sells green cleaning products, admitted that doing *less harm* is not the same as doing *good*. As stakeholders gain legitimacy and leaders who are more visionary take the helm of organizations, businesses will need to turn their attention to proactively maximizing their positive impacts on society and the environment, usually at the expense of short-term profitability. This constitutes a fundamental change in how to think about sustainability: from a mainly negative approach of minimizing unwanted externalities to a more positive approach focused on maximizing the value that products and services can render to society and natural ecosystems. Driving change to transform an organization is a challenging task that requires clear ideas along with the ability of leaders to inspire others while generating energy and passion within the organization. Changing the focus from minimizing harm to maximizing positive impacts will require addressing many complexities. We need to let go of old mental models where we assumed that resources and the capacity of our ecosystems to absorb waste are unlimited; instead, we need to develop new mental models where we change the way we interact with our natural environment, modify our patterns of consumption, and create a new way of doing business. We need to find a sustainable way to generate products and services according to the capacity of our ecosystems even as we take into consideration the uncertain socioeconomic environment in which we live.

In order to be successful, pioneering organizations need to adopt a new business model. That is, they need to move away from the *business case for sustainability* and toward a sustainable business model. Traditional frameworks and strategies fail to serve organizations in efficiently pursuing nonfinancial goals. This book aligns academic theory with practical frameworks to assist responsible businesses in moving toward the sustainable enterprise—an organization that pursues a viable, profitable business model to maximize social and environmental well-being. In a sustainable enterprise, profitability is used as a means to achieve a mission rather than being an end in itself. Getting to that point is not an easy process but instead a journey that evolves over time where business has to face many complex situations in the different economic and social contexts where it operates. Important economic challenges that business needs to address include the tension that exists between the pressure to produce short-term financial results and need to invest in sustainability initiatives that will provide profits in the long term. While some companies have already started down that road, there are significant challenges.

At the core of the book, we emphasize that sustainability is an ever-moving target and ideal.[8] There are two important claims made by this statement: sustainable best practices will continuously evolve, and sustainability is not a minimum threshold or set of requirements but rather an optimal outcome. From the outset, these two statements distinguish our book and its ideas from the vast majority of sustainability books and current practices. The first statement infers that practices considered sustainable ten years ago, such as strategies to decrease waste and reduce ecological footprints, are no longer sustainability best practices; they are the norm. Take the case of household detergents, which are a major source of phosphorus input into our aquatic environment. These detergents were responsible for almost half the phosphorus in water supplies. Phosphorus, together with nitrates, causes eutrophication—a leading form of water pollution that can deplete oxygen in water and potentially kill aquatic animals. The German company Henkel voluntarily launched Persil—the first phosphate-free detergent—in 1986. To address the evidently transboundary challenge of phosphate discharges in Europe, the European Commission banned the use of phosphates in detergent in all twenty-seven countries of the European Union in 2010. Today, phosphate-free detergents in Europe are not considered a sustainability best practice but instead the norm in the detergent industry.[9]

Current sustainable practices need to go beyond the status quo. It is this sentiment that sets us apart from other books on the topic. What most authors consider *best practices*, we regard as present-day common sense. The second statement adopts an abundance or positive approach for sustainability, arguing that companies that pass minimum thresholds are not sustainable. Instead, sustainable companies are those that continuously push the frontier between business and society, aiming to achieve the greatest idealized outcome. Therefore, frameworks such as the Global Reporting Initiative (GRI) fail due to their emphasis on compliance and surpassing minimum requirements as opposed to stressing the optimal way to have an impact on all of an organization's stakeholders. In particular, there is not enough attention given to weak or silent stakeholders, such as producers, the environment, or future generations.

The focus of this book is to provide tangible and practical strategies with frameworks—ways to look at particular situations—to help businesses and organizations tackle the challenges of becoming more sustainable. Beginning with the core mission and vision of an organization, and extending to building networks for sustainability innovation, this book explores the key problems organizations face when pursuing sustainability agendas. The purpose of this book is not to *convert* people and organizations so that they become more sustainable; there are plenty of books on the topic. Instead, it aims to guide business leaders through the dilemmas they face in making corporate sustainability a reality in their organizations, such as how to reconcile sustainability and profitability as well as how to maximize societal and environmental well-being through a profitable, viable business model designed for the long term.

Sustainability is not what an organization is but rather what an organization does over time to become sustainable. Thus, it can be seen as a journey where organizations face significant challenges that make them change and adapt in order to respond to emerging social and environmental needs in a somewhat-volatile economic environment. In order to understand the sustainability journey, it is necessary to review the historical journey of organizations. In the next section, we map the historical stages of sustainability, focusing on the relationship between business and society at each stage. Next, we explore the structure of this book—a strategic journey to help businesses grapple with transitioning from sustainability agendas that minimize *harm* to business models that maximize *good*.

Stages of Sustainability

While the terms *sustainability* and *sustainable development* did not formally arise until the twentieth century (particularly in the context of business), their ideals have been rooted in various religious traditions, dating back thousands of years. Many Eastern and Western religions promote respect toward nature, people, and society.[10] Traditional African and Polynesian religions in particular advocated for a balanced harmony between humans and nature in order for life to flourish and thrive.[11] When sustainability concepts were reignited millennia later to form the modern sustainability movement, the ideal of a thriving society was absent. In its place was a direr agenda: enabling society to survive. The following is a map of the stages of sustainability and evolution from unregulated businesses to the sustainable enterprise ideal. It is important to note that many of these movements occurred in parallel with anachronistic starting points.

Stage 1: Survival
In 1798, Thomas Robert Malthus wrote a book titled *An Essay on the Principle of Population*. It remains the most influential book on population to date. Through six editions of his work, Malthus stresses the limits to growth caused by resource scarcity. His line of reasoning goes like this: there is a limit, albeit an undefined one, to the amount of the earth's resources. He argues that if left unchecked, the populations in areas that have plenty will expand, thereby increasing the demand for a limited supply of goods. This will increase the price of goods, making it harder for the poor to survive. At the same time, the population increase will make labor cheaper, causing people to need to work much harder (or longer) to earn the same as before to afford the increased price of goods. The limits to growth would soon be reached. Hence, the primary framing for sustainability was survival: How do we ensure society will survive?

Malthus proposed two forms of checks to limit the size of the population: positive checks that increase the death rate (i.e., hunger, disease, war, etc.) and preventive checks that decrease the birthrate (i.e., birth control, celibacy, etc.). The limits to growth or population that Malthus's mathematical models attempted to estimate were later coined the *carrying capacity*, defined by Robert Riddell as "the population that can be sustained by an ecosystem."[12] Malthus's population theory has influenced the work of many scholars, leading to fears of a *population explosion* beginning in the 1950s. These worries became increasingly sensationalized with publications such as *Population Bomb* by Stanford University's Professor Paul Ehrlich that warned of mass starvation during the 1970s and 1980s due to overpopulation.[13]

While Malthus discussed the critical role that technology could play, he discounted its efficacy in curbing the resource scarcity problem due to the increase in consumption that would accompany it and limits to efficiency that it could provide. To defend his latter point, Malthus argued, "No man can say that he has seen the largest ear of wheat, or the largest oak that could ever grow; but he might easily, and with perfect certainty, name a point of magnitude, at which they would not arrive. In all these cases, then, a careful distinction should be made, between an unlimited progress, and a progress where the limit is merely undefined."[14]

Contesting Malthus, Robert Solow asserted that technology was the solution. He attempted to explain long-run economic growth by looking at capital accumulation, labor or population growth, and increases in productivity, commonly referred to as technological progress.[15] Moreover, Solow took issue with the idea that the productivity increase associated with technology was the most significant contributor to sustained economic growth. The model he developed was capable of describing how industrialized economies had been able to sustain growth and held that technology was the single most important factor. Solow received a Nobel Prize in Economics in 1987 for his contributions. Many other scholars agreed with Solow, pointing to the improved quality of life that technology had afforded. Technology has been able to decrease death rates (through medical innovations) and increase consumption (two factors that should technically result in the limit of growth according to Malthus), yet it can also sustain growth through vast improvements in energy sources, genetically modified crops, highly efficient machines, and so on.

But what about the *dark side* of technology? Technology also contributes to pollution, increases in consumption, crowding, and resource depletion. Jay Forrester used these variables to build on Malthus's theory of the relationship between food supply and population. Through a model grounded in system dynamics (the field he founded), Forrester published *World Dynamics* in 1971 to demonstrate how pollution, crowding, and resource depletion significantly hindered population growth as well as food supply.[16] In many ways, he set the context for sustainability agendas that would ensue in the decades that followed his seminal work. A year later, in 1972, Donella Meadows, Dennis Meadows, Jørgen Randers, and William Behrens III published *The Limits to Growth*, expanding on Forrester's model to make future predictions.[17] Nearly every scenario that was played out spelled uncertain doom unless drastic steps were taken immediately.

The works by Erlich, Forrester, Meadows, and others that raised caution about population growth spurred the *no-growth* or *slow-growth* movement, whereby philosophers and economists alike began stressing the improved quality of life that could be obtained by curbing population growth. This normative stance distinguished the no- or slow-growth theorists from the scholars in the *limits-to-growth* or *carrying-capacity* disciplines; the former studied how human life could thrive, rather than merely survive, given the factors hindering it (not merely its growth). This important theme underpins the modern *positive* sustainability movement we champion in this book.

Barry Commoner developed the general I = PAT equation to guide the sustainability debate during this stage.[18] I = PAT captures the impact (I) on the environment as a function of population (P), affluence (A), and technology (T). Furthermore, as population and the average consumption (represented by affluence) increases, the impact on the environment also increases (at an exponential rate). Technology (T) therefore has to increase productivity and efficiency at an exponential rate to counter the other two factors while curbing the total impact on the environment.

It is essential to point out that the negative impacts of businesses on society were largely ignored during this stage. Regulations were basically nonexistent, and the only implications of the impacts of businesses on sustainability were at the industry level. This was not to last, however. Technology, after all, is not an abstract wonder but rather usomething developed, innovated on, and employed by firms.

Stage 2: Environmentalism and Compliance
What precisely are the roles of technology and firms on environmental degradation? This question is at the cornerstone of the second stage of sustainability, which is still a prominent theme today. While firms can improve society through productivity and efficiency, on the one hand, they can also harm it, on the other hand, through the negative

externalities that result. A biologist named Rachel Carson was one of the influential figures responsible for bringing this debate to the mass public with her 1962 publication, *Silent Spring*.[19]

In 1939, Paul Hermann Müller, a Swiss chemist, made a remarkable discovery on the insecticidal properties of dichlorodiphenyltrichloroethane (DDT). He was awarded the Nobel Prize for his research less than a decade later as DDT became extensively used during World War II to curb malaria and typhus among troops. DDT's efficacy soon led to its adoption in the United States as an insecticide. Its initial success was quickly dampened by its unforeseen harmful side effects, including toxicity to animals and humans. DDT was capable of causing genetic mutations and disrupting the hormone system, and scientists demonstrated that it had terrible effects on wildlife and humans. In addition, it was found that DDT is a *persistent organic pollutant*—organic compounds that are resistant to environmental degradation through chemical, biological, and photolytic processes. This means that DDT can remain toxic in soil for up to thirty years, as it slowly gets absorbed into various ecosystems. It can also cause eggshell thinning among birds, and given this, some argue that it has been the primary contributor to the decline of various bird populations including the bald eagle. DDT is likely one of the most famous and controversial inexpensive pesticides ever manufactured. About four billion pounds have been applied worldwide from 1940 to 2012.[20] Its use posed a sustainability dilemma to society and decision makers. Is it socially acceptable to make use of a toxic product, which helps to save lives—by controlling malaria and typhus—while at the same time creating health and environmental impacts? Is this sustainability?

Despite the various press releases on the topic, Carson's *Silent Spring* was largely responsible for starting the environmental movement in the United States. Her *The Sea around Us* and *The Edge of Sea*, which were published in 1951 and 1955, respectively, had the poetic ability to bring life to the ecosystems we inhabit.[21] But *Silent Spring* took a different tone, as Carson provided scientific evidence of the harmful effects chemicals have on both wildlife and human populations. The findings that Carson compiled in conjunction with the direct implications for the readers of *Silent Spring* caused a national storm, which led to the successful campaign by various activist groups to ban DDT in the United States in 1972 except for emergency cases.

Silent Spring and the various publications and activist campaigns that followed were directly responsible for the National Environmental

Policy Act that was signed into law on the first day of 1970. Often coined as the modern-day environmental Magna Carta, the act led Richard Milhous Nixon to establish the US Environmental Protection Agency (EPA) in the same year. This monumental legislation put an end to largely unregulated industries in the United States, ensuring that businesses met certain levels of compliance so that they did not permanently damage ecosystems. Consequently, the EPA passed significant amendments to the Clean Air Act (initially established in the 1960s as a research initiative) in 1970, 1977, and 1990 to protect society from hazardous airborne contaminants. In 1973, the EPA also worked with the Nixon administration to help pass both the Clean Water Act and Endangered Species Act.

Silent Spring ushered in an era of regulating businesses to prevent their impacts on the environmental integrity of ecosystems in the United States. It also served as an anchor for a larger global movement to pass significant regulations on businesses and establish agencies to protect important ecosystems. As H. Patricia Hynes said, "*Silent Spring* altered the balance of power in the world. No one since would be able to sell pollution as the necessary underside of progress so easily or uncritically."[22]

While the environmental movement in the United States was primarily spurred through awareness, its parallel movement in Europe was triggered by tremendous crises. The first Clean Air Act was in fact passed in the United Kingdom in 1956 in response to the Great Smog of 1952. Airborne pollutants from the burning of coal became trapped in the air above London during a period of cold weather and nearly windless conditions. This resulted in a thick layer of smog that engulfed the city for five days. Medical reports released by the government and later studies demonstrated that the event caused anywhere from between four and twelve thousand people to die prematurely, while leading to over a hundred thousand people falling ill. Environmental laws and voluntary business emission reduction initiatives have not been sufficient to protect people from the effects of air pollution. A recent 2014 Organization for Economic Cooperation and Development study indicated that in 2014, air pollution killed more than three million people around the world and caused health problems ranging from asthma to heart disease for many more. This is costing Organization for Economic Cooperation and Development societies plus China and India US$3.5 trillion a year in terms of the value of lives lost and ill health, and the trend is rising.[23]

Later events, including the first major oil leak in 1967 from the Torrey Canyon supertanker, prompted the United Nations to create a more significant and overarching environmental program, resulting in the creation of the UN Environmental Programme (UNEP) agency in 1972. Further crises, such as the nuclear disaster at Chernobyl, caused the breadth of UNEP to increase. As a result, UNEP later established the Intergovernmental Panel on Climate Change, which shared the Nobel Peace Prize in 2007.

But are environmental regulations sufficient to control the harmful effects of business activities on the environment? Although banning pollutants was an important measure, what about the trees felled for industry or the tons of carbon dioxide (CO_2) expelled by its operations? Contesting the population theorists, who were primarily concerned with overpopulation being the greatest threat to society, others argued that the lack of accountability on the negative externalities of business were the primary dangers to society.

Wassily Leontief, a Russian American economist who developed input–output matrices during the 1930s and 1940s while at Harvard University, became one of the first economists to clearly align the relationship between the outputs of organizations and industries with their inputs.[24] Rather than being developed in black box machines, all goods required raw materials, labor, and energy to be manufactured. Leontief earned a Nobel Prize in Economics for his work, but Commoner applied it to the field of corporate responsibility. In particular, Commoner contended that capitalism and the technologies it embraced were responsible for the environmental degradation that was largely going unchecked, not overpopulation. In his book *The Closing Circle*, Commoner lays out "four laws of ecology":[25]

- Everything is connected to everything else.
- Everything must go somewhere.
- Nature knows best.
- There is no such thing as a free lunch.

These laws continue to set the tempo for the debates concerning the relationship between business and society. Most important, they expand on Carson's critique of chemicals and the chemical industry by implicating all businesses as contributing to the environmental crisis and ultimate demise of the planet unless significant measures are taken. Thus began the movement toward *ecoefficiency*, as popularized by Stephan Schmidheiny in *Changing Course*.[26] Moreover, by lowering the amount of resources consumed in relation to the outputs provided, businesses could lessen their negative impacts on the "natural capital" or finite stock of natural resources.

The ideal organization would adopt a *cradle-to-cradle* (C2C) or circular economy approach.[27] C2C champions a waste-free approach as organizational processes mimic biological ones. It uses renewable energy to develop products that over time, are consumed or transformed into future inputs. The by-products from each of the cycles are also captured under this approach, and they are used as inputs in future processes. The adaptation of C2C in an industrial approach is illustrated in figure 1.1.[28]

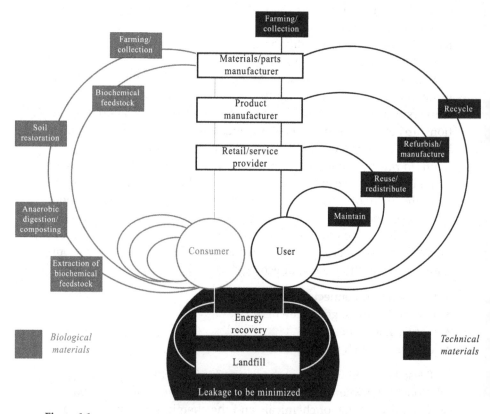

Figure 1.1
The circular economy
Source: "Circular Economy System Diagram," Ellen MacArthur Foundation, www.ellenmacarthurfoundation.org/circular-economy/circular-economy/interactive-system-diagram (accessed May 7, 2016). An interactive version can be found at the link.

The circular economy has become not only a necessary but also an urgent sustainability approach today. Plastics and plastic packaging, for example, have many applications in a variety of industries, including pharmaceuticals, health care, food, construction, automobiles, and aerospace. As a result, the plastics industry has been growing steadily and is financially successful—but at a cost. While plastics deliver many benefits to modern society, they have important drawbacks, too. A recent study of the plastic economy reported that "plastics production has surged over the past 50 years, from 15 million tonnes in 1964 to 311 million tonnes in 2014, and is expected to double again over the next 20 years."[29] Most plastics have a short life span, however, so they soon end up in landfills,or are dumped in the natural environment and key ecosystems like the oceans. The problem is not only the waste that is produced but also the loss of the economic value that the plastics industry creates. The plastic packaging industry—which represents 26 percent of all the plastics used today, and has an economic value of between $80 and $210 billion annually—loses 95 percent of its economic value because less than 15 percent of plastic is recycled today. In addition to this, UNEP estimates that 8 million tons of plastic enter the oceans every year and that there are 250 million tons of plastic waste in the oceans that have an impact on marine diversity, such as killing thousands of seabirds, sea turtles, seals, and other marine mammals each year after they ingest plastic or get entangled in it.[30] Endangered wildlife like Hawaiian monk seals and Pacific loggerhead sea turtles are among the nearly 300 species that eat and get caught in plastic litter.[31] It is apparent that the plastics industry needs to develop a new sustainable business model based on the circular economy.

The concept of *natural capital* encourages the use of an environmental lens when operationalizing accounting theory. Moreover, as suggested by Robert Gray in the input–output analysis, organizations should measure all the natural resources used as inputs for the products and services they provide along with all the outputs during the manufacturing phases.[32] As such, an organization can measure its environmental impact, and then develop practices to minimize or repay it. This process has various flaws, as Gray himself has admitted. It is also difficult to calculate all the inputs and outputs of an organization, and even more difficult to repay the resources used.

Stage 3: Corporate Social Responsibility

In the late 1980s, the United Nations tasked the World Commission on Environment and Development (WCED) with discussing the ideal path for development. After a nine-hundred-day international exercise that involved leading scientists, political figures, research institutes, nongovernmental organizations, and the general public, the initiative culminated with a report titled *Our Common Future*. In the report, the WCED (chaired by Gro Harlem Brundtland) married the concepts of economic development with a long-term horizon and coined the concept *sustainable development*, which it defined as "development that meets the needs of the present without compromising the ability of future generations to meet their own needs."[33] The WCED recommended that all social actors, businesses included, promote a growth strategy that is sustainable in the long term.

In addition to its impacts on the environment, what is the extent of a business's responsibility to society? Stakeholder theory, developed by R. Edward Freeman in 1984, is a pivotal contribution to management theory and practice. Through the theory, Freeman strategically frames the various actors that have a stake in the impacts of businesses by defining a stakeholder as "any group or individual who can affect or is affected by the achievement of the firm's objectives."[34] Freeman therefore argues that firms have a social responsibility to cater to the needs of stakeholders, which not only includes its shareholders but also extends to its employees, customers, the broader community, and various silent stakeholders such as future generations and the environment. Figure 1.2 illustrates the stakeholder view of the firm, which has been adapted from Freeman's original 1984 diagram. In this framework, stakeholders are not external to an organization but instead are actually considered an extension of it.

In addition to Gray's input–output framework, the stakeholder view of the firm was adopted by John Elkington to form the notion of a *triple bottom line* (TBL) whereby organizations should not only measure their economic but also their environmental and social bottom lines.[35] The GRI provides guidelines or key performance indicators to help organizations measure their bottom lines. Nevertheless, under the TBL approach and GRI framework, the social domain largely remains a mystery due to a lack of meaningful and relevant indicators on how organizations actually have an impact on societal well-being. It is also difficult to capture the complete impact of an organization's practices and products on the environment. While the TBL and GRI have been

A stakeholder view of the firm

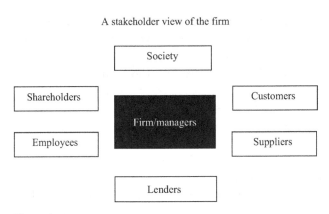

Figure 1.2
A stakeholder view of the firm
Source: Adapted from R Edward Freeman, *Strategic Management: A Stakeholder Approach* (Boston: Pitman, 1984).

adopted by nearly every large organization, chapters 4 and 6 describe their shortcomings, and present alternative strategies for measuring and communicating sustainability performance.

It is in this stage of sustainability that current best practices and books on the topic are entrenched. Businesses championing "corporate social responsibility" are largely concerned with minimizing harm toward stakeholder groups and doing so in a fiscally responsible way. Furthermore, proponents of responsible business highlight the business case for sustainability achieved through cost savings over the short and long terms. For example, a reduction in energy usage, materials, and waste can lower short-term costs while the availability of resources can help sustain the long-term viability of a business. Take the case of energy consumption in the cement industry. The production of cement is an energy-intensive process. Energy consumption typically accounts for 20 to 40 percent of the production costs. In 2008, the US cement industry spent about $1.7 billion to purchase energy; around $0.75 billion of this was for electricity and $0.9 billion was for fuels. The production of cement results in the emission of CO_2 from both the consumption of fuels and calcination of limestone. ENERGY STAR®, a voluntary program operated by the EPA, provides guidance, energy management tools, and strategies for successful corporate energy management. Through the ENERGY STAR industrial program, the 2011 overall energy efficiency improvement in ninety-six US cement plants that participated in the program represented a 13 percent change in total source energy, equivalent to an annual reduction of 5.4 billion kilograms of energy-related CO_2 emissions.[36] Companies can also avoid costly smear campaigns by being more proactive about their impacts on the environment. Nonetheless, the business case for sustainability can be reduced to a euphemism from Milton Friedman's famous *New York Times* article, "The Social Responsibility of Business [to Shareholders] Is to Increase Its Profits."[37] While there is a business case for social responsibility, we contend that it is a much more evasive topic.

Stage 4: The Sustainable Enterprise
The primary distinction between stages 3 and 4 of the sustainability movement is the primary objective of a sustainable organization as well as the role of the leader in changing the organization to become more sustainable. Rather than maximizing profitability while reducing harm (stage 3), the sustainable enterprise maximizes societal and environmental well-being through a profitable, viable business model designed for the long term. Moreover, while environmentalism and corporate social responsibility focus on minimizing the negative externalities of organizations on the environment, they do not spend much time on how organizations proactively improve and develop society. Alternatively stated through the stakeholder view of the firm, we define a sustainable enterprise as an organization that *positively* impacts *all* stakeholders. It is this transformational shift that organizations have a much more difficult time grappling with—namely because the business case for sustainability becomes less obvious. Instead, organizations concentrate on a business model for sustainability. As such, new frameworks and strategies need to be adopted. In order to achieve this stage of sustainability, leaders will have to make many changes as well as address many challenges to implement and lead a sustainable enterprise. They will have to change their ways of thinking, their attitudes toward stakeholders, many business processes, and shareholders' expectations. Rather than focusing mainly on short-term profits, robust sustainable organizations will adopt new sustainable and profitable business models where long-term profitability is obtained.

The visionaries in this field largely stem from the positive psychology and positive organizational ethics fields. Positive psychology was a response to the psychology field, which has mainly concerned itself with solving mental illnesses since the 1940s as opposed to understanding when and how human beings are capable of positive phenomenon. Similarly, the positive organizational ethics field assesses how organizations can achieve their highest potential versus focusing on solving problems and filling deficits. The deficit (or problem-solving) approach is characteristic of previous stages of sustainability, but it was abandoned in the fourth stage in lieu of an abundance or positive approach. John Ehrenfeld offers a positive definition for *sustainability*: "The possibility that human and other life will flourish on the planet forever."[38] Rewinding back to the limits-to-growth stage of sustainability, flourishing is the polar opposite of an emphasis on enabling humans to achieve long-term survival. The positive deviance continuum (figure 1.3) illustrates how sustainable practices are positively different from the ethical norms or socially responsible practices. This provides a framework consistent with the framing for sustainable practices discussed earlier as being a constantly evolving target and ideal. Given this, what was considered a sustainable best practice fifteen years ago (i.e., reducing material usage and lowering emissions) has become the ethical norm today. While these practices are socially responsible or ethical, there are better ways for businesses to impact society and the environment.

Sustainability is a key business issue that must lie at the heart of any business strategy. The reason for this is that sustainability allows organizations to define their mission and long-term vision to utilize as

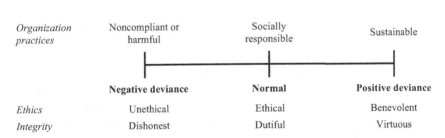

Figure 1.3
Positive deviance continuum
Source: Derived from Arran Caza, Brianna A. Barker, and Kim S. Cameron, "Ethics and Ethos: The Buffering and Amplifying Effects of Ethical Behavior and Virtuousness," *Journal of Business Ethics* 52, no. 2 (2004): 169–178; Gretchen M. Spreitzer and Scott Sonenshein, "Positive Deviance and Extraordinary Organizing," in *Positive Organizational Scholarship*, ed. Kim S. Cameron, Jane E. Dutton, and Robert E. Quinn (San Francisco: Berret-Kohler Publishers Inc., 2003), 207–224; Gretchen M. Spreitzer and Scott Sonenshein, "Toward the Construct Definition of Positive Deviance," *American Behavioral Scientist* 47, no. 6 (2004): 828–847.

well as conserve resources in a way that will allow them to remain in business for the long term, develop new business opportunities by innovating products and services that respond to social needs, eliminate unnecessary risks, and create new partnerships with stakeholders. Some scholars have attempted to include sustainability in existing business strategy models such as Michael Porter's "Five Forces," Alexander Osterwalder's "Business Model Canvas," and W. Chan Kim and Renée Mauborgne's "Blue Ocean Strategy," to mention a few.[39] These business models, however, do not capture the concept of the sustainable enterprise because their main stress is on achieving competitiveness and profit maximization while generally complying with environmental regulations and undertaking some social initiatives. In other words, the focus here is on maximizing profit generation, minimizing environmental impact, and undertaking selected social initiatives. What these traditional business models miss is the big picture of sustainability whereby the organization strives to maximize and conserve the environment plus improve the quality of life of people while remaining profitable. For example, take the case of Nespresso—an operating unit of the Swiss-based Nestlé Group, which sells machines to brew espresso and coffee from coffee capsules. The company announced an ambitious 2020 sustainability strategy in which it committed to 100 percent sustainably sourced coffee, 100 percent sustainably managed aluminum, and 100 percent carbon-efficient operations.[40] No doubt, these are good environmental targets. Yet Nespresso uses the traditional business strategy model to promote profitable growth and minimize harm. The espresso pods that Nespresso uses are made of aluminum, which is highly energy intensive and ends up in landfills. As of 2012, Nespresso had sold more than twenty-seven billion pods worldwide.[41] In addition, the pods consume energy, generate CO_2 in their production, and create significant amounts of waste. While the product has been remarkably profitable, coffee producers earn a tiny fraction of the total revenues. By using a traditional business strategy, Nespresso will continue to grow and expand its market, but its strategy does not capture the concept of a sustainable enterprise from a strategic perspective.

The majority of books on the topic of sustainability simply extend traditional business models to make sure that the organization is environmentally compliant and more socially responsible—making the business case for sustainability. Instead, organizations need to move toward the business model for sustainability. The primary shift required is a switch in the objective of an organization, from profitability and return on investment only to addressing societal needs while making profits, followed by a transformation across every other aspect of the traditional business model (in which all previous stages of sustainability are entrenched). Rather than developing a need and creating demand around it, sustainable enterprises center on the needs of society and the environment, and then proceed to develop business models around them. While it is an arduous, uphill journey for businesses to transform their business models, we are already seeing promising signs. It is an important and critical journey for all businesses to take in order to remain relevant and pioneering in the years to come. Like all things, there will be leaders and followers. This book is a guide for those organizations that want to be leaders.

The Sustainability Journey: Toward a New Business Model

How do you transform your current business model into a sustainable business model? To begin with, there needs to be a shift from maximizing profits to maximizing the positive societal as well as environmental impacts that your organization delivers. Although profitability should still be maintained in a sustainable enterprise, fixating on profitability often results in short-term gains at the expense of long-term impact. Rather than creating something that people would want to buy, a sustainable enterprise is driven by a specific shortcoming in society and/or the environment that it aims to address through an innovative business model. In this book, we provide a strategic framework for the sustainability journey, which starts at the core of an organization (which we refer to as the *sustainable DNA*) and continues in a cyclic manner.

Figure 1.4 highlights the current process behind developing business models, informed by the Business Model Canvas proposed by Osterwalder.[42] Despite the use of a canvas to diagram the relationships between nine essential business building blocks, the business model is based on a linear, nine-step process, as illustrated in figure 1.4. Through this process, an organization identifies the customers it wishes to serve, chooses the products and services to sell to meet their demands, determines how to deliver its products and services, selects the type of relationship it wants to have with its customers, establishes how it plans to make money from each customer segment, calculates the resources it needs in order to support the business, defines the core set

Figure 1.4
Current business model (based on the Business Model Canvas)
Source: Alexander Osterwalder and Yves Pigneur, *Business Model Generation: A Handbook for Visionaries, Game Changers, and Challengers* (Hoboken, NJ: Wiley, 2013).

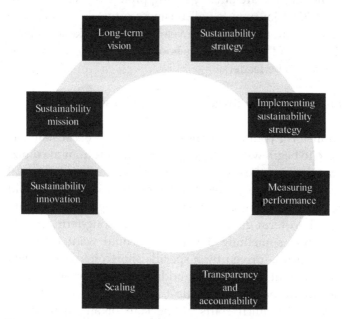

Figure 1.5
A new eight-step business model for sustainability

of activities to achieve the value proposition, creates partnerships with suppliers, buyers, and other strategic partners, and assesses the cost structure associated with the key activities. This model does not explicitly include guidance on how organizations can use resources in a sustainable manner nor how they can maximize their societal contribution.

The alternative model—specifically the business model for sustainability—that we propose is depicted in figure 1.5. The cyclic process that we espouse has eight core stages, and we argue that sustainability, as an ever-improving target and ideal, needs to be reassessed constantly.

Each stage or step in the business model for sustainability has a dedicated chapter in the book, as outlined in the following pages.

Chapter 2: Sustainability Mission

What is the purpose of your organization? The business model for sustainability begins with this critical question. The focus of a sustainable enterprise needs to be entrenched in improving society in a particular way. Profitability, then, becomes the means and not the end. Moreover, sustainability needs to be an integral part of the DNA of a company. But what exactly makes a sustainable mission, and how does a company actually put it into practice? In this chapter, we assess how Johnson & Johnson (J&J) recalled Tylenol in the 1980s in the pursuit of its mission. We also explore the recent automobile recall failures to impart the importance of not only developing a strong mission but also following it. Some businesses will need to adopt new missions or purposes in order to embark on the sustainability journey. For instance, if we look at Pepsi or Coca-Cola, each has an impressive portfolio of charitable activities, and are taking actions to minimize their footprints. If the core purpose of each company is detrimental to society because it contributes to various health issues, however, can either company ever have a sustainable business model? Making the sustainable leap can sometimes require a complete revision of a firm's mission. We acknowledge that this is a major undertaking for any existing organization. Still, just because it is difficult, does not make it impossible. We look at how Ray Anderson overhauled the mission of Interface in the 1990s along with the critical change in mission made by Hollender of Seventh Generation. We conclude with the following thought exercise: What matters most?

Chapter 3: Long-Term Vision

What is the time frame for sustainability? Sustainability gains are not achieved overnight. While low-hanging fruit exists, the major hurdles in becoming more sustainable require time and money. A 1994 study undertaken by the prestigious consulting firm McKinsey&Company concluded that sustainability generally requires economic resources that diminish the net profits of the firm.[43] This thinking has prevailed for many years. Many companies concentrate only on immediate, annual gains, and therefore resort to reactionary measures when dealing with sustainability. Although companies are beginning to be more proactive, their time frame (which is often influenced by share-holders and the price of their stock) is nearly always too short. We present the case of General Motors (GM) and the electric vehicle to demonstrate our argument. In order for companies to become truly sustainable, they need to stop focusing on quarterly earnings, and develop ten- and twenty-year plans instead. Here's a good rule of thumb: if you can achieve it within a year, it is not the most sustainable option. In contrast to GM, Tesla Motors is a prime example of a company pursuing a long-term plan to improve the sustainability of the automobile industry (its mission). San Patrignano and Amazon are others that we examine. If you had a twenty-five-year time frame, what could your organization do to maximize its positive impact on society and/or the environment?

Chapter 4: Sustainability Strategy

Do you consider/include all stakeholders in your business model? Do you know who all your stakeholders are? Does each stakeholder group have a voice and forum in which to speak? Are sustainability agendas based on stakeholder desires? And how do you create value for them? Not money, but value? Plus who captures the value that the firm creates? Alternatively, what is it that you do, how do you do it, and who profits from it. In this chapter, we explore the direct and indirect impacts of an organization on society. We define sustainable organizations as those that positively impact all stakeholder groups in the short and long term. This requires a new strategy that does not conform to traditional business models. All too often, the sustainability strategies of organizations are entrenched in activities focused on mitigating negative externalities. For instance, Walmart—the largest retailer in the world with 11,500 stores in 27 countries and 2.2 million employees—has as inspirational goal of achieving zero waste across its global operations. By working with suppliers, Walmart is developing product-packaging solutions that cut unnecessary waste and save customers money. It has introduced the four "Rs" packaging model: reduce, reuse, recycle, and rethink.[44] The initial results are promising. In Japan and the United Kingdom, Walmart has managed to divert 90 percent of its waste from landfills. In the United States, more than 81 percent of the materials that flow through Walmart stores, clubs, and distribution centers are being diverted, and in Canada and Mexico, it is more than 70 percent. Yet Walmart's emphasis on sustainable packaging is still on creating less harm (stage 2—environmentalism). A sustainable organization is one that not only minimizes harm but also attempts to maximize positive outcomes. Walmart and other retailers need to think differently to properly address sustainable packaging. They need to adopt a dynamic systems approach in order to involve all the actors related to packaging: producers of raw materials (the plastic and paper industries), manufacturers of packaging (companies such as Tetra Pak), brand owners (companies such as Unilever and Nestlé), retailers (such as Walmart, Kroger, and Tesco in the United Kingdom), the logistics industry (transporters of goods), and consumers. The joint collaboration of all the actors in the packaging supply chain will help to maximize the resource utilization by making use of the circular economy concept in which one will achieve zero waste not by reducing it but rather by not producing it in the first place. While the TBL and other frameworks suggest that firms can make up for negative performance through positive outcomes, this is simply not accurate. Sustainability, after all, is not a zero-sum game. We therefore look at best practices among companies for positively impacting various stakeholder groups including TOMS shoes, Warby Parker, Patagonia, and Triodos Bank. We also address the efficacy of certain initiatives, such as Fairtrade, and look at the strides companies are making to improve their impacts including McDonald's in Europe. We conclude with the following exercises: How do your current core products impact society? How do you begin implementing your sustainable mission and long-term vision?

Chapter 5: Implementing Sustainability Strategy

As stressed in this chapter, companies cannot drive sustainability agendas internally. Instead, leaders require stakeholder engagement to not only implement sustainable practices but also understand what precisely to implement. We start with caution stories of lead paint and DDT, emphasizing the dangers of not understanding who your stakeholders are. We then highlight the disasters that can occur when organizations fail to effectively engage with stakeholders such as the Rana Plaza collapse in Bangladesh, Nestlé palm oil case, and Shell crisis in Nigeria. On the other hand, we feature success cases such as Panera Bread in which organizations have collaborated with stakeholder groups to achieve optimal outcomes.

Chapter 6: Measuring Sustainability Performance

How do you determine the sustainability performance of your organization? Do the TBL and GRI's guidelines effectively measure the sustainability performance of your organization? We explore the challenges faced by Nike, Coca-Cola, Nestlé, Unilever, and countless others grappling with various frameworks to effectively measure sustainability performance. Despite being the common best practice, the TBL and GRI as well as other frameworks fail to measure the sustainability performance of an organization due to a firm-centric level of analysis, deficit-based conceptualization of sustainability, and reductionist approach to measuring performance. After examining the challenges of measuring the impact that the investing and sustainable banking sectors were up against, we propose sustainability performance should be determined by stakeholders, framed on a continuum, and assessed holistically. We conclude with a stakeholder-driven framework for determining sustainability performance.

Chapter 7: Transparency and Accountability

Can you pass the newspaper test? Would your company be ready to highlight every aspect of its performance on the front page of the *Financial Times* or *New York Times*? If not, what does it need to do in order to be comfortable being completely transparent?

Many sustainable organizations grapple with the difficulty of conveying their sustainability performance to their stakeholders while their less sustainable counterparts frequently benefit through greenwashing practices. While the previous chapter defends the stance that stakeholders should be the determinants of sustainability performance, this chapter emphasizes the responsibility organizations have to their stakeholders for communicating sustainability information. We explore the leading best practices by Patagonia, Triodos Bank, Honest by, and PUMA to improve reporting frameworks. Located in the Netherlands, Triodos Bank, which extends loans solely to sustainable initiatives, utilizes a Google Maps platform to publish details of every investment it makes. In this way, stakeholders can keep an active record of Triodos's activities and ensure it aligns with their expectations of the firm. Similarly, Honest by details the precise costs of every item in its clothing, along with information about the factories that helped produce it.

Chapter 8: Can Sustainability Scale?

Can sustainability scale? How do you scale in a sustainable manner? Social enterprises and sustainable movements frequently face a difficult time maintaining their mission and values as they attempt to scale their operations. Oftentimes, profit-seeking behavior dilutes the motivation to create a larger impact. In this chapter, we assess the setbacks faced by Ben & Jerry's and Seventh Generation after achieving rapid growth. Yvon Chouinard from Patagonia questions whether growth is necessary when it comes to sustainable enterprises. Organic Valley's CEO George Simeon cautioned against growth opportunities and instead opted to ensure its sustainability mission. We conduct a historical analysis of the Mondragon cooperative movement to understand how a champion in the social enterprise space has strategized during periods of growth and recession. One common element we identify is the types of actors who assist with growing an organization, and the characteristics of those who do not. Therefore, growing organizations must carefully select stakeholder partners when scaling and developing a plan for upholding their sustainability mission.

Chapter 9: Sustainability Innovation

How do you promote sustainability innovation? While a lot of work has been conducted to understand innovation, what has been done about innovations that specifically target a societal problem? Are there any unique characteristics of sustainability innovations—that is, how do they arise, and who are the various stakeholders that make them possible? We assess sustainable financial innovations such as microfinance and socially responsible investing, and demonstrate that sustainability innovations are triggered by crises (economic, social, or environmental) and facilitated through the creation of social networks driven by the opportunity to improve society. Hence, organizations must be on the lookout for crises outside the bounds of their organizations and build strategic partnerships to foster sustainability innovations. As the adage goes, never waste a crisis.

We look at the most transformative innovations from electric cars to making plastic out of thin air to highlight the leadership necessary to further illuminate the process. What is a current, impending, or evolving crisis to which your organization can help respond? Who are the strategic partners necessary to foster a solution?

Chapter 10: Making It Happen

Sustainability is a new paradigm for business. Companies and executives confront a significant challenge when attempting to develop sustainable organizations. Embracing the sustainable approach requires more than *cosmetic* organizational changes to the way business operates today. A different way of thinking and the adoption of new business models are needed. Sustainability requires business leaders and organizations that are ready to challenge the status quo to change the existing mental models (assumptions) with which they have been working for many years. In this chapter, we examine the changes that leaders and organizations need to make in order to embark on the highest level of the sustainability journey. We present the results of our research derived from sustainable leadership in action and identify the four key competencies that leaders need to develop to promote a sustainable business model in their organizations. To change these mental models, it is necessary to question the status quo of the present economic model in which business operates so that more effective ways can be found to achieve profitability in a sustainable manner.

How This Book Is Structured

This book provides the framework—or a coherent structure of ideas—on how to develop a new business model for sustainability. It is best used by reading the introductory chapter first so the reader gains an understanding of the different stages of the sustainability journey, and can then assess where the reader and their organization are located on the journey to sustainability. The reader should then focus on the eight steps of the new business model—which are described in chapters 2 through 9—to understand how the model works and how it can be used in the reader's organization. Each of these chapters includes the following:

• A business dilemma for sustainability that steers the chapter.
• At least one exercise—typically asking specific questions about how you and your company are approaching the issues discussed in the chapter.
• A strategic framework that is theoretically grounded and applicable to industry.
• Case studies that illustrate the dilemmas of the concepts presented

and demonstrate best practices, with the acknowledgment that the case studies are limited learning tools that represent specific situations in specific socioeconomic and cultural contexts.

• Key learnings derived from the concepts and case studies discussed in the chapter, and reiterating the actions leaders and organizations must undertake to become sustainable; these can be used to better understand the concepts in the chapter so that you can apply them in the context of your organization and your own professional journey to sustainable leadership.

Chapter 10 summarizes the findings of our research, describes the experiences of many practitioners, and focuses on how to implement the new business model for sustainable leadership. We present the exercises from each chapter as a guide for starting or transitioning to a sustainable organization. While the frameworks from the book are theoretically grounded and have been industry tested, the sustainability dilemmas that organizations face are challenging and complex. The strategic frameworks presented are not meant to be quick, easy fixes; instead, they will take many years of commitment and resources to implement. In many cases, a sustainable version of your organization will bear little resemblance to its present state. Corporate sustainability is a continuously evolving process that should never cease from steering the core of an organization.

2 Sustainability Mission: What Is the Purpose of Your Organization?

While the question is a simple one, referring to why the company exists, the answer can be quite complex. The common answer by many executives is often profitability. But should *profitability* be the core purpose of an organization? If so, how can one organization be distinguished from the rest? Milton Friedman, a Nobel Prize winner from the Chicago school of economics, developed the concept that the purpose of business is to maximize profit for the shareholders.[1] Friedman was responding to the economic context of his time when competition was starting to become global, and it was becoming more difficult for companies to increase their profits. In the 1970s, organizations were focusing on making money. This narrow concept had numerous implications for consumers, employees, and the environment because they were not a priority for many companies.

Years later, this limited notion was challenged. General Electric CEO Jack Welch changed his mind two decades later, stating, "On the face of it, shareholder value is the dumbest idea in the world. Shareholder value is a result, not a strategy. ... [Y]our main constituencies are your employees, your customers and your products. Managers and investors should not set share price increases as their overarching goal. ... Short-term profits should be allied with an increase in the long-term value of a company."[2]

Yet many organizations still seem to be guided solely by the bottom line. As David Packard once said to a Hewlett-Packard training group, "I want to discuss why a company exists in the first place. In other words, why are we here? I think many people assume, wrongly, that a company exists simply to make money. While this is an important result of a company's existence, we have to go deeper and find the real reasons for our being."[3]

Companies exist for a particular reason: to provide a particular set of goods and services for society. An organization's mission statement guides the actions of the organization by outlining its values and answering the following questions: What business is my company in? What do we do? For whom do we do it? And how do we do it? A corporate mission exists to serve as a compass. But how many executives and employees know the mission of their organization? And how many follow it? Finally, are all corporate missions adequate for organizations to begin the journey toward the sustainable enterprise? Although some organizations need to realign with their missions, others need to realign their missions with a more sustainability-oriented purpose.

Before continuing, it is essential to establish what we mean by a sustainability-oriented mission. As diagrammed in the first chapter, sustainable practices are best categorized on a positive deviance continuum (reproduced in figure 2.1). Based on business and organizational ethics theory, this framework distinguishes between three types of organizational practices: noncompliance, social responsibility, and sustainability. Sustainable practices are those that are positively different from the ethical norm. Norms are established standards of conduct that are expected and maintained by society and/or professional organizations. Ethics is the science of morals that deals with human

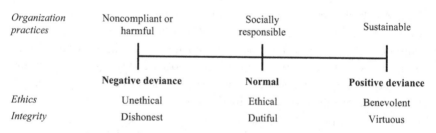

Figure 2.1
Positive deviance continuum
Source: Derived from Arran Caza, Brianna A. Barker, and Kim S. Cameron, "Ethics and Ethos: The Buffering and Amplifying Effects of Ethical Behavior and Virtuousness," *Journal of Business Ethics* 52, no. 2 (2004): 169–178; Gretchen M. Spreitzer and Scott Sonenshein, "Positive Deviance and Extraordinary Organizing," in *Positive Organizational Scholarship*, ed. Kim S. Cameron, Jane E. Dutton, and Robert E. Quinn (San Francisco: Berret-Kohler Publishers Inc.), 207–224; Gretchen M. Spreitzer and Scott Sonenshein, "Toward the Construct Definition of Positive Deviance," *American Behavioral Scientist* 47, no. 6 (2004): 828–847.

character and conduct. Ethical norms establish "right behavior," and represent the collective conception of what people find desirable, important, and morally proper (for instance, honesty, fairness, respect, transparency, and responsibility). In well-regulated industries (particularly in North America and Europe), the ethical norm is equivalent to the industry norm. As such, a sustainable organization is one with practices (i.e., core products and services) that are positively different from the industry's norm. Rather than mitigating harm or even promoting ethical behaviors, sustainable practices are those that proactively improve society through a system of *positive* ethics. A sustainability-oriented mission is therefore one that aims to differentiate a company's core products and services by how they improve society. Such a mission needs to be embedded in the DNA of a company to steer it toward improving society, not maximizing profitability. In this way, the mission and the positive ethical framework of a sustainable organization are synonymous.

What does a sustainable mission actually look like? To operationalize this, the following are examples of four mission statements for a household goods manufacturer that parallel the four stages of sustainability introduced in chapter 1:

• Stage 1 (survival): Foster innovation to create quality consumer goods at affordable prices with fair returns to our investors.
• Stage 2 (environmentalism): Create environmentally friendly household products while meeting the needs of our customers.
• Stage 3 (social responsibility): Promote healthy homes and happy communities through a restorative economic system.
• Stage 4 (sustainability): Improve the lives of people, health of their environments, and quality of our communities through transformative household solutions.

The first stage of sustainability, survival, is primarily concerned with staying in business. Thus, the key terms of innovation, quality, affordability, and returns are included, highlighting the two critical stakeholders being addressed: customers and investors. Despite the eloquence of mission statements in this sector, many can be reduced to this.

The next stage represents the inclusion of another stakeholder, albeit a silent one: the environment. An organization championing this mission is careful about its supply chain, ensuring that harmful chemicals are minimized and the negative environmental impacts from its organization are mitigated.

The third stage of sustainability begins moving an organization toward the stakeholder system perspective, viewing itself as part of the broader ecosystem it impacts and by which it is impacted. The long-term impacts are assessed in a restorative economic system (or circular economy, as described in chapter 1), whereby the earth is returned to the state it was in before it was first impacted by the company. This net-zero ideal is currently the goal of the most responsible organizations, which are generally shooting for 2020 or 2025 targets.

The fourth mission listed represents the final stage of sustainability, on which this book is focused. Rather than surviving or even maintaining the status quo, organizations in this realm of sustainability strive to improve society and the natural environment for present as well as future generations through transformative solutions. That is, organizations exist to solve a particular problem over the long term and do so in a systemic way that maximizes the positive impact on every stakeholder.

Seventh Generation, founded by Jeffrey Hollender in 1988, is an actual household goods company that largely began at what we have coined stage 2 sustainability. Its original aim mirrored the second mission statement above, focusing on all natural, environmentally friendly cleaning products (and laundry detergent specifically). To be precise, an early goal for Seventh Generation read, "Our mission is to provide high-quality, environmentally responsible products that are safer for your home, your neighborhood, and the Earth's environment. We are dedicated to providing products that work as well as or better than traditional brands, fit effortlessly into your everyday life, and put a smile on your face whenever you use them."[4] Through its engagement with Whole Foods during the 2000s, however, Seventh Generation made a profound shift in its mission—moving from a company that sold all-natural cleaning products to one that concentrated on creating healthy homes. Honing in on the sustainable DNA at its core and broadening its scope positively altered the purpose of the organization. It represented a shift in mission from stage 2 to 3. Although Seventh Generation took an important first action, there is still some question about how well it is fulfilling its mission. Its products no longer dictate the mission; instead, its mission dictates its products. As such, Seventh Generation sells anything from cleaning products to diapers, and aims to "inspire a consumer revolution that nurtures the health of the next seven generations."[5] This change represented an entire reorganization on the part of Seventh Generation as to how to conduct its business. Far from promoting innovation geared toward diminishing the environmental footprint of cleaning products, the organization launched an internal revolutionary thinking process to answer the questions, What is a healthy home, how can we contribute to building one, and whom should we partner with in this endeavor? By asking these questions, Seventh Generation was in fact addressing the central query of this chapter: What is a sustainable mission? While products sometimes change, a great mission is timeless and focuses on purpose, not products. For instance, Google's mission is to "organize the world's information and make it universally accessible and useful."[6]

Action 1: Establish your sustainability mission by explicitly indicating how the raison d'être of your company answers a sustainability need.

In 1994, Ray Anderson began questioning the business model on which his successful business was centered. Anderson founded Interface when he realized that there was a need for modular carpets in ever-changing office environments. Using a new process Anderson discovered called *fusion bonding*, Interface soon became one of the leading sellers of modular carpets, or carpet tiles that could be transported, placed, and moved easily when necessary. Beginning with a $1.5 million investment in 1973, Interface grew to become the world leader in carpet tiles by the late 1980s. In 1992, sales totaled $594 million. Yet customers started asking about Interface's impact on the environment. As a task force began investigating the company's supply chain in 1994, Anderson began reading *The Ecology of Commerce* by Paul Hawken to gain inspiration for a speech.[7]

Building on the theories of Barry Commoner and others in the circular economy, Hawken implored businesses to look toward ecological systems in order to abandon capitalist-driven processes that harm the environment and instead replace them with "human-centered enterprises that are sustainable producers."[8] Anderson was overwhelmed by the "restorative economy" that Hawken championed, and decided to transform the mission of Interface to "become the first name in commercial and institutional interiors worldwide through its commitment to people, process, producer, place, and profits."[9] He led Interface on a journey toward what his company called the "Mission Zero" commitment, or the "promise to eliminate any negative impact

Interface has on the environment by 2020."[10] Interface has identified seven fronts of sustainability, as itemized below, to fulfill its Mission Zero aims:[11]

- Eliminate all forms of waste.
- Eliminate all toxic substances from products and the supply chain.
- Obtain 100 percent of energy from renewable sources.
- Use recycled and bio-based materials to "close the loop" of the circular economy.
- Make the transportation of people and products more efficient.
- Improve the lives and livelihoods of all stakeholders.
- Create a new business model to redesign commerce.

Interface has made significant progress on many fronts, and it is a good example of a company that is on its way to stage 4—the sustainable enterprise—because the fourth stage of sustainability begins precisely after companies have minimized their negative impacts on stakeholders, and started developing strategies and business models to maximize their positive impacts on consumers, society at large, the government, and future generations.

Its website and annual reports highlight its efforts in each of the categories listed above, including easy-to-interpret charts, as illustrated below. Each sustainability front is tracked and discussed to inform others of ongoing progress. Waste to landfill has decreased from 12.5 million pounds in 1996 to 1.2 million pounds in 2013, as depicted in figure 2.2. While Interface was initially reliant on fossil fuels, figure 2.3 demonstrates how 35 percent of its energy used in 2013 came from renewable sources. Of all the raw materials used, 49 percent were from recycled and bio-based sources. Innovations in this area include glue-free tiles (coined "TacTiles") and bio-based nylon (coined "Fotosfera"). Alongside its success as a sustainability leader, Interface has performed well financially. In 2013, its sales reached $960 million.

The concept of the restorative economy evolved over time. In response to a world that started confronting scarcity of materials in the late 1980s, two British economists—David Pearce and Kerry Turner—developed the concept of the circular economy in which they expressed that a traditional open-ended economy was developed by treating the environment as a waste reservoir. "The circular economy is grounded in the study of feedback-rich (non-linear) systems, particularly living systems."[12] On December 17, 2012, the European Commission published a document titled "Manifesto for a

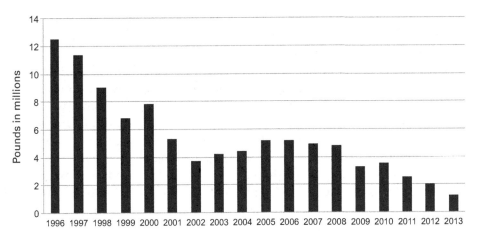

Figure 2.2
Decrease in waste to landfill at Interface
Source: "Waste," Interface, http://www.interfaceglobal.com/Sustainability/Environmental
-Footprint/Waste.aspx(accessed May 30, 2015).

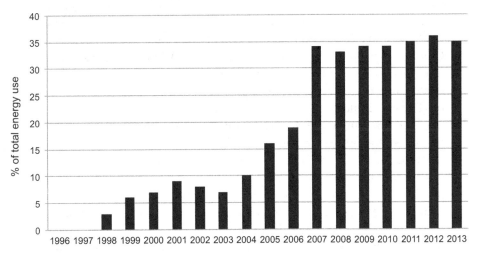

Figure 2.3
Increase in renewable energy use
Source: "Energy," Interface, http://www.interfaceglobal.com/Sustainability/Environmental
-Footprint/Energy.aspx(accessed May 30, 2015).

Resource-Efficient Europe." This manifesto clearly stated that "in a world with growing pressures on resources and the environment, the EU has no choice but to go for the transition to a resource-efficient and ultimately regenerative circular economy." The document stressed the importance of "a systemic change in the use and recovery of resources in the economy."[13] Subsequently, in 2015, the European Commission adopted an ambitious "Circular Economy Package," which includes revised legislative proposals on waste to stimulate Europe's transition toward a circular economy to boost global competitiveness, foster sustainable economic growth, and generate new jobs. The package also contains measures covering the entire business cycle—from production and consumption to waste management and the market for secondary raw materials.[14]

Action 2: Translate your sustainability mission into concrete indicators and measure them to determine success.

How important is an organization's mission? Perhaps the alternative question is more meaningful: How powerful can an organization's mission be? Only as important as the core values that uphold it. On September 29, 1982, May Kellerman, a twelve-year-old girl near Chicago, passed away. A short while later, Adam Janus also died. Then his brother and sister-in-law, who were both mourning Adam's death, also died. Mary McFarland, Paula Prince, and Mary Reiner died from similar causes, too—poisoning from potassium cyanide. The Federal Bureau of Investigation (FBI) quickly stepped in and identified the source of the deaths based on two similarities of all the victims: they were all near the greater Chicago area and all had unknowingly ingested acetaminophen capsules (branded Tylenol) laced with potassium cyanide. Once the cause of the deaths was confirmed, the FBI launched a full-scale inquiry. In addition to announcements over all major television and radio stations, police vehicles drove through Chicago's neighborhoods to broadcast the warning over their loudspeakers.

As a subsidiary of J&J, Tylenol accounted for 17 percent of the pharmaceutical company's income in 1982. Besides halting all production and advertising, J&J issued the largest and arguably first recall at the time, on October 6, 1982—approximately a week after the first death. It had already begun recalling ninety-three thousand bottles of pills a day after the first death, but recalling thirty-one million bottles across the whole of the United States was a move that no one anticipated or expected. The heads of the FBI and US Food and Drug Administration (FDA) considered J&J's response to be an overreaction. James Burke, the chair and CEO, disagreed. At the time, Tylenol controlled 35 percent of the market for over-the-counter pain medicine—more than the market share of the next three biggest brands combined. Industry analysts and marketing experts were convinced that the "Chicago Tylenol murders" were the end for Tylenol and J&J as a whole.

Burke, however, knew that a company or brand was much more significant than short-term profitability. After obtaining an MBA from Harvard Business School in 1949, Burke worked for Procter & Gamble before starting his career at J&J in 1953. Rising through the organization, Burke championed the over-the-counter sales of Tylenol in addition to selling to its existing market of hospitals and physicians. In 1976, Burke became CEO. While it is the historic decision of 1982 he is remembered for, many pundits focus on an event six years prior. In an intense argument around the same time he became CEO, Burke told other J&J executives to either recommit to the company's credo or "tear it off the wall."[15] Developed in 1943 by General Robert Wood Johnson II, the son of the founder and first chair, Robert Wood Johnson, the credo for J&J begins as follows: "We believe our first responsibility is to the doctors, nurses and patients, to mothers and fathers and all others who use our products and services. In meeting their needs everything we do must be of high quality." The credo goes on to prioritize, in order, J&J's employees, "the communities in which [they] live and work and … the world community as well," and finally, the stockholders, who "should realize a fair return."[16]

It is the adherence to this credo that inspired Burke to make the most significant corporate recall at the time, costing Tylenol $100 million at the onset alone. Furthermore, the company invested in circulating national broadcasts warning consumers not to ingest any acetaminophen products. To serve its existing customers, J&J allowed them to trade in their previously purchased capsules for tablets. It also distributed forty million coupons with a face value of $2.80 each to reimburse customers for the Tylenol they had discarded. Finally, J&J researched and developed a tamper-proof seal to protect its products in the future—a current industry standard enforced by the FDA.

Through its various efforts, J&J paid an enormous amount to protect the well-being of its customers—the primary stakeholder, as emphasized in its mission to this day. While it is difficult to summarize the total cost of all the company's actions, it is straightforward to state the outcomes. Of the eight million capsules that J&J tested, seventy-five contained cyanide. The stock price plummeted following the news of the deaths associated with cyanide-laced Tylenol, but it rebounded within two months. Finally, Tylenol, which still remains a household name, recovered 85 percent of its original market within a year and completely recovered it by the mid-1980s.

Burke continued to run J&J until his retirement in 1989. *Fortune Magazine* named him one of the top-ten greatest CEOs of all time. After leaving J&J, Burke launched the Partnership for a Drug-Free America, the largest public service campaign in history against illegal drug use by teens. President Bill Clinton commended Burke's work with the partnership by bestowing on him the United States' highest civilian honor, the Presidential Medal of Freedom.

As we learn from the specific successful sustainability initiatives of selected companies, it is important to understand that companies face many sustainability challenges, and they do not make progress on every front at the same time. J&J, say, might not be an example of sustainability performance in other areas of the company, thus highlighting the complexity of the sustainability journey.

Not all organizations have a Burke, though. Toyota, a Japanese company, has the following mission: "We deliver outstanding automotive products and services to our customers, and enrich our community, partners and environment." It first communicated its core principles of continuous improvement and respect for people in 2001, summarizing them as the "Toyota Way." As shared on its website, Toyota's vision is to be the "most respected and admired company" based on four core values: customer first, respect for people, international focus, and continuous improvement and innovation. In addition, Toyota has a code of ethics and a set of seven guiding principles.[17] As we learned from Burke at J&J, it is one thing to have a strong credo, but something entirely different to follow it.

Although Toyota had received various reports of sudden, unintended acceleration potentially as early as 2002, the first major incident occurred on August 28, 2009, when a family of four was killed in a deadly car accident after its 2009 Lexus began accelerating uncontrollably to speeds over a hundred miles per hour (mph) before hitting another car at the intersection of a dead-end road, flipping over a fence, tumbling downward, and catching fire. Mark Saylor, a California Highway Patrol officer who had served twenty years in the air force, was the operator of the vehicle. He was driving his daughter to her soccer practice along with his wife and brother-in-law. When the Toyota-manufactured vehicle began accelerating uncontrollably, the brother-in-law called 911, and informed the operator that the accelerator of their car was struck and they were approaching an intersection. The recorded 911 call led to an investigation into the source of the crash. It turns out the same vehicle, which was a rental, had previously been rented by Frank Bernard, who reported having the same unintended acceleration problem. Bernard was able to control the vehicle by shifting it into the neutral position before returning it to the Toyota/Lexus dealership and reporting the problem. Unfortunately, the matter was not resolved.

After a two-week investigation, it was revealed that incorrect floor mats were the source of the unintended acceleration, causing interference with the gas pedal. Toyota announced its first recall two weeks later, on September 29, 2009, of 4.2 million vehicles. Owners were instructed to remove the floor mats until dealers could zip-tie them appropriately in order to prevent them from interfering with the gas pedal. Many cases of unintended, sudden acceleration did not involve floor mats, however. Toyota denied these claims, and attributed the cases to driver error or the previously identified problem with the floor mats. On December 26, 2009, a Toyota Avalon was seen going through a stop-sign-controlled intersection at over forty-five mph before crashing through a fence and flipping upside down into a pond. All four people in the car were found dead. The floor mats had been removed and were discovered in the trunk of the vehicle. As further investigations determined, there were problems inherent in the accelerator pedal itself, not merely the floor mat issue. On January 21, 2010, Toyota issued an additional recall for 2.3 million vehicles in the United States along with almost 2 million in Europe and Asia. It then suspended sales five days later.

In comparison to J&J, it took Toyota months to make the decision to issue the appropriate recall. And perhaps it took years. The National Highway Traffic Safety Administration reported that it received over sixty-two hundred complaints between 2000 and May 2010 of unintended, sudden acceleration in Toyota vehicles. These cases are linked to eighty-nine deaths. Many others could have fallen outside the time frame. In one instance, a thirty-two-year-old man was wrongfully imprisoned for four years after killing three people when his 1996 Toyota Camry accelerated uncontrollably off an exit ramp of a highway into an intersection. The jury dismissed his plea of innocence although he tried to explain he could not brake or control his car. As a result of "blatant misrepresentations" and a "cover-up" according to one senior justice official, Toyota was fined $1.2 billion for hiding the deadly, uncontrolled acceleration problem—the most significant fine levied against an auto manufacturer. This does not include Toyota's costs for recalling cars and loss of sales, estimated at over $8 million for each day that sales were halted. Attorney General Eric Holder reported that "Toyota confronted this public safety emergency as if it was a public relations problem."[18] The eighty-nine deaths were nearly equivalent to the ones J&J would have been responsible for had it not acted in a timely manner.

Of the Toyota memos released, some included the "favorable recall outcomes" and savings of "$100 million" through the recall strategy of mats. These short-term savings now pale in comparison to the billions it cost the company to fix the inevitable.

Action 3: Use your core values to uphold your mission even if there are short-term costs involved in addressing crisis situations.

It is clear that Toyota lost its way. In 2004, before the crisis, Jeffrey Liker published a book titled *The Toyota Way* that highlighted the four overarching categories that led Toyota to eventually surpass GM in the US market: adopt a long-term philosophy; employ the right process to produce the right results; develop people, as key to bringing value to the organization; and become a learning organization by solving the root problems in every process. Toyota has consequently begun to return to these principles and realign its operations with its mission.[19]

In this chapter, we identify three important actions when developing a sustainability mission: connect your mission to a sustainability need, operationalize your mission by developing concrete initiatives, and uphold your mission and sustainability initiatives through a set of core values. A notable example of an organization that has followed this approach is Nestlé.

Nestlé, the largest food and beverage company in the world, has been under significant fire from a variety of stakeholder organizations. These allegations date back to 1977, when Nestlé was boycotted globally for aggressively advertising baby formula as being more advantageous than breast milk. Greenpeace launched another significant campaign against Nestlé's rapid deforestation practices via its palm oil plantations. These practices were not only harmful to the environment due to the massive amounts of CO_2 released but also to various habitats and ecosystems, threatening species such as orangutans. Other issues included traces of horse meat found in food, greenwashing to promote the purchasing of bottled water, and the secondhand employment of child labor.

Launching a new era of sustainability to address these various deleterious practices and become more proactive in improving other impacts it has on its stakeholder system, Nestlé has embraced the following statement: "Nestlé is ... committed to enhancing the quality of consumers' lives through nutrition, health, and wellness. Our mission of 'Good Food, Good Life' is to provide the best tasting, most nutritious choices in a wide range of food and beverage categories and eating occasions, from morning to night."[20]

This is a shift from Nestlé's previous mission: "Nestlé is dedicated to providing the best foods to people throughout their day, throughout their lives, throughout the world. With our unique experience of anticipating consumers' needs and creating solutions, Nestlé contributes to your well-being and enhances your quality of life."[21]

In addition, in 2010, Nestlé updated its "Corporate Business Principles," which it also calls "Creating Shared Value," as follows: nutrition, health, and wellness; quality assurance and product safety; consumer empowerment; human rights in business activities; leadership and personal responsibility; safety and health at work; honest and fair supplier standards; socioeconomic development of farmers and rural communities; environmental sustainability; and responsible water management.[22]

Nestlé has addressed the various stakeholder critiques with its sustainability mission and principles, thereby defining its initiatives moving forward. The core, guiding values it has established around this mission are: nutrition, health, wellness, and you (customers). Nestlé needs to continue making progress on its sustainability journey to fulfill its mission. But it starts with taking ownership for impact and taking the leap to become a more sustainable organization.

Now reflect on your organization's mission. Can you recall it offhand? Does it focus on products or on the purpose of your company? Is it incorporated into making tough decisions? How do you measure success around your mission to ensure that your organization's practices are always in line with its purpose? Most important, however, are you willing to take the leap?

Here is a concluding thought exercise: What matters most? In other words, what is the most significant aspect of your organization? What does it really want to spend all its efforts working on and pursuing? What makes it different from every other organization? These questions, with the actions crafted in this section, will help you and other leaders at your organization determine its purpose or sustainable mission.

In box 2.1, we introduce the key lessons from this chapter and enumerate the actions leaders can take when establishing their organizations' sustainable missions:

Box 2.1
Sustainability Mission: Key Lessons and Actions

• The key lesson from Seventh Generation is that an organization can better address sustainability by focusing on the social need that its products and services are attempting to fulfill rather than only on product/service, price, and differentiation.

Action 1: Establish your sustainability mission by explicitly indicating how the raison d'être of your company answers a sustainability need.

• The key learning from Interface's experience is that sustainability is about thinking big when it comes to sustainability goals, taking into account every actor and aspect of the business ecosystem, and then proceeding to measure progress in a tangible and accountable way. The selection of sustainability goals and process for achieving them are crucial for sustainability. CEO Anderson did not decide to simply reduce the waste Interface was generating by a certain percentage; he instead decided to solve 100 percent of the problem. This goal represented the guiding light in all the actions while creating inspiration, engagement, and pride for the staff at Interface. The organization has been working steadily and incrementally to achieve the goal.

Action 2: Translate your sustainability mission into concrete indicators and measure them to determine success.

• The J&J and Toyota cases clearly demonstrate that living the mission and values of the company pays in the long term even if the organization has to incur financial costs in the short term. The contrary is also true: ignoring the mission of the company for the sake of short-term gains jeopardizes both the short- and long-term financial performance as well as reputation of the firm.

Action 3: Use your core values to uphold your mission even if there are short-term costs involved in addressing crisis situations.

As the next chapter explores, a sustainable mission is the first part of an arduous journey on the path toward a sustainable enterprise. Some organizations have already begun the process while others are just starting. Before continuing to the next chapter, on long-term vision, try working through the following two cases, which we will examine further in the next chapter.

Case 1: GM

In the 1980s, Australia invited GM to participate in the world's first solar-powered race. Striving to pave GM's path into the future, Roger Smith, the chair and CEO at the time, invested $2 million into subcontracting AeroVironment to build a solar vehicle. AeroVironment, founded by Paul MacCready in 1971, already had an impressive portfolio of vehicles, including the Gossamer Condor, the first (successful) human-powered airplane, and Solar Challenger, a solar-powered electric aircraft that flew from France to England. While MacCready was more than capable of developing an aerodynamic, solar-powered vehicle, he contracted Alan Cocconi to develop an AC motor and electric power train to drive it. Cocconi also used regenerative braking to help recharge the vehicle's battery. The team was successful. In 1987, the Sunraycer took the lead in the World Solar Challenge; traveling 1,867 miles at an average speed of 41.6 mph, it was never surpassed. The second-place vehicle completed the race two days later.

A year later, the Sunraycer (see figure 2.4) shattered the solar-powered record, with a top speed of 48.7 mph. To provide perspective on this feat, this record was held for over twenty years until it was finally surpassed in 2011 by the Sunswift IV, which reached a top speed of 55.2 mph.

In January 1990, GM introduced the Impact (see figure 2.5), a concept electric car, at the Los Angeles Auto Show. The car had been developed by AeroVironment, based on the AC motor and electric power train that Cocconi had developed for the Sunraycer. The Impact was met with immediate praise, and later that year, Smith announced that it would become a production vehicle. Based on the proof-of-concept electric vehicle, the California Air Resources Board passed a mandate in 1990 that required all major automobile suppliers to the United States to develop zero-emissions vehicles.[23] In response, GM began investing in research and development for the EV1—a fully electric automobile.

Figure 2.4
GM Sunraycer car at the GM Heritage Center, November 2009
Source: "GM Sunraycer," photographed by Dshakes, http://commons.wikimedia.org/
wiki/File:GM_Sunraycer.JPG(accessed June 11, 2015).

GM became the world's first mass-produced electric vehicle retailer
when it released the EV1 (see figure 2.6) in 1996. The 127-horsepower
AC motor installed in the first-generation car enabled it to go from zero
to sixty mph in approximately eight seconds with a top speed (which
was electronically limited) of eighty mph. The lead-acid batteries gave
the car the ability to travel between seventy and a hundred miles on a
single charge. To offset the weight and maximize the distance capable
of being traveled on a single charge, the form factor was optimized and
had a drag coefficient of 0.19—the lowest among any mass-produced
vehicle. While it took approximately ten hours to recharge the battery
using standard 110-volt outlets, GM 220-volt systems could charge
the car in five hours. And even though the original EV1 had lead-acid
batteries, some Gen II versions, released in 1999, came with nickel
metal-hydride ones.

The EV1 could only be leased, despite requests by many customers
to purchase the car. Due to the EV1's limited availability, the waiting
list of customers who wanted one was long. Demand for the car was

Figure 2.5
GM Impact concept electric vehicle
Source: Stephen Eldestein, "How Does GM's Fabled EV1 Stack Up against the Current Crop of Electrics?" *Digital Trends*, February 2013, http://www.digitaltrends.com/cars/how-does-gms-fabled-ev1-stack-up-against-the-current-crop-of-electrics/(accessed May 2, 2016).

further amplified by the list of high-profile individuals, such as Tom Hanks, Sylvester Stallone, and Mel Gibson, who were proud lessees of the EV1. Despite the strong following along with rave reviews from customers and car reviewers, GM did not consider the EV1 a viable solution because it was expensive to produce. The company cited that the leasing rates ranging from $399 to $549 significantly understated the actual costs of producing the EV1. Place yourself in the shoes of Rick Wagoner, the CEO of GM. What should GM do?

Case 2: Philip Morris International

Can all companies take the journey toward becoming a sustainable enterprise? Philip Morris International (PMI) is the second-largest tobacco company in the world, with reported revenues in 2013 of $80

Figure 2.6
The GM EV1
Source: Kurt Ernst, "Cars of Futures Past—GM EV1," *Hemmings Daily*, June 2013, http://
blog.hemmings.com/index.php/2013/06/27/cars-of-futures-past-gm-ev1/(accessed
May 2, 2016).

billion and $7.7 billion in net earnings.[24] Yet PMI represents an interest-
ing case to study in terms of sustainability. While PMI champions its
sustainability strategy, which in 2013 contributed $39 million to charity,
reduced its CO_2 emissions by 30 percent, recycled over 80 percent of
its waste, and engaged in fair agricultural practices toward tobacco
producers, its core products are cigarettes and other tobacco products,
which of course are highly detrimental to the health of consumers as
well as those nonconsumers who frequently share the same geographic
space as tobacco consumers. Defenders will argue that the company is
simply meeting a market need, and is doing so in a more sustainable
way than its competition. Through marketing its products, however,
PMI can also be accused of encouraging harmful habits such as
smoking.

As published on its site, PMI's goals are "to provide high quality
and innovative products to adult smokers, generate superior returns
for shareholders, and reduce the harm caused by smoking while operating our business sustainably and with integrity."[25] With a global

workforce of ninety-one thousand people, a collection of eighty thousand tobacco producers, and a customer base many multiples larger, PMI has a tremendous impact on the environment and society. The company also states that it wants to reduce the harm caused by smoking. Consequently, PMI is investing in four different reduced-risk platforms, as described below:[26]

- Platform 1: An electronic holder that heats tobacco rather than burning it, thereby creating a nicotine-containing aerosol with significantly fewer harmful constituents compared to cigarette smoke.
- Platform 2: A pressed-carbon heat source that once ignited, heats the tobacco without burning it in order to generate a nicotine-containing aerosol.
- Platform 3: A chemical process to create a nicotine-containing aerosol.
- Platform 4: An e-cigarette—a battery-powered device that produces an aerosol by vaporizing a nicotine solution.

In addition, PMI is moving toward aggressive 2020 goals to reduce the negative externalities its operations have on the environment. Are its current actions and investments enough to become a sustainable enterprise? If you were André Calantzopoulos, the current CEO, what would you do? What would be your long-term vision for PMI to make it a sustainable enterprise? Would you keep the same mission? Is it possible for PMI to become a sustainable enterprise, or are all businesses in the tobacco industry doomed with regard to pursuing stage 4 sustainability?

3 Long-Term Vision: What Will Your Organization Look Like in Twenty-Five Years?

This question quickly stumps many executives. It is perhaps the most important question that organizations need to grapple with, though, particularly those that pursue the sustainability journey. It is true that all companies will be *somewhere* in twenty-five years, but where they will be matters a whole lot on the sustainability journey.

First, ask yourself, What is the capacity of my organization? Now imagine that every machine your company owns suddenly stops. Imagine that every product your company makes disappears. Imagine your supply chain instantly dissolves. Imagine everything that occupies your buildings vanishes, except for your coworkers. They are all standing idly by, anxious. *This* is the capacity of your organization. It is independent from all the machines, goods, services, materials, and even bottlenecks that often distract us during our daily business processes.

Returning to the sustainable, purpose-driven mission statement that you developed in chapter 2, if your organization had twenty-five years to work toward fulfilling that mission, what should it do? In this chapter, we explore how to pursue a sustainability-oriented mission with a long-term perspective. We look at two organizations that have taken a long-term perspective in their business models, Amazon and Tesla Motors, before returning to the two case questions we concluded with in the previous chapter. Then we'll look at two cases: Triodos Bank and McDonald's in France.

It is hard for many people to remember that the largest online retailer in the world, Amazon, began as an online bookstore in 1994. Not for Jeff Bezos, however. Working at D. E. Shaw, he realized that the data transmitted over the Internet had increased by a factor of approximately twenty-three hundred. Nothing to date had grown so fast, and Bezos did not want to miss out. Before many people knew what the

Internet was (Bezos had to in fact explain it to his father), he had a vision—*the everything store*—a store that would get things from manufacturers to customers. While some were seeing the decline of the middleperson, Bezos realized that there would always be a middleperson; the question was who and how. The Internet was his solution.

An online bookstore was never Bezos's ultimate goal. He just needed to start somewhere, with his long-term vision of being the everything store always intact. After developing a list of twenty product categories, Bezos honed in on books as the initial product. With over three million published books, no physical bookstore could possibly have title. In addition, books were a commodity, and so were worth the same amount no matter where you purchased them. For the first time, the Internet could be used with little overhead to show an unlimited offering to customers. Books were therefore a case in point for the much broader value proposition Bezos wanted to offer. With the vision of becoming the biggest conduit in the world for anything, Bezos selected Amazon as the name for his company. The arrow from the *a* to *z* in Amazon was introduced in 2000 to communicate its large selection.

The unique aspect of Amazon is that by 2014, it resembled Bezos's original vision from twenty years earlier. In a 2013 interview on the *Harvard Business Review*'s blog, Bezos remarked, "If we had always needed to see significant financial results in two or three years, then some of the most meaningful things we've done would never have been started—like Kindle, Amazon Web Services, Amazon Prime." As such, Bezos is never worried about the day-to-day fluctuations in the stock price. He quotes economist Benjamin Graham as saying, "In the short term, the stock market is a voting machine. In the long term, it's a weighing machine."[1] Bezos thus titled his first shareholder letter, in 1997, "It's All about the Long Term." While this is a constant point of contention with shareholders, who generally take a short view of investments, it is the source of Amazon's success.

In another interview, Bezos explains that if you work on a three-year horizon, you are competing with everyone. He continues:

But if you're willing to invest on a seven-year time horizon, you're now competing against a fraction of those people, because very few companies are willing to do that. Just by lengthening the time horizon, you can engage in endeavors that you could never otherwise pursue. At Amazon, we like things to work in five to seven years. We're willing to plant seeds, let them grow—and we're very stubborn. We say we're stubborn on vision and flexible on details.[2]

Despite its rapid success and stronghold in the market, Amazon is unique in that Bezos does not intend to abandon his philosophy over the long term. Whereas many other companies in Amazon's position would focus on cementing their market share, Bezos knows that this is impossible—new companies will constantly disrupt markets and force them to evolve.

With its significant arsenal of resources and constantly evolving long-term vision, Amazon is probably best situated to pave the way forward. Amazon, for example, recently launched Amazon Fresh, delivering fresh groceries and produce on the same day they are ordered. Perhaps the most intriguing concept in its pipeline, however, is Amazon Prime Air. Using unstaffed aircraft systems or drones, Amazon plans to get products into its customers' hands within thirty minutes. Amazon even has a video that demonstrates this technology.[3] While Amazon is still waiting for new Federal Aviation Administration regulations to be passed, it says that it will be ready when it happens. This is a refreshing point about companies that pursue the journey to become sustainable enterprises: they do not wait for regulations to begin innovating; they wait for them to catch up and constantly lead the way. This is a point that is repeated when we look at Tesla and GM in terms of electric vehicle regulations.

We are confronted with an intriguing question to ponder: Is Amazon a sustainable enterprise? From the onset, Amazon's mission has been "to be Earth's most customer centric company."[4] This mission can have many different levels, and it is capable of being anywhere from a stage 1 to 4 level of sustainability. With its recent hire of a chief sustainability officer, Amazon may begin to tweak this mission statement. Nonetheless, the important takeaway is that by having a long time frame that is stakeholder-centric *and* constantly reassessed, you can become a sustainable enterprise. The reason for this goes back to the positive deviance continuum, which places sustainable practices as being positively deviant from the norm. Hence, if you always take a long-term approach with your customer's interests at heart, you are constantly attempting to offer products and services that are better than the status quo. Had Bezos remained complacent with selling books (and thereby satisfying the demands of short-term investors), Amazon would most likely be a relic of the past.

Action 4: Focus on the long term.

While Bezos may not have had sustainability in mind when starting his company, Vincenzo Muccioli did. Sustainability practices entrenched in stage 4 are distinct from previous stages of sustainability in that they directly address societal needs and prioritize them over short-term profit maximization. In 1976, Muccioli had a vision for curbing the increasing population of drug addicts in Rimini, Milan, and the greater Romagna region. Born to a wealthy family in 1934, he had acquired a two-hundred-hectare estate called San Patrignano, located in the hills above Rimini. The primary activities conducted in San Patrignano were agriculture, wine harvesting, and animal breeding. On a trip to the neighboring city, Rimini, Muccioli saw two things that affected him deeply: local youths lying on the streets, weak with malnutrition from drug use; and locals who walked past them with condescending attitudes and comments. Instead, Muccioli's reaction was that these youths were sick and needed help recovering.

After establishing a tradition of inviting various drug addicts to his estate in San Patrignano for Christmas, Muccioli developed a more concrete, long-term vision. He felt that the best way to curb drug addiction was not through state subsidies, rehabilitation centers, or even therapists. Instead, Muccioli believed that people who had addiction problems should feel as though they were a part of something larger, such as a family or community, and become functioning, contributing members within it. Muccioli thought that even if people addicted to drugs were cured, their long-term future was uncertain. Would they be accepted by society? Who would give a job to individuals who had been under the influence of drugs for a long time and in a rehabilitation center for months or years? Muccioli decided to look at the big picture of drug addiction. He decided that focusing on the long-term situation of drug addicts would be the key to their sustainable, long-term rehabilitation. He then decided to develop a long-term approach for rehabilitation that started by creating a family for the drug addicts and giving them a potential future for their lives. After discussing this plan with his wife, Muccioli invited a few drug addicts to live in San Patrignano, referring to them as his *ragazzi*, or kids. Yet he had three conditions: they had to discontinue all drug use, they were not allowed to ask for any money from the state, and they had to choose from a list of approximately thirty activities in order to make San Patrignano a self-sustaining community. There were no therapists in San Patrignano, merely small support groups among the previous drug users. Traditional therapy was replaced with community building and productive activities. From producing wine and cheese to soap and detergent, Muccioli's *kids* were able to support themselves and contribute to a greater community. Those who had not completed school had the option of sharing an apartment in a larger city to pursue their education.

From eight members in 1980, San Patrignano rapidly increased over the years, reaching six hundred members in 1985 and two thousand members in 1994. What began as a small family evolved into a community, and eventually became a completely sustainable society. Beginning in the 1980s, guests at San Patrignano went beyond producing the goods and services they needed, and started producing excess quantities to sell to markets. The number of industries San Patrignano competes in is astounding, ranging from agriculture to horse racing to furniture, and almost everything in between. Guests are able to suggest new work activities as well, which further contributes to the diversity. The revenues from these activities are reinvested into the community, which has expansive living quarters, a communal dining area, sports facilities, a medical center, and other facilities in addition to the workshops, agricultural plots, and equestrian areas. Members of the community can therefore have their full suite of needs met and participate in a variety of activities outside their daily workload.

The efficacy of this approach has been astounding and extremely successful. It is estimated that until 1994, San Patrignano had curbed the Italian government's spending on incarceration costs by approximately $80 million. While only a few longitudinal studies have been conducted to compare the efficacy of San Patrignano to other drug rehabilitation programs, those that have been done affirm the success of Muccioli's approach. Consequently, a variety of programs has been carried out to rehabilitate drug users through jobs—something that drug users have a difficult time attaining. San Patrignano has ushered in a revolutionary approach to dealing with drug addicts—one that involves no therapists. Whereas the majority of treatments for drug addicts focused on incremental changes to type of stay (outpatient versus residential) and length of therapy, Muccioli transformed the landscape by constructing a new system altogether.

A long-term vision is essential for long-term business results. A recent McKinsey study on the call to reform capitalism after the 2008 economic crisis states, "One issue is particularly essential: shifting markets and companies from 'quarterly capitalism' to a true longer-term way of thinking, thereby renewing the fundamental ways we govern, manage, and lead today's corporations. Achieving that change, however, requires wide-ranging shifts in both mind-set and practice sustainability."[5] Unilever CEO Paul Pollman related this concept to achieving sustainability in organizations. He explained how capitalism must evolve from a culture of "short-termism":

Thinking in the long term has removed enormous shackles from our organization. I really believe that is part of the strong success we have seen over the past five years. Better decisions are being made. We don't have discussions about whether to postpone the launch of a brand by a month or two or not to invest capital, even if investing is the right thing to do, because of quarterly commitments. We have moved to a more mature dialogue with our investor base about what strategic actions serve Unilever's best interests in the long term versus explaining short-term movements.[6]

In a recent discussion about long-term vision with executives from a major European oil and gas company, we asked them to think what their company would look like in thirty-five years. What would the company be doing differently from now, and which economic, environmental, social, and technological trends should they be presently concentrating on in order to prepare their company to be a leader in its industry in the year 2050? The answers were surprisingly unanimous:

There will be little oil and gas in the world; thus, our company will have changed its business model and will be a renewable energy company.
   Our company will become a renewable energy company working in the European market as well as in Latin America.
   We will be the biggest providers of solar technology and best designers of wind farms.
   Our company will be in the business of providing cities and industries with electricity from renewable energy sources.[7]

The three things their company will be doing differently in 2050 are developing solar and wind technology, working in the field of smart grids, and engaging with new stakeholder groups and partners. Nevertheless, when asked what the company is doing in each of these domains, the participants were silent. While some eventually said that they were following important trends (such as solar and wind efficiency, nuclear energy development, and emerging markets for alternative energy), the company cannot stop there. Too many companies, such as GM, which we describe in the next section, focus on following trends rather than being the transformational leaders that are necessary for creating those trends. If you know that your company or industry will evolve in the next thirty years, be the trailblazer.

Significant obstacles to change, though, remain in place. "Most companies are still focused on the relatively short term, on the next quarter's numbers," said David Symons, director of consultancy at WSP | Parsons Brinckerhoff. As long as company boards emphasize short-term profit and shareholder returns, the longer-term demands of a more sustainable business will suffer.[8]

Action 5: Adopt a systems perspective to pursue transformational as opposed to incremental changes.

It is sometimes easy to take the game changers of the past for granted, as we bask in the realized vision of transformation leaders. Elon Musk, for example, is one of the few corporate leaders who can tell you where his company will be in twenty-five years. His long-term vision is one where the entire global car fleet is electric, his activities are powered from renewable energy sources, and he is colonizing Mars. Whether or not his predictions will come to fruition, one thing is true: Musk is leading the charge and has been successful so far. After selling PayPal to eBay for $1.5 billion in 2002, Musk helped found and grow three innovative businesses: SolarCity, SpaceX, and Tesla Motors. Each of these initiatives is what we call a game changer in its respective industry. While customers wanting to make the switch to solar power often have to face steep, up-front costs to purchase solar panels, SolarCity makes them available for free by leasing panels to customers at rates comparable to their current utility bills. Once the panels have been paid off, customers enjoy free electricity.

The value proposition for SpaceX has been even more dramatic. Space expedition has been extremely costly in the past, forcing National Aeronautics and Space Administration to halt its space program. The current item attributed to the cost of missions was fuel. But Musk noted that the principle cost was something most organizations took for granted: the cost of the actual rocket. By returning rockets back to Earth, SpaceX is able to reduce the price point of a shuttle launch from $450 to $60 million.[9] SpaceX has already successfully proven its value proposition by delivering a payload to the International Space Station and successfully bringing the rocket back to Earth. It currently offers twice the payload of the next-best solution at a third of the cost. Musk's goals are to begin sending staffed missions to Mars in the mid-2020s in an effort to start colonizing the planet.

Perhaps the most effective case that demonstrates long-term vision is Tesla Motors. While its vision is more modest than that of SpaceX, Tesla highlights the dangers of becoming too entrenched in the short term. Interested in electric cars since the age of fourteen, Musk jumped on the opportunity to lead Tesla's Series A financing round with a personal investment of $7.5 million. Although electric vehicles were invented in the mid-nineteenth century, they suffered from three problems: high cost (primarily attributed to batteries), low top speed, and short range.

That all changed with Tesla. Whereas other companies were unwilling to make the up-front investment for developing electric vehicles, a handful of visionaries were ready. Tesla raised $187 million through five rounds of financing, largely led by Musk, who became chair of the board. Tesla's vision was for a high-performance fleet of electric vehicles—vehicles that could outperform their gasoline and hybrid peers in every category. Its primary innovation was investing in lithium-battery technology—the same batteries that power many modern consumer electronics such as laptops and cell phones. Lithium batteries benefit from high energy density, minimal capacity loss over many charges, and little loss in charge when not in use. They are the most optimal battery technology for electric cars, but were not used until Tesla entered the field due to their high cost point. Tesla worked tirelessly to innovate on lithium-ion cells, redesigning them to make them lighter and cheaper to manufacture.

On August 2, 2006, Musk wrote a memo titled "The Secret Tesla Motors Master Plan (Just between You and Me)." In it, Musk described how the first goal of Tesla was to build a high-end sports car, the Tesla Roadster, which could go head-to-head with a Porsche or Ferrari yet still have twice the energy efficiency of a Prius. With a price point of approximately $110,000 for the Roadster, Musk admits that there will only be a small supply, but they will serve as a proof of concept, and allow Tesla to draw enough revenue and backing to begin building a more affordable car. With retail sales beginning in 2012, the Model S fell into this category, starting at just under $70,000. After selling enough of these units, Musk stated that Tesla's plan was to launch an even more affordable car. This car, code-named BlueStar, and now referred to as the Model 3 or Model E, was launched on April 1, 2016. It will be priced at $35,000 (about half the cost of its predecessors), and delivery to customers will start at the end of 2017. The new electric vehicle has a five-star safety rating, 215 miles of range, goes 0 to 60 mph in less than six seconds, and all versions will have Tesla's famed autopilot and supercharging capabilities as standard features.[10] Tesla aims to produce 500,000 of these vehicles a year with the aid of its massive lithium-ion Gigafactory in Sparks, Nevada, thereby cutting the cost of the car's battery pack and enabling a lower-priced car. In the first twenty-four hours after announcing the Model 3, Tesla received 115,000 preorders. Just six days later, on April 7, Musk reported that Tesla had received more than 325,000 reservations.[11] This means that his goal of selling 500,000 cars a year is already well on its way. He also plans to increase Tesla's storefront locations, service stations, and supercharging stations to prepare for Tesla's new drivers. Tesla's ability to follow Musk's road map and eleven-year vision is impressive to say the least.

In addition to revolutionizing the use of lithium-ion battery cells, Tesla has taken a long-term systems approach with its electric fleet— from the cars themselves to the charging stations that are available when traveling long distances. The Model S scored a perfect five National Highway Traffic Safety Administration safety rating, with *Consumer Reports* giving it a score of ninety-nine out of a hundred—the highest rating the publication has ever awarded to a car. It is hard to disagree with this rating because on a single charge, the cars can travel 300 miles, and they have the ability to go from 0 to 60 mph in 4.2 seconds on a 302-horsepower motor, or 5.9 seconds on a 416 horse- power motor. By placing the batteries in the floor of the car, the Model S maximizes interior space, making it capable of seating five adults and two kids (with child-rated jump seats in the cab space.) A drag coeffi- cient of 0.24 makes the Model S one of the most aerodynamic cars on the market, with a fuel economy of 89 miles per gallon of gasoline equivalent. For customers traveling long distances, the Model S can be recharged for no cost at a supercharger station in approximately thirty minutes. Otherwise, the batteries can be charged overnight in a regular socket. Tesla has strategically placed superchargers across the United States to create a complete network of charging stations.

Tesla's success can be attributed to the long-term vision of Musk, just as its market penetration can be credited to the short time frames in which long-standing auto manufacturers are entrenched. In a 2009 interview, the vice chair of GM, Bob Lutz, remarked, "All the geniuses here at General Motors kept saying lithium-ion technology is 10 years away, and Toyota agreed with us—and boom, along comes Tesla. So I said, 'How come some tiny little California startup, run by guys who know nothing about the car business, can do this, and we can't?'"[12]

The question posed to leaders is this: If a game-changing technology is another ten years away from being realized, why are you not already working on it? Ten years is the minimum timeline that companies should adopt in order to remain competitive. And they need to continuously look ten years ahead every year. Even though Tesla has not finished ramping up production of its current Model S series, in April 2016, it launched its more affordable Model 3/E series—which will go to the market in January 2017—and has already demonstrated a prototype for the autonomous driving technology that it plans to incorporate into all its vehicles in the future. Tesla also has invested in developing the largest factory in the world for lithium-ion batteries. Ironically, when competitors do finally develop comparable electric vehicles, they will most likely purchase the batteries from Tesla— batteries that account for over 8 percent of the cost of developing the vehicle. In a bold move to help expedite this process, Tesla released all its patents and made them publicly available. Through his approach for continuously innovating and looking ten years out, Musk plans for Tesla to be the biggest supplier to its competitors while boasting cars that drive themselves.

Action 6: Make sure you are always ten years ahead of the competition.

Why is Tesla and not GM leading the electric vehicle market? Returning to the case question posed at the end of the previous chapter, GM was in fact the first automobile manufacturer to mass-produce an electric vehicle—the EV1. It was primed to become the leader in the electric vehicle market, having without doubt the latest and most advanced technology at the time. GM maintained that the actual cost for producing electric vehicles was too high to market. It therefore decided to terminate the EV1, in one of the most controversial moves in business history. Despite the appeal from many lease owners, who mailed checks and letters claiming that they would assume all risk for the vehicle, GM declined all requests, and instead repossessed all EV1s only to scrap and crush them. In addition, GM and other automakers were notoriously blamed for spending millions of dollars to lobby against regulations that would require the auto industry to produce a certain percentage of electric vehicles in each fleet.

Consequently, GM is largely targeted in the famous documentary titled *Who Killed the Electric Car*, which argues that the oil industry and large automobile companies are to blame for the failure of electric vehicles to take off during the 1990s and early 2000s.[13] Moreover, the efforts by automobile companies to begin selling electric vehicles in the early 1990s were weak at best and generally unsupported in spite of moderate consumer demand. A study financed by the automobile industry to defend its actions in the electric vehicle market found that consumers were only willing to purchase electric vehicles if they were $28,000 less than the sticker price of an equivalent, gasoline-powered automobile. Yet an independent study financed by the California Electric Transportation Coalition found widely different results. The commissioned survey instead discovered a significant market for electric vehicles, ranging between 151,200 and 226,800 people in California alone, as long as the range of electric vehicles improved and the price point was comparable to their gasoline-equivalent peers.[14] Many critics argue that automobile manufacturers did only the bare minimum to advance electric vehicles so that they could appease the California Air Resources Board and continue selling their existing fleets to the highly profitable Californian market. After all, why change what works?

Rick Wagoner, the CEO of GM at the time, stated that ending the EV1 program was the worst decision he ever made. It may have also been the costliest one. In retrospect, GM would gladly have financed the $187 million that Tesla Motors raised in order for it to have Tesla's present fleet of vehicles. It would also have been able to avoid the costly fees associated with lobbying regulators and protecting its brand image through various public relations and marketing campaigns. Ironically, it could have invested much less than Tesla Motors did and reached the market much sooner. Furthermore, Tesla's electric power train is based on prototypes developed by Alan Cocconi, one of the principal contractors GM hired to develop the EV1. In 1992, Cocconi had cofounded AC Propulsion, the company that Musk first tried to per-suade into commercializing electric vehicles after test-driving its updated TZero prototype in 2003. Powered by lithium-ion batteries, the prototype could go from zero to sixty mph in under four seconds and had a three-hundred-mile range. This was six years before the Tesla Roadster was released.

Nevertheless, with a range between seventy and a hundred miles, the ability to go from zero to sixty mph in eight seconds, and a top speed of eighty mph, the EV1 was clearly ahead of its time in 1996—and that was with traditional lead-acid batteries. If GM had opted to continue investing in the electric vehicle, it would be in a drastically different position today. GM arguably would have had a much superior model to the Chevy Volt if it had started production ten years earlier, and had significant iterations every two to three years. Moreover, if a small company, AC Propulsion, was capable of developing lithium-ion-powered vehicles, one can only imagine the capabilities of GM. GM research and development chief Larry Burns wished in 2007 that his company had not killed the plug-in hybrid EV1 prototype his engineers had on the road since 1997. More recently he said, "If we could turn back the hands of time, we could have had the Chevy Volt 10 years earlier. Just like that old prototype, the Volt will not generate immediate profits. However, times have changed."[15]

Musk admits that the team at Tesla, as newcomers to the automobile sector, spent five times more money than necessary when learning how to make an automobile. To this day, Tesla Motors is trying to increase capacity to meet demand—throughput that GM could have easily managed. Instead, GM took the short-term approach and abandoned the EV1 program due to the high costs associated with it. GM felt the full weight of its decision (and failure) in 2009, when it filed for Chapter 11 bankruptcy. While this was largely a result of the 2007–2008 recession, an underlying cause was that GM had no competitive edge in the automobile industry. After all, sales of Tesla vehicles continued to increase over this span of time. GM's failure to invest a figure less than $187 million into electric vehicles resulted in a record bailout of $49.5 billion that came from the pockets of taxpayers. While the government recovered $39 billion, taxpayers still had to pay $10.5 billion for GM's mistake. This $10.5 billion was alongside a deteriorated environment from CO_2 emissions of gasoline-powered vehicles that GM chose to prioritize.

GM is not alone. Many organizations shy away from sustainability-oriented initiatives comparable to GM's decision not to pursue electric vehicles. While lack of a long-term perspective is bad business, it also significantly hinders societal progress. If GM had embraced a sustainable mission and championed a long-term perspective, we would have been fifteen years closer to a more efficient and environmentally cleaner fleet of vehicles. Instead, the short-term thinking adopted by leaders at GM caused it to spend money in the opposite direction of progress. How many other sustainability initiatives have been halted due to high costs? Sustainability does not always pay, particularly in the short term. But over the long term, new business models can be developed to make sustainability a viable and profitable option while forcing traditional models to play the costly game of catch-up. Need proof? With $187 million, Tesla's market cap reached $36.3 billion in 2014–2011, years later. Alternatively, GM, which was the largest US corporation from 1954 to 1973, and from 1985 to 1999, was valued at $66 billion in May 2000 and has steadily declined to $51 billion in September 2014. Despite being valued at over half the value of GM, Tesla sells fewer cars in a year than GM sells in a day.

Action 7: Prioritize long-term goals over short-term profit maximization.

The case of PMI presented at the end of the previous chapter presents a challenging question: Can all companies become sustainable? Notwithstanding its efforts to curb emissions, decrease waste, and contribute to charity, PMI's core business is the sale and distribution of tobacco products. PMI has begun to make significant investments to reduce the harm that smoking causes, but are these enough. As stated earlier, doing less harm is not equivalent to doing more good. So how could PMI embark on the sustainability journey?

As evidenced by GM and others, many companies spend a lot of time focusing on how to continue doing what they are doing. As such, they become increasingly shortsighted. These companies, however, have an incredible amount of resources and capacity. As mentioned in PMI's case, it has a global workforce of ninety-one people and eighty thousand tobacco producers. Rather than improving on the cigarette, is there a more transformational change PMI could make that would move it away from stage 2 sustainability (environmentalism), and toward stage 3 or 4? The thought exercise at the beginning of this chapter is meant to push the boundaries of what the actual capacity of an organization is when a long-term vision is pursued.

Recent studies have identified the promise of genetically modified tobacco as a source of biofuel. By increasing the amount of oil in the leaf, which has a high sugar content, by twenty times, scientists believe tobacco can be a more efficient biofuel than existing sources. In addition, unlike the current sources of biofuel, such as soybean and corn, utilizing tobacco for fuel does not affect the food supply. As the demand for tobacco has decreased dramatically in the United States and around the globe, genetically modified tobacco could be a significant game changer.[16] Experts caution that this process can take up to five years, but if PMI adopts a long-term strategy, it may be able to begin using tobacco to positively improve society rather than harm population subsets.

PMI could also begin venturing beyond tobacco. With its extensive network of tobacco growers, it could repurpose land for other crops or uses by simply creating markets for them. One way to go about this process is to project what the leading sectors will be in twenty-five years and then begin shifting toward them. With the increasing regulation in the tobacco space and decreasing demand for tobacco worldwide, it is viable to ask if PMI's present business model can even survive over the long term. Whether it is using tobacco for alternative energy sources, converting tobacco crops to agricultural crops to meet the demands of our growing population, or constructing solar and wind farms to harvest renewable energy, PMI has the capacity and labor force to move into any industry it wishes by adopting a long-term vision.

Action 8: Use your organization's full capacity to pursue long-term, sustainable objectives.

The actions for achieving the second step of our sustainable business model, a long-term vision, as described in this chapter, are enumerated in box 3.1, along with some key lessons.

A long-term vision is necessary to embark on the sustainability journey and ensure your enterprise remains competitive. Translating that into a business strategy to offer core goods and products, though, is not a simple undertaking. The following two cases demonstrate the challenges that exist when developing a sustainability strategy. They will be explored further in the next chapter.

Case 1: Triodos Bank

In the early 1970s, a working group developed the idea of "using money for good." In response to the various financial crises of the times, this group of individuals and institutions wanted to develop a new way of investing whereby they only invested in sustainable enterprises. While many banks and investment groups have socially responsible umbrellas, the Triodos Foundation was one of the first institutions to invest only in activities that positively improved society. By pooling their money together, the Triodos Foundation members were able to receive a higher interest rate on their savings, which they relinquished to their sustainable investment fund. Based on the large

Box 3.1
Long-Term Vision: Key Lessons and Actions

• Sustainability is a journey that organizations travel over time. The story of Bezos and his long-term vision for Amazon offers a crucial lesson for sustainability. Focusing on the long-term allows the organization to work toward a defined future as well as address the challenges and difficulties that can be encountered in the short term

Action 4: Focus on the long term.

• The key lesson from Unilever is the benefit of looking ahead and designing the kind of long term that an organization wants to create for its future, and using a systems approach to determine what that desired future would look like.

Action 5: Adopt a systems perspective to pursue transformational as opposed to incremental changes.

• The Tesla case shows clearly how a company that looks forward and aligns its vision with the future needs of society can become sustainable. Musk understood that the fossil-fuel-powered car would not be the transportation mode of the future mainly because even if fuel engines become more and more efficient, they generate CO_2, which in turn contributes to an increase in climate change. By sharing his patents with competitors, Tesla is moving the entire automobile industry into the future.

Action 6: Make sure you are always ten years ahead of the competition.

• The story of GM and the electric vehicle shows that an organization can miss significant opportunities by only focusing on short-term gains. The sustainability journey requires organizations to develop and adopt sustainable missions with a long-term perspective.

Action 7: Prioritize long-term goals over short-term profit maximization.

• The main takeaway from GM, Tesla, and PMI is that organizations can only achieve becoming sustainable enterprises by having a clear vision of where they are going, and anticipating and "living" a bit in the future. Sustainability is about looking forward and outward. In addition, it is a moving target. Only by being in close contact with societal needs and different groups of stakeholders can organizations favor initiatives that revolve around the future.

Action 8: Use your organization's full capacity to pursue long-term, sustainable objectives.

success and growing demand for the funding of social enterprises, the Triodos Foundation became a full-fledged banking institution in 1978 and one of the first *sustainable banks* in the world. Sustainable banks can be defined as value-based banks that prioritize people over profitability.

Over the years, Triodos Bank has been a pioneer not only in the sustainable banking sector but also in sustainability best practices across industries. It was one of the first banks to make its entire portfolio transparent—publishing every loan it makes on a Google Maps platform. It can also be credited with helping finance the first wind farm, the first Fairtrade organization (Max Havelaar), and a microfinance investment fund through the unique savings accounts it offers retail clients, which enables them to decide how their money is invested.

In the interest of being a sustainable enterprise, Triodos Bank does not offer any credit cards. Moreover, cognizant of the growing consumer debt crisis, Triodos Bank managers do not want to become enablers or contributors to unsustainable debts. As an organization that is in close contact with its stakeholders, however, Triodos Bank needs to find a way to appease the increasing pressure from its retail clients to offer credit accounts. If you were Peter Blom, who sits at the helm of Triodos Bank, how would you appease the present needs of stakeholders with the long-term vision and mission of Triodos Bank to use money for good? What is the most sustainable business strategy that Triodos can employ for this market segment?

Case 2: McDonald's in France

Notwithstanding its success in North American markets, McDonald's faced considerable challenges when attempting to scale up its European penetration. In 1972, Raymond Dayan, a French restaurateur, convinced McDonald's headquarters to allow him to open franchises in France. Beginning with a location just outside Paris, Dayan was able to expand to fourteen locations by 1978 despite the critiques of French experts that fast food eaten with hands would never be culturally accepted in France. Yet McDonald's repossessed the franchise locations after legal battles with Dayan ensued. Nonetheless, by 1988, McDonald's opened its first drive-through locations in the outskirts of the city.

In 1992, however, tensions finally reached a breaking point between the US franchise and local French farmers when the Blair House Accord was enacted. The accord's passage, which McDonald's lobbied for heavily, facilitated the importation of US agricultural products into France. These imports threatened the demand for French agricultural products such as beef and cheese, and jeopardized the livelihoods of many French farmers. To protest the Blair House Accord, French farmers lit a bonfire outside a McDonald's location. Tensions continued to increase during the 1990s, culminating with the 1999 riots led by José Bové, a sheep farmer and cheese producer, to protest the sanctions the United States passed on imported French cheese and foie gras. The US restrictions passed by the Clinton administration were retaliation for the European Union's reversal of the Blair House Accord through its restriction on hormone-enhanced US beef. Bové was sentenced to three months in prison for vandalizing and destroying a McDonald's location that was being constructed in southern France. His acts were largely supported by French locals and even considered "just" by the French prime minister, Lionel Jospin.

To improve its brand in the French markets, McDonald's hired Jean-Pierre Petit—the founder of a successful French ad agency. Imagine you are Petit. McDonald's has approximately a thousand locations in France, making it the second-biggest market after the United States. What should its long-term vision be in order to become a sustainable enterprise? Similar to the case of PMI, is it possible for a fast-food chain to become a sustainable enterprise? Lastly, what strategy should it adopt in France to begin pursuing its sustainability journey? While meeting the needs of stakeholders is a pivotal aspect of stage 3 sustainability (corporate social responsibility), positively improving society is critical to stage 4 sustainability efforts. In lieu of the protests and opposition to McDonald's in France, how can Petit *transform* McDonald's?

4 Sustainability Strategy: Identify Your Stakeholders and Develop a Plan to Impact Them in a Positive Way?

We define sustainable organizations as those that positively impact all stakeholder groups in the short and long term (a stakeholder view of the organization is reproduced in figure 4.1). Doing so requires a new strategy that does not conform to traditional business models. The question that organizations have to ask themselves is how they positively and negatively impact all stakeholder groups in the short and long term. All too often, the sustainability strategies of organizations are entrenched in activities focused on the negative externalities of the firm (i.e., reducing harm or minimizing negative externalities on stakeholder groups). A sustainable organization, however, is one that not only minimizes harm but also attempts to maximize positive outcomes. While the TBL and other frameworks suggest that firms can make up for negative performance through positive outcomes, this is simply not accurate. Sustainability, after all, is not a zero-sum game. If an organization pollutes the environment, does it actually reverse its impact by paying for CO_2 offsets? Similarly, if a company pays its producers below minimum wage, will donating a portion of its profits toward a nonprofit ameliorate the situation? In short, sustainability should not be an afterthought or public relations maneuver; instead, it should be integrated from the outset into the core strategy and business model of an organization. This chapter explores the best practices of sustainable organizations and the innovative ways they manage to impact stakeholders positively through their business strategies.

We attempt to debunk two important trends. The first is the *business case for sustainability*. Proponents of this modus operandi champion the various ways businesses can become more sustainable while increasing profitability.[1] The notion of becoming more sustainable is largely reduced to minimizing negative externalities, particularly environmental ones. Instead, sustainable organizations should internalize

A stakeholder view of the firm

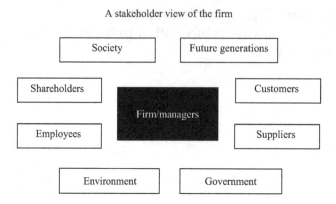

Figure 4.1
Stakeholder view of the firm
Source: Adapted from R E. Freeman, *Strategic Management: A Stakeholder Approach* (Boston: Pitman, 1984).

externalities and maximize positive outcomes, viewing stakeholders as integral parts of the firm.

Figure 4.1 shows a stakeholder view of the firm. Although there are many stakeholder groups that the firm needs to interact with, the economic stakeholders of the firm seem to get more attention. Business strategies espousing the business case for sustainability positively improve the same stakeholder group that almost all traditional businesses serve—that is, shareholders. Moreover, by minimizing harm while increasing profitability, only one stakeholder is impacted positively even as others are not harmed as much. When examining the impact of British Petroleum's (BP) spill of two hundred million gallons of oil in the Gulf of Mexico starting on April 20, 2010, for example, the International Finance Corporation made the business case for sustainability by indicating how much money BP could have saved had it had a sustainability strategy for the Gulf of Mexico. While assessing the cost of the disaster, the IFC only focused on the financial cost to BP and its shareholders: "BP has lost more than $32 million a day in brand value. BP's market value had dropped from $184 billion to $96.5 billion, roughly 48% in a period of two months. Developing a good environmental and social reputation can contribute to a willingness among customers and investors to pay a price premium, which directly affects the company's bottom line."[2] The IFC report failed to assess the significant impact that the oil spill and the two hundred million gallons of toxic dispersants on a thousand-mile shoreline had on other key stakeholders, such as the local residents and marine environment. A Center for Biological Diversity study also reported that eleven people were killed during this disaster, along with more than eighty-two thousand birds, about six thousand sea turtles, and nearly twenty-six thousand marine mammals including dolphins, and an unknown massive number of fish and invertebrates may have been harmed by the spill and its aftermath.[3]

Our view is that a sustainable business strategy should aim to impact all stakeholders positively.

The second trend in sustainability is the stress on environmental sustainability. While this is important, the primary emphasis for sustainability efforts is placed on minimizing an organization's environmental footprint. Although not enough focus is spent on improving the environment, the social dimension of sustainability remains largely elusive. Coca-Cola, for instance, has made a significant effort to reduce by 33 percent the water needed to produce one bottle of Coke. This approach, which is also shared by other companies in the beverage industry, highlights Coca-Cola's efforts to reduce its environmental footprint. Another example is PepsiCo; the company reports significant improvements in the amount of water resources it uses to produce its beverages and other food products: "During 2014, we decreased absolute water use by approximately one billion liters and realized approximately $17 million in cost savings."[4] Nevertheless, these companies do not seem to adopt similar initiatives to minimize the negative social impact that their products might have—more specifically, the impact that the high sugar content of their products has on society, particularly in terms of the link between the consumption of their products and increase in obesity. Research shows that high rates of obesity worldwide have been attributed to a combination of genetics and environment including calorie-rich diets. A Harvard University School of Public Health Study reports that "two out of three adults and one out of three children in the United States are overweight or obese, and the nation spends an estimated $190 billion a year treating obesity-related health conditions. Rising consumption of sugary drinks has been a major contributor to the obesity epidemic. A typical 20-ounce soda contains 15 to 18 teaspoons of sugar and upwards of 240 calories. People who drink this 'liquid candy' do not feel as full as if they had eaten the same calories from solid food."[5]

Looking at the stakeholder view of the organization, a whole host of nonenvironmental actors is largely ignored in sustainability discussions. We therefore draw on best practices that demonstrate how societal sustainability should be integrated into an organization's sustainability strategy while largely skipping the environment and shareholders—two stakeholder groups that have already received attention in the sustainability literature and news. Instead, we concentrate on how organizations have been able to positively impact key stakeholders including society, suppliers, employees, customers, and the government. While this list of stakeholders is not exhaustive, it shows the areas of improvement organizations can strive toward when developing a comprehensive sustainability strategy that emphasizes the social dimension of sustainability.

Society

Business has largely made positive contributions to society over time, improving various quality-of-life measures through products and innovations. From transportation to food, communication and housing, businesses produce almost every good and service we consume. Of course, not every individual has the same capacity; so while some enjoy the luxuries businesses provide, many are unable to do so. To address this problem, many organizations engage in some level of philanthropic contribution toward a marginalized subset of society. These contributions usually are made to nonprofit organizations, which are valuable and should be encouraged because they target various social needs.

We argue, however, that businesses can be much more effective in contributing to meeting social needs by leveraging their firms' knowledge, experience, products, and services. Some businesses are effective providers of those social needs. For instance, various technology companies have worked to decrease the digital divide in developing countries. Additionally, pharmaceutical companies such as Pfizer and Novartis develop drugs required by people from all subsets of society, yet not every member can afford them. Rather than donating money toward nonprofit organizations to improve society, a pharmaceutical company's greatest contribution would be to deliver its drugs at a reduced cost or free of charge to populations in need. The pharmaceutical company GlaxoSmithKline recently announced a positive sign in this direction. In March 2016, the company unveiled plans to make its latest drugs available to the world's poorest people at a fraction of the commercial price. Glaxo will no longer seek patents for medications launched in countries classified by the United Nations as "least developed" or "low income," allowing generic drugmakers the freedom to manufacture and supply cheap, copycat versions of Glaxo's latest medicines to the world's most deprived countries.[6]

While the Glaxo initiative has become a best practice in the pharmaceutical industry, it has faced a series of obstacles, and has come under intense scrutiny and debate, raising the following questions: Which customer segments should receive such benefits? Is it fair to other customer segments that essentially subsidize the cost of the medicine? What if there is not enough demand for a certain medicine to be developed, or if the demand were in a poor region with customers who are unable to afford the medicine that would require an investment by the pharmaceutical company?

While some of these hurdles continue to challenge the pharmaceutical sector, there are other business models that have evolved when organizations focus on how to address social needs. A good example of this is the *buy one, give one* model. Under this scheme, for every product that a customer purchases, the company gives one away to someone in need. Blake Mycoskie, who founded TOMS shoes in 2006, was one of the early pioneers of this model.[7]

During a visit to Argentina, Mycoskie was introduced to a type of local shoe called *alpargatas*, or espadrilles. The shoe style has been in existence for thousands of years, but it was first produced on a large scale in the Catalan and Basque regions of Spain. The sole was traditionally made from jute rope, but modern designs use a rubber sole. The upper design is fashioned as a slip-on shoe, made out of cotton or similar material. After purchasing a pair for himself, Mycoskie also realized how many children in Argentina lacked shoes. He therefore devised a new business model, which he named "One for One," whereby TOMS would donate a pair of shoes to a child in need for every pair of shoes it sold. The new style of shoe along with its sustainability mission has made TOMS a rapid success. As of 2014, TOMS had given away more than thirty-five million pairs. At an average price of $75 per pair, that means that TOMS has earned approximately $328 million per year since its inception, not to mention the significant impact TOMS has made on the social problem it identified.[8] The TOMS experience, though, has generated some criticism from theorists. Some people believe this approach is paternalistic and hinders development. Economist Dambisa Moyo suggests that aid can end up replacing local markets, thereby hampering development.

Another study looked at used-clothes imports to Africa and concluded that they provoked a depression in local apparel industries.[9] A study in El Salvador on the effect of giving free TOMS shoes to poor people stated that receiving TOMS shoes had a negative impact on future shoe purchases.[10]

The buy one, give one model has expanded greatly to almost every sector imaginable. Warby Parker, an eyewear company founded by graduates from the Wharton School of Business at the University of Pennsylvania in 2010, is another great example. Incidentally, TOMS has also expanded into the eyewear segment. Championing a new business model, Warby Parker was able to become a significant player in the eyewear space, which amounts to an estimated $18 billion market. Moreover, a sustainability mission was not enough to bolster Warby Parker. It instead was an innovative redesign of all the elements in that space. Rather than using traditional retail channels, Warby Parker brought the entire process of manufacturing and sales in-house. By producing its own frames and lenses, and selling to customers directly through its website, Warby Parker is able to charge $95 per pair for many prescription glasses. Not too many optical stores can provide the same value. To facilitate the traditional process of choosing a pair of frames, Warby Parker ships up to five frames at a time directly to customers, who can try the pairs of glasses at no charge. Most important, Warby Parker's frames are extremely well built and well designed, based on vintage-inspired styles. The fashion trend has become widely recognizable, and the brand is sported by many public figures.[11]

To date, Warby Parker has raised $56 million through three rounds of financing. In June 2014, four years after its inception, Warby Parker had sold a million pairs of glasses, and consequently distributed the same number to populations in need.[12] TOMS, Warby Parker, and other successful enterprises attempt to impact society positively through their products by including their social contribution in the price of their products and marketing their contribution through their value proposition. These enterprises do not rely entirely on their sustainability missions, strong as they may be, but rather incorporate them into their corporate strategies.

Action 9: Incorporate societal contribution into the core business strategy as opposed to treating it as an afterthought.

Suppliers

While Warby Parker, TOMS, and others have developed ways to price their social impact into their business models, is there a more direct way to positively improve society's marginalized populations? Recognizing that the world's poorest populations often produce products that wealthier global citizens consume, the notion of *fair trade* emerged post–World War II. While initiatives that championed fair trade principles were in practice as early as the eighteenth century, the movement materialized significantly after the Second World War with the help of various religious groups and nongovernmental organizations (NGOs). Early initiatives, whereby handicrafts were imported from developing countries, and sold to customers through catalogs or stores by the Mennonites and Oxfam, created livelihoods for some of the world's poorest citizens. These initiatives led to the slogan "trade not aid," which was adopted by the UN Conference on Trade and Development in 1968. Empowerment, as opposed to philanthropy, is an integral concept to sustainable organizations.

One of the largest sectors for fair trade products is the coffee industry. Others include tea, cocoa, sugar, nuts, and spices. In 1988, the first widely recognized fair trade label was developed in the Netherlands. The label's name, Max Havelaar, was based on an 1860 novel written by Eduard Douwes Dekker under the pen name Multatuli. The novel was a harsh critique against the Dutch government based on its practices and laws in Java, a Dutch colony at the time. Protesting the policies being instituted, Multatuli raised European awareness of the suffering caused to producers by the wealth many Europeans enjoyed. In order to help eliminate the inequity that still existed, the Max Havelaar label was developed. Van Weely was one of the first coffee roasters to adopt the label. It purchased coffee at a higher price per pound from a cooperative in Mexico and sold it through many retail outlets across the Netherlands.

The Max Havelaar label and many others were soon established around the world, leading to the development in 2002 of a universal Fairtrade mark, which was introduced by the Fairtrade Labeling Organization—an umbrella for the various fair trade labels that existed globally. By 2013, Fairtrade sales amounted to approximately €5.5 billion worldwide.[13] While Fairtrade has grown significantly, it represents a tiny fraction of the global products that are traded. For instance, researchers estimate that only 1 percent of the coffee sold worldwide is Fairtrade certified.[14]

Various studies have additionally demonstrated that the high certification costs and unethical management on behalf of cooperative managers led to producers being hardly better off in fair trade schemes.[15] Moreover, Fairtrade producers need to pay licensing costs regularly, thereby enabling the Fairtrade organization to pay for its overhead (including the costs associated with sending licensing officials to physically verify producers). Further still, the profits from Fairtrade revenue streams rarely trickle down to producers. A study conducted in Finland suggests that only 11.5 percent of the amount consumers paid for Fairtrade coffee went to exporters.[16] Of that, even less is returned to producers because managers frequently control finances and hoard profits. A UK study calculated that of the 18 percent premium that customers paid for Fairtrade coffee, only 1.6 percent made its way to producers.[17]

Finally, Fairtrade is not synonymous with high quality. Producers are also incentivized to sell their lowest-quality products through fair trade markets, where they are guaranteed a minimum price, and then sell higher-quality goods on mainstream markets, where goods are priced based on their quality. Consequently, many companies, including Starbucks, carry only a small percentage of Fairtrade-certified coffee.

How, then, can producers earn more and receive greater wages? In other words, is there a more sustainable solution than Fairtrade labeling to increase the value in a value chain? Michael Porter introduced the concept of the value chain in his 1985 best seller, *Competitive Advantage: Creating and Sustaining Superior Performance*.[18] Porter describes a value chain as a series of activities that a firm in a specific industry performs to deliver a valuable product or service to the market. In response to pressure from NGOs to minimize negative impacts on the environment and pay fair wages, many companies adopted the value chain framework and focused on how to increase value in this chain. The value chain framework remains popular to this day, as firms determine how to ameliorate their ecological footprint and increase value to the end customer while benefiting all actors in the value chain. As highlighted by the shortcomings of the Fairtrade movement, however, we need a better solution. Perhaps the challenge is not to increase value but rather to redistribute it. After all, even if Fairtrade were optimized, would it make a significant difference in the lives of producers? The challenge for sustainable companies thus becomes, How can we redistribute value in a socially sustainable way?

Employees

One promising option for redistributing value can be through the cooperative form of organization. This was established in northwest England during the nineteenth century in response to harsh working conditions, and the Fairtrade movement and other sustainable development initiatives have recently adopted it. Cooperatives have a unique structure, in which their members (including producers and workers) are also their owners. As such, profits are returned to the members of the cooperative as opposed to external shareholders.

Still, as observed in the argan oil sector, even cooperatives have their limitations. Argan oil, which has traditionally been used for cosmetic and culinary purposes by the Berbers in southwest Morocco, is pressed using an excruciating process that begins with the fruit of the argan tree. An eighty-million-year-old species, argan trees once spanned across the whole of North Africa, helping prevent desertification and providing numerous benefits to those who cultivated it.[19] During the last Ice Age, the number of argan trees declined so dramatically that they are now mainly concentrated in the Sous Valley region in southwest Morocco where the particular conditions allowed it to survive. These argan forests are estimated to have diminished by a further 50 percent during the twentieth century due to overharvesting of wood because of a heightened demand for fuel, overgrazing by goats, and land conversions for exportable crops. In 1998, the UN Educational, Scientific, and Cultural Organization declared the region a biosphere reserve, or an area "that seek[s] to reconcile conservation of biological and cultural diversity and economic and social development through partnerships between people and nature."[20]

Zoubida Charrouf, who is presently a professor in the science faculty at Mohamed V. University in Morocco, wanted to commercialize argan oil to incentivize local populations to protect the argan forests. An increase in the demand for argan oil would raise the price, which in turn would act as a financial motive for local communities to disengage from harmful practices in the forests. After studying in France, Charrouf used scientific processes as part of her doctoral dissertation to affirm local Berber knowledge regarding the medicinal and beautification properties of argan oil, which increased global interest in the product. Yet the process of producing the oil was still too arduous at the time to generate a significant and consistent supply. By mobilizing the mechanization of the process, Charrouf addressed another important issue central to rural Morocco: the socioeconomic status of women.

In 2013, 44 percent of Morocco's population lived in rural areas, where the annual gross domestic product per capita was estimated to be €1,325, or 60 percent less than the national average. Access to resources in the country's desert and mountain regions is severely limited, further exacerbating the problem. Most women in southwest Morocco are illiterate and do not speak Arabic, which makes it difficult for them to leave the countryside.[21] The argan oil sector offered women and their families, with no alternative employment options in this patriarchal society, a much-needed additional source of income.

In southwest Morocco in 1996, Charrouf developed the first argan oil enterprise, structuring it as a female cooperative. The Amal cooperative had a mechanized system for pressing and filtering argan oil—procedures that were previously performed by hand. The more efficient production process, combined with the growing awareness of the health and beauty benefits of argan oil, generated interest from cosmetic companies in Europe and North America. This led to the birth of other, privately owned argan oil enterprises with superior managerial and technical skills, and they soon outperformed the cooperatives.

With grants from various countries, Charrouf founded the Ibn al Baytar association in 1999 to finance the growth of cooperatives under its umbrella. The injection of donor funding also attracted good managers to run cooperatives in the countryside. By 2009, Ibn al Baytar had helped organize eighteen hundred women into 20 cooperatives. At the time, there were an estimated 150 cooperatives in Morocco employing approximately seven thousand women, with each member earning an average annual income of €617. This was over three times higher than the income of argan oil producers at private enterprises. Despite investing twenty hours of manual labor to produce one liter of oil, producers earned only 0.8 percent, or €5, of the final retail price (the oil is sold in fifty-milliliter bottles with a retail price of approximately €32 each, totaling €640 per liter). And this was in cooperatives—which again, paid women three times more than they would otherwise earn in traditional argan oil companies.

The rise of associations presented a strong alternative to labeling solutions, but it still returned a small proportion of value to producers—the members in the value chain that work the hardest. What was needed was a redistribution of value in this chain. One innovative solution in the space is the Argan Tree, which brands itself as a beauty cooperative.[22] Few argan oil cooperatives sell directly to the market because they lack the direct connection to retailers, and have poor branding and marketing skills. Instead, they sell to cooperative associations, which then sell to distributors connected to cosmetic labs and brands in global markets. By connecting directly to cooperatives instead, the Argan Tree eliminates middlepersons while increasing the amount returned to cooperatives and their members. The Argan Tree, which has developed a brand around five product offerings, sources argan oil directly from its own sixty-woman cooperative in Morocco and returns 100 percent of the profits to the members. By doing so, the sustainable enterprise helps transform the relationship between organizations and argan oil producers, treating them as employees and owners of the Argan Tree.

Action 10: Eliminate unnecessary middlepersons to ensure value is appropriately distributed in value chains while empowering important actors.

Customers

Thus far, we have focused on sustainability strategies that improve how value is distributed in the value chain as initiatives aim to increase the wages and, in the case of cooperatives, equity that producers receive. What about the other side of the value chain, however? What strategies improve the value returned to consumers? For instance, the proposed case solution for PMI in the previous chapter suggested that in order for the company to become more sustainable, it needed to undergo a radical transformation that required it to abandon the tobacco cigarette sector. That is, PMI's greatest opportunity to improve the lives of one its most critical stakeholders, the customer, was to stop selling what it was selling. We instead argue that PMI could leverage its vast network of tobacco farms and farmers to either shift the tobacco market toward sustainable biofuels or change how the land is used altogether to more positively impact the needs of society.

Not all companies are selling products that can be harmful to customers and other stakeholders. So how can these companies have a more positive impact on their customer stakeholder groups? Patagonia adopted a daring approach to this question, launching one of the most impressive campaigns in advertising history. US consumers spend more on Black Friday, which begins at midnight following Thanksgiving Thursday, than any other day of the year. Over the course of the Thanksgiving weekend, the National Retail Foundation expects approximately 45 percent of the US population to visit stores.[23] It was quite shocking, then, to see Patagonia ads in the Black Friday edition of the *New York Times* in 2011 with the following printed in a large, bold font under a photo of a Patagonia fleece "R2 Jacket": "Don't Buy This Jacket" (the ad is reproduced in figure 4.2):

It's Black Friday, the day in the year retail turns from red to black and starts to make real money. But Black Friday, and the culture of consumption it reflects, puts the economy of natural systems that support all life firmly in the red. We're now using the resources of one-and-a-half planets on our one and only planet.

Because Patagonia wants to be in business for a good long time—and leave a world inhabitable for our kids—we want to do the opposite of every other business today. We ask you to buy less and to reflect before you spend a dime on this jacket or anything else.

Environmental bankruptcy, as with corporate bankruptcy, can happen very slowly, then all of a sudden. This is what we face unless we slow down, then reverse the damage. We're running short on fresh water, topsoil, fisheries, wetlands—all our planet's natural systems and resources that support business, and life, including our own.

The environmental cost of everything we make is astonishing. Consider the R2® Jacket shown, one of our best sellers. To make it required 135 liters of water, enough to meet the daily needs (three glasses a day) of 45 people. Its journey from its origin as 60% recycled polyester to our Reno warehouse generated nearly 20 pounds of carbon dioxide, 24 times the weight of the finished product. This jacket left behind, on its way to Reno, two-thirds its weight in waste.

And this is a 60% recycled polyester jacket, knit and sewn to a high standard; it is exceptionally durable, so you won't have to replace it as often. And when it comes to the end of its useful life we'll take it back to recycle into a product of equal value. But, as is true of all the things we can make and you can buy, this jacket comes with an environmental cost higher than its price.

There is much to be done and plenty for us all to do. Don't buy what you don't need. Think twice before you buy anything. Go to patagonia.com/CommonThreads or scan the QR code below. Take the Common Threads Initiative pledge, and join us in the fifth "R," to reimagine a world where we take only what nature can replace.

Figure 4.2
Patagonia ad from the Black Friday edition of the *New York Times*, 2011
Source: Patagonia, "Don't Buy This Jacket, Black Friday, and the New York Times," Cleanest Line, November 25, 2011, http://www.patagonia.com/blog/2011/11/dont -buy-this-jacket-black-friday-and-the-new-york-times/ (accessed July 3, 2016).

The "fifth 'R'" that the ad refers to is "reimagine," which Patagonia champions in addition to the four other Rs: reduce, repair, reuse, and recycle. Few companies have the audacity to tell consumers to think twice about their purchase decisions and buy less. Even fewer companies explain in excruciating detail the negative environmental impact of a single product. Most intriguing is that Patagonia does not boast its industry-leading environmental and sourcing practices. Patagonia goes further still by offering to colist the used Patagonia items that customers want to sell rather than throw garments away or let them gather dust. While some critics will contend that Patagonia's famous "Buy Less" campaign was a public relations strategy and point to the increase in sales that Patagonia has achieved since placing the advertisement, Patagonia's more recent efforts suggest otherwise.

Yvon Chouinard, a rock climber and environmentalist, founded Patagonia to provide outdoor enthusiasts with technical clothing as well as create an outstanding workplace. He soon transformed the company into a pioneer in the corporate social responsibility movement by committing 10 percent of its profits or 1 percent of its sales (whichever is greater) toward environmental causes. He also helped propel the organic cotton industry in California during the 1990s after discovering how bad cotton was for the environment.[24] Turning to the social side of sustainability, Chouinard launched Patagonia's buy less campaign. In the face of increasing sales, Chouinard is taking his campaign to help curb unsustainable consumerism one step further: limiting growth.

While the buy less campaign resulted in a 30 percent increase in sales, and thereby an increase in products sold, Patagonia's next move is more aggressive. Chouinard plans to limit sales by limiting the number of products Patagonia produces—that is, Patagonia will make fewer products. In addition, Patagonia has expanded on the Common Threads initiative it references in its 2011 ad by beginning to sell *refurbished* clothing in its stores. It purchases used articles of Patagonia-produced clothing from its customers, and then repairs and sells them. After rebranding Common Threads into the new "Worn Wear" initiative, Patagonia has begun branding worn items for clothing. In an ad published in the *New York Times* during Fashion Week, Patagonia captions a torn pair of surf trunks from 1994 as "Better Than New" (see figure 4.3). The company also features Worn Wear stories on its website, encouraging people to show off their used clothes rather than new ones. To help customers refurbish their damaged articles of Patagonia

Better Than New

Patagonia® Surf Trunks from 1994

It's Fashion Week, when the design world turns its attention to what's new. We'd like to point out something better: what lasts. While we're proud of the quality and performance of Patagonia clothes, every new thing we make—everything anyone makes—costs nature more than we now know how to repay.

That's why Patagonia has chosen to celebrate our old stuff as well as our new. We've asked customers to send in photos and stories for our Worn Wear™ blog, which chronicles Patagonia clothes that have lasted for years or decades and become old friends. The Patagonia Surf Trunks from 1994 you see here belong to Christo Grayling, who has worn them paddling and surfing everywhere from India to Baja to Ecuador. They're still in use, though beat up, scratched up and altered. Fabric from a beach umbrella now makes up the rear. The missing strip at the hem serves as a patch on another pair of Patagonia shorts.

This fall we're opening Worn Wear used-clothing sections in several of our stores. Here you can find high-quality Patagonia clothes still on their way toward gaining the character to become great Worn Wear stories. It's part of our Common Threads Partnership with our customers to reduce consumption, repair what breaks, recirculate what we no longer use, recycle or repurpose what wears out, and reimagine a world where we take only what nature can replace.

patagonia

Join us at patagonia.com/commonthreads

Figure 4.3
Patagonia ad in the *New York Times* Fashion Week edition
Source: Kasey, comment on Patagonia, "Better Than New," Cleanest Line, September 10, 2013, http://www.thecleanestline.com/2013/09/better-than-new-fashion-week-new -york-times-worn-wear-patagonia-common-threads-partnership.html (accessed April 19, 2019).

clothing, Patagonia has free online manuals for fixing clothes, and it is building a repair truck to traverse the United States and refurbish damaged articles of Patagonia clothing.

Patagonia's efforts to become a sustainable company, shifting from minimizing environmental impact to improving how consumers consume, may not silence all critics. Some will still point to the profits Patagonia is earning through these efforts. But that's OK. The sustainable enterprise does not preclude profitability. It is important for sustainable companies to make money, just so long as they do so as a means rather than the penultimate goal. Many companies only pursue practices that will guarantee a financial return, falling short of their potential to maximize their positive impacts on stakeholder groups.

Increasing the rates of economic growth has long been the holy grail of conventional economics and business success. But does economic growth bring about a higher standard of living? The lessons to be learned from Patagonia are that you can improve your sustainability performance and increase the profitability of the organization by focusing on improving the experiences and needs of consumers, not only by concentrating on growth.

Action 11: Reimagine your business strategy by selling customers what they need versus what they want, and promote awareness to help customers distinguish between the two.

In the previous chapter, we presented the Triodos Bank case. Heralded as a pioneer in the sustainable banking sector, Triodos only invests in initiatives that positively impact society and present no harm. While its banking customers appreciate knowing where their money goes, which Triodos Bank publishes on a Google Maps platform, they began requesting lines of credit. This presented a challenging dilemma for Triodos, which did not want to contribute to the consumer debt crisis. Therefore, the CEO, Peter Blom, and other executives wanted to determine how they could more positively impact the lives of their customers without harming them in the long term.

The solution? Triodos decided to offer a sustainable checking account without traditional credit cards or consumer loans, but with a credit line based on the monthly income of the customer with a few exceptions for sustainable purchases such as an electric car. In this way, Triodos could extend credit to its retail customers based on their means rather than their desires. This enabled Triodos to appease its customers and expand its retail segment while avoiding the risk of propagating consumer debt.

Achieving this was not an easy feat, however. At the same time that Triodos launched its sustainable retail-banking program, a new law was passed in the Netherlands requiring Dutch banks to have one ATM for every four thousand customers. This law was extremely costly to abide by for small banks such as Triodos and others. Triodos worked with other small and medium-sized banks to lobby the European Commission to drop the law, arguing that it was discriminatory against small banks. They were successful. Nonetheless, ATM machines were an important resource for retail clients. So Triodos Bank collaborated with another sustainable bank, Rabobank, to enable its customers to use a Rabobank ATM as often as eight times per day to withdraw up to €1,500.

After various media outlets applauded Triodos for its innovative strategy in the consumer banking space, Triodos had an application volume of about six times greater than normal.

Within three years, Triodos Netherlands had opened thirty thousand checking accounts serving thirty-six thousand customers. It is crucial to note that checking accounts that cannot be linked to credit cards or consumer loans are not profitable financial products for banks. Yet they are a sustainable solution for countering the growing consumer debt crisis. They also provide an avenue for increasing the funds that go toward Triodos Bank's sustainable loans and funds. Similar to the Patagonia case, there is not always an obvious revenue stream or case for profitability associated with a particular sustainability strategy. After all, unlike Patagonia, Triodos would have been much more profitable if it offered credit cards and consumer loans. Other positive linkages, though, can happen by actively pursuing positively deviant initiatives that impact stakeholder groups. Through its sustainable checking accounts, Triodos was able to partner with another sustainable bank to make the initiative cost-effective while dramatically increasing the number of customers that could invest in its sustainable portfolio.

Action 12: Pursue sustainability strategies even if there is not an obvious business case for them.

Government

One significant measure that Triodos Bank took was to work with other banks in lobbying the European Commission to overturn the Dutch law requiring retail banks to have an ATM machine for every four thousand customers. If Triodos had not lobbied the commission, there is a strong chance that it would not have been able to introduce the sustainable checking account at all due to the steep costs required to develop only a small number of ATMs. The steep barrier of entry associated with certain sustainability initiatives sometimes makes them completely infeasible. Often the differentiating aspect between a sustainable organization and an unsustainable one is the pursuit of such initiatives. For example, in the GM case presented in chapter 3, due to the high cost point of electric vehicles, GM elected to invest millions of dollars in lobbying against the California Air Resources Board legislation that required automobile manufacturers to produce electric vehicles.[25] What if it had instead elected to lobby the US government to introduce a tax incentive for electric vehicle purchases? In fact, the US government eventually passed this legislation, providing a $7,500 tax rebate that it started issuing for electric vehicles sold beginning in 2010. If GM had opted to lobby the government for this rebate years earlier, it may have been able to achieve an even greater rebate amount, especially if the state of California offered an additional tax incentive. As the first mass producer of electric vehicles, GM would have benefited much more significantly than any other player in the space. It could also have lobbied for more public charging stations, which were eventually developed as well, to improve the infrastructure for electric vehicles. But GM chose to be on the wrong side of history and paid dearly for its decisions, along with every other GM stakeholder groups including customers, society, the environment, and future generations.

In stark contrast to GM, Triodos Bank wanted to create a new market for renewable energy in the 1990s. Along with other banks and politicians, Triodos proposed a tax break for green investments in the Netherlands to spur investment activity for wind and solar farms. Two members of Parliament in particular developed the legislation, which was heralded by the press and other key stakeholders in the Netherlands. As a result of the strong support and popularization of the green tax incentive, Parliament passed the law one year later, in 1995. Consequently, green funds became popular financial products that are now offered by a majority of banks in the Netherlands and the rest of the world.

Action 13: If there is not a business case for sustainability, promote legislation to make one.

The second case in chapter 3 explored the sustainability challenges of McDonald's, especially when entering the French market. If McDonald's wants to become a sustainable enterprise, what would it take? In the 1990s, McDonald's faced significant opposition in France from various stakeholder groups, including farmers and consumer activist organizations. Things worsened further with the 2004 documentary *Super Size Me*, in which Morgan Spurlock, the film's director, only consumes food from McDonald's for an entire month, during which he gains 24.5 pounds, reaches an LDL cholesterol level of 230 (anything above 190 is considered high), and suffers from significant mood changes and fat accumulation.[26] The results took over a year to reverse.

In light of this, McDonald's hired Jean-Pierre Petit to transform its franchises in the European markets, particularly in France. McDonald's in France is now hardly recognizable from its US counterparts. For one, the logo has been completely altered, changing the background from red to green, denoting a departure from its past. Responding to the critiques of farmers, Petit completely overhauled the purchasing and quality of beef. Today, 95 percent of the beef served at McDonald's France is purchased within France, from grass-fed (as opposed to corn-fed) cattle that are hormone free. Due to the tracking systems in France, every burger can be traced back to the cow and farm it came from.

Through the thirteen hundred franchises it operates in France, McDonald's has become the biggest purchaser of beef in the country, where a recent survey by Gira Conseil found that the new favorite food in France has become the burger. France is now the second-biggest market for McDonald's after the United States. Whereas Burger King has slowly been closing down its locations in France, McDonald's continues to expand.

Although McDonald's restaurants in the United States have made slight revisions, including offering healthier substitutes such as salads and fruit, McDonald's chains in Europe have followed the McDonald's France model more closely. McDonald's United Kingdom, for instance, uses organic semiskim milk that it sources from organic farms in Britain and Ireland in all its products, with the exception of milkshakes and ice cream. The company cites that the supply for semiskim organic milk is limited, with media reports estimating that McDonald's alone purchases 5 percent of the organic milk sold in the United Kingdom. McDonald's has gone even further with its sourcing of eggs, purchasing only free-range, cage-free eggs across all locations in the European Union.

All this being said, McDonald's still faces significant challenges on its journey toward becoming a sustainable enterprise. In addition to improving its supply chain, McDonald's may require a complete shift in the types of food that it offers to customers. While this seems far-fetched for the McDonald's brand many Americans are familiar with, it may not be implausible. The following is a comparison of ingredients used in the most commonly purchased item at McDonald's—french fries:

U.S. ingredients: Potatoes, Vegetable Oil (Canola Oil, Soybean Oil, Hydrogenated Soybean Oil, Natural Beef Flavor [Wheat and Milk Derivatives]*, Citric Acid [Preservative]), Dextrose, Sodium Acid Pyrophosphate (Maintain Color), Salt. Prepared in Vegetable Oil (Canola Oil, Corn Oil, Soybean Oil, Hydrogenated Soybean Oil with TBHQ and Citric Acid added to preserve freshness). Dimethylpolysiloxane added as an antifoaming agent. CONTAINS: WHEAT AND MILK. *Natural beef flavor contains hydrolyzed wheat and hydrolyzed milk as starting ingredients.[27]

U.K. ingredients: Potatoes, Vegetable Oil (Sunflower, Rapeseed), Dextrose (only added at beginning of the season). [The restaurants use nonhydrogenated vegetable oil.][28]

The case of McDonald's changing its french fries recipe, along with how the ingredients are sourced, shows how a company can use sustainability to redesign its products and make the company more competitive. Sustainability, or at least the pursuit toward it, has become a significant competitive advantage.

The sector as a whole is moving in a more sustainable direction, and McDonald's needs to continue its surge. McDonald's has already excised the "Super Size" option from its menus, coinciding with the release of *Super Size Me* in 2004, and introduced a variety of healthy options such as fruit and salad on its menus.

To pursue a holistic sustainability strategy, McDonald's also needs to determine how it can more positively impact other stakeholder groups. Can it begin lobbying the government to start supporting healthier food options? For instance, McDonald's has eliminated trans fat from its food offerings and can support legislation to force other companies to do the same. New York became the first city in the United States to ban trans fats in 2006 while the FDA openly declared in 2013 that it plans to do so at the national level. As of December 10, 2014, Argentina banned trans fat from all its food and estimates that the government will save US$100 million in health care costs.[29] In addition, McDonald's can brand healthier items on its menu as delicious or even warn consumers about how unhealthy various menu items are for them. The fourth stage of sustainability begins precisely at this intersection, after companies have minimized their negative impacts on stakeholders, and start developing strategies and business models to maximize their positive impacts on consumers, society at large, the government, and future generations.

Action 14: Adopt a holistic sustainability strategy that positively impacts all stakeholder groups rather than minimizing harm or only targeting specific groups.

Box 4.1 introduces the key lessons from this chapter and reiterates the actions.

Box 4.1
Sustainability Strategy: Key Lessons and Actions

• The lessons derived from both companies—TOMS and Warby Parker—is that the social contribution of organizations should not be an afterthought but rather a core aspect of a sustainable business model. This is what distinguishes them from companies that engage in philanthropy. This is not to discount philanthropic practices but instead to challenge companies to determine how they can integrate societal causes within their business strategies. For instance, a computer company can focus on developing products to meet the societal needs of underprivileged and marginalized communities versus solely donating money toward causes that alleviate such conditions.

Action 9: Incorporate societal contribution into the core business strategy as opposed to treating it as an afterthought.

• To benefit suppliers, an organization's focus should not be limited to increasing the value in the value chain; instead, it should concentrate on capturing the added value and equitably distributing it across the value chain—with a greater emphasis needed at the beginning of the value chain.

- The argan oil case shows that one way to increase the value to the members of the supply chain is to empower producers and other actors to take on greater responsibility while eliminating transactional actors who do not create substantial value.

Action 10: Eliminate unnecessary middlepersons to ensure value is appropriately distributed in value chains while empowering important actors.

- As seen in the case of Patagonia, an organization can develop sustainable products and services by shifting its definition of success from "growth" to the "satisfaction of social needs."

Action 11: Reimagine your business strategy by selling customers what they need versus what they want, and promote awareness to help customers distinguish between the two.

- The Triodos and Patagonia cases show that organizations engage consumers when they authentically pursue positive initiatives. Triodos created a new type of sustainable checking account, while Patagonia created a buy less campaign—both aimed at curbing consumerism and creating more responsible customers. They did so with complete transparency of their rationale and before there was an obvious business model behind either. Many organizations have to make the leap to the sustainable enterprise, the fourth stage of sustainability, before developing business cases behind them—but stakeholders, like consumers, tend to rally behind them.

Action 12: Pursue sustainability strategies even if there is not an obvious business case for them.

- Sustainability strategies cannot always be profitable; sometimes they require assistance from other parties, such as legislators. Companies attempting to meet social needs will often have similar objectives as government organizations, as demonstrated by the Triodos Bank case. Triodos was therefore able to leverage this common goal by proposing a strong strategy that helped all stakeholders.

Action 13: If there is not a business case for sustainability, promote legislation to make one.

- The case of McDonald's in France provides an important lesson. By acknowledging that some of its products can contribute to increasing the cholesterol levels of its customers, the company moved forward in its sustainability journey by redesigning its products to positively impact the well-being of its customers and aligning with society's sustainability demands for healthier products, which in turn is making McDonald's more profitable.

Action 14: Adopt a holistic sustainability strategy that positively impacts all stakeholder groups rather than minimizing harm or only targeting specific groups.

Developing a sustainability strategy is a challenging task, especially for existing companies that need to transform or shift away from the current strategies in place. Even more challenging, however, is actually implementing that sustainability strategy. Sustainability leaders quickly discover that putting a sustainability strategy into practice does not simply reside at the leadership or even organizational level. Moreover, it extends to the stakeholder network to which an organization belongs. Engaging stakeholders, then, is paramount to implementing a sustainability strategy and making it happen.

Before moving on to the next chapter, we encourage you to attempt to solve the following two cases that highlight the challenges of implementing sustainability strategies in companies.

Case 1: Panera Bread

Originally named St. Louis Bread (which is still the case in St. Louis), Panera Bread was purchased in 1993 by Au Bon Pain, a Boston-based company founded by Ron Shaich. Beginning in 1999, Panera Bread began expanding across the United States, achieving approximately eighteen hundred stores in forty states and a market capitalization of $4.6 billion as of February 2014. As a fast-casual restaurant, Panera Bread was a pioneer in the fast-food industry for providing customers with healthy food options, ranking first in Zagat's 2009 rankings for the "Best Healthy Option" and "Best Salads" categories.[30] In 2010, Panera became one of the first national US restaurant chains to post calorie information for each of its options at every location.[31]

Despite his company's rapid growth and expansion, Shaich realized that not everyone could necessarily afford the healthy meals that Panera sold. This problem was further exacerbated by the financial crisis in 2007–2008. In 2009, Shaich began brainstorming how Panera could develop a nonprofit called Panera Cares to assist with the growing lack of affordability for healthy food options. While Panera could dedicate a significant portion of its revenues to supply food for those less fortunate, Shaich was convinced his efforts would go a lot further if he could somehow engage stakeholders and particularly customers. If you were Shaich, what would you propose to the board of Panera?

Case 2: Triodos Bank

As discussed earlier in this chapter, Triodos Bank is a pioneer in the sustainable banking sector. Despite the bank's strong mission from the outset and a best-in-class sustainable strategy, its employees have been particularly helpful in upholding Triodos's sustainability mission and practices. An early challenge that Triodos Bank faced was how to reward its employees and specifically its bankers. In the financial services industry, employees are rewarded with large bonuses at the end of every year. These bonuses are tied directly with an employee's performance, particularly the amount of money they earn for their bank. According to the New York State Comptroller's Office, executives on Wall Street earned $23.9 billion in bonuses in 2006.[32] Bonuses were largely blamed as a factor that propagated the global financial crisis, as "Wall Street traders were thinking of the bonus at the end of the year, not the long-term health of their firm," according to Larry Tabb, the founder of the TABB Group.[33]

There is a critical lesson to be learned from the Triodos case: performance is not based on how much money an employee earns for a firm; instead, it is focused on how well the employee helped the company achieve its sustainability mission. As a sustainability mission is assessed over the long term and largely measured through nonfinancial indicators, Blom and other executives were trying to determine how to engage employees at Triodos Bank. If you were Blom, how would you motivate and incentivize employees at Triodos?

5 Implementing Sustainability Strategy: How Can You Engage Your Stakeholders for Maximum Impact?

As we discussed in chapter 4, sustainable organizations are those that positively impact all stakeholder groups. Richard Freeman formalized the notion of stakeholders in 1984 in an attempt to extend the bounds of responsibility that firms had to society. Freeman argued that firms were required to go beyond maintaining compliance with the law and had a social responsibility to their stakeholders. He defined stakeholders as "any group or individual who can affect or is affected by the achievement of the firm's objectives."[1] Through this framework, Freeman was able to propose a better perspective for firms and their relationships with various stakeholders.

Yet it is not always obvious how organizations can impact all stakeholders positively, or how they can maximize this impact. In fact, it is not uncommon for organizations to antagonize certain stakeholder groups while completely ignoring others. In this chapter, we implore organizations to engage with their stakeholders. Organizations can become sustainable only by interacting with their stakeholders to understand and respond to their needs. By harnessing stakeholder input, organizations can focus on what is important to them and thus strengthen their sustainability strategies. Take, for example, the Mexican multinational Gruma, the global leader in corn and flour tortilla production. Gruma adopted a sustainability program centered on the health of its customers. Accordingly, it engaged with nutrition organizations that suggested Gruma develop a fat-free tortilla in order to contribute to reducing the growth of obesity among its customers. Gruma then developed the 98 percent fat-free and 0 percent cholesterol "baked tortilla." This initiative was a risky undertaking for Gruma because it changed the flavor of the product, which could have resulted in customer rejection. The product, however, became a market success because customers rewarded the company by buying it due to its healthier implications.[2]

Perhaps the most significant barrier that hinders stakeholder engagement is the varying degrees of importance that organizations place on different stakeholder groups. One of the most notable distinctions is that of a primary stakeholder versus a secondary one. Namely, primary stakeholders are those who are directly tied to an organization through financial transactions. These include shareholders, managers, employees, customers, and suppliers. Secondary stakeholders, on the other hand, include those indirectly impacted by or have an impact on an organization. These include the environment, society at large, and the communities connected to primary stakeholders. The current prioritization of stakeholder groups is further tiered than the traditional two-group characterization implies. As depicted in figure 5.1, most organizations prioritize primary over secondary stakeholders, but they make further distinctions within each category.

Our first contribution to the stakeholder engagement dialogue is to prioritize all stakeholders equally. Moreover, there should not be a distinction between the attention given to primary and secondary stakeholders, or between stakeholders within each grouping. Despite not sharing direct financial ties, secondary stakeholders have the same stake in an organization as do primary stakeholders. Stakeholder theory also is based on the premise that it is not a financial interest that gives a group a stake in an organization; instead, it is the sum of various impacts between the group and organization. By making all stakeholders equitable, a firm's financial objectives will not be achieved at the expense of a firm's societal and environmental objectives. Thus, the first and most important element of stakeholder engagement is making all stakeholder groups equitable in the eyes of the firm. The next step is to develop a process to interact with each stakeholder. This could be in the form of a dialogue, participation in the stakeholders' initiatives, or by working with the stakeholders of your stakeholders. This could be a dialogue organized by the firm, or the firm participating in the activities of other stakeholders. For example, one of the coauthors, Francisco Szekely, in his role at the Ministry of Natural Resources and Environment of the federal government of Mexico, where he was responsible for Mexico's sustainability agenda, identified the private sector as one of the ministry's key stakeholders that needed to be fully engaged for the successful implementation of the sustainability agenda. More specifically, local and international companies working in water

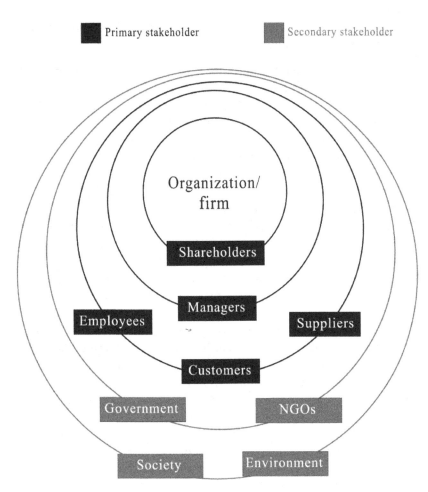

Primary stakeholder   Secondary stakeholder

Organization/
firm

Shareholders

Managers

Employees   Suppliers

Customers

Government   NGOs

Society   Environment

Figure 5.1
Traditional characterization of stakeholder groups

supply as well as water treatment and sanitation had to be involved.
As government authorities called for a dialogue with these and other
stakeholders, it became clear that the government had to participate in
initiatives led by the private sector in which companies were making
their own plans and partnerships to develop their business strategies
with the participation of their own stakeholders. By participating in the
water companies' initiatives, the Ministry of Natural Resources and the
Environment could establish connections with farmers' associations
that were working with technical company experts on issues of water
conservation.

Action 15: Identify the interests and needs of all your stakeholders, and pay equal attention to them.

Before understanding the interests of an organization's stakeholders, however, it is first important to identify who an organization's stakeholders are. Executives should spend a significant amount of time understanding the full gamut of stakeholders that belong to their company's ecosystem. While we focus extensively on stakeholders impacted by the supply chains of organizations, which often leave a longer trail of impact than organizations realize, it is also crucial to look at the end users of your products and beyond. A whole host of companies, for instance, have been able to expand to new markets due to the unintended use of their products. Many of these expansions have been largely positive.[3] In other examples, Play-Doh, a putty that can be molded into different shapes, was originally designed to clean wallpaper. Text messages, which dominate the way we communicate today, were initially designed solely for telephone carriers to communicate network problems to customers. And Rogaine, which aids hair growth to prevent balding, was invented to treat high blood pressure. As there are a number of other products that have resulted in unintended consequences, though, companies should make sure that they understand how their products are impacting society.

One case in point is lead paint. Although lead is an element that can be found in the air, water, food, and soil, a high concentration inside the body can be extremely harmful. Although the toxicity of lead has been known for over a century, the ban of paint containing more than 0.06 percent of lead was not put in place in the United States until 1978. Furthermore, the most common victims of lead poisoning were not workers applying the paint but rather children, who would ingest paint chips based on their sweet taste. Therefore, Louis Wade Sullivan, the secretary of the US Department of Health and Human Services, stated that lead was "the number one environmental threat to the health of children in the United States."[4] As such, various paint companies, including Sherwin-Williams, have had to pay for the cleanup and retrofitting of places painted with lead paint. Their damages to a key stakeholder constituent, which were unbeknownst to them at the time, cannot be recuperated.

Another illustration is DDT. Discovered by Paul Herman Müller in 1939, DDT was extremely effective during World War II in controlling malaria and typhus. Müller was awarded the Nobel Prize for his discovery. But as described in the first chapter, once DDT became repurposed as an insecticide that farmers used for spraying large areas, there were many harmful impacts on wildlife populations and humans. When Müller launched DDT, he was not aware that his product had unintended stakeholders such as people, wildlife, and other living and nonliving elements of the natural environment. This suggests that it is essential for companies to thoroughly think through who or what their stakeholders are, and who or what their future stakeholders are likely to be. Rachel Carson exposed the impact of DDT on nature in her famous and passionate 1962 publication, *Silent Spring*.

There are countless other implications in other sectors, including weapons (which should never be in the hands of children or the mentally handicapped but frequently are) or even alcohol (with the dangerous effects it can have on newborn children if ingested during pregnancy). Not all the unintended consequences of an organization's impacts are obvious initially. Some take many years to manifest. For instance, when automobile companies in China were developing, they may not have realized how much smog and pollution their vehicles would contribute because they were unable to predict how many vehicles would be sold. The Chinese automobile market has increased 500 percent in the last ten years. In 2004, China was selling 5 million passenger and commercial vehicles.[5] By 2015, the numbers of vehicles sold in China was 24.6 million.[6] This number is equivalent to the vehicles that all the countries in the European Union and Japan consume together in one year.[7] Any picture of a congested Chinese city highlights the impacts of automobile manufacturers on stakeholder groups. These stakeholder groups include, at the local level, bicycle commuters, pedestrians, and the public. The stakeholders, however, extend far beyond their customers and other groups that automobile manufacturers may have originally accounted for. The CO_2 generated by this elevated number of vehicles has a global impact on climate change, making every citizen on the planet and the natural environment a stakeholder of Chinese automakers. If the Chinese manufacturers had thought more about their stakeholders, they could have pursued vehicles that are more efficient or introduced electric fleets. The presence of these new stakeholder groups also demonstrates how the stakeholders of an organization are not static, and that an organization's stakeholder network increases as an organization expands—and it often expands at a much faster pace.

It is thus important for organizations to identify the various intended and unintended stakeholders that they impact, both at present and in the future, to begin meaningful collaborations. They need to be specific and deliberate in this process so that they can prepare for strong, healthy relationships in the future.

Action 16: Know thy stakeholders; identify every current, primary, and secondary stakeholder group, and anticipate future stakeholder ones.

To determine the needs of stakeholders, it is important to *get close* to your stakeholders and create open forums for dialogue with them. As companies scale, it is easy to lose track of the various groups that constitute the stakeholder system of an organization. Bureaucracy and efficiency frequently dictate the types of relationships that managers have with various stakeholder segments rather than sustainability objectives. This was sadly learned the hard way on April 24, 2013, in Dhaka, Bangladesh, when an eight-story commercial building, Rana Plaza, collapsed, killing 1,129 people.[8] It was the deadliest accident in the history of the garment sector. The building, which had been purposely built for shops and offices, was not designed for the rigors of the many factories it housed. In addition, there was no permit for the upper four floors of the building. A news story featured the day before the accident revealed cracks in the structure, causing a building-wide evacuation. There were 122 unions in Bangladesh's garment industry in 2012. The unions, which represented the interests of workers—a critical stakeholder for the companies that had garment factories in Rana Plaza—had voiced their concerns to the company owners about the unsafe building conditions. The companies unfortunately ignored the warnings, and informed employees that the building was safe and it was all right to return to work the following day.[9] Some employees were even threatened with the loss of a month's pay if they did not come to work.[10] On the day of the collapse, there was a power outage in the grid. Diesel generators that were started on the top floor to provide electricity are cited as the probable source of the collapse.

The garment factories in Rana Plaza produced apparel for many famous brands including Walmart, Mango, United Colors of Benetton, Bonmarché, the Children's Place, Joe Fresh, Matalan, El Corte Inglés, Monsoon Accessorize, and Primark. Most, if not all, had never heard of Rana Plaza until April 24, 2013. If any of them had, consistent dialogues with employees or managers could have alerted them to the building safety issues and workplace environment. Unfortunately, this is not the first time that such an incident has occurred. In 2005, a factory that produced garments for Zara collapsed and killed sixty-four workers. In fact, estimates suggest that a majority of the three thousand garment factories in Bangladesh have structural issues.[11] While companies have begun to sign various agreements to ensure the structural integrity of buildings, there is a vast variety of issues that harm stakeholders.

The overwhelming majority of companies rely on corporate social responsibility reports to identify various issues, develop key performance indicators (KPIs) to measure them, and then track performance. Indeed, most of the companies that were affiliated with the Dhaka tragedy were guilty of this. This is a mistake, though, and evidently a deadly one. Corporate social responsibility reports only serve as a one-direction communication system. Instead, companies need to get closer to stakeholders and actually hear what they have to say. Before attempting to measure performance, companies need to listen to stakeholders to understand what it is that they should be measuring.

Action 17: Get closer to your stakeholders and listen to what they have to say.

Companies are largely unaware of all the impacts their actions have on stakeholders. In the case of the garment industry in Bangladesh, purchasing companies knew who their suppliers were, but they developed bureaucratic structures to manage them and failed to see all the impacts they were having on stakeholders. While some may argue that the large fashion brands were not directly affecting stakeholders, the indirect impacts of a company's actions are often the most detrimental to society. Engaging with these stakeholders is paramount to understanding what the actual impacts of your organization are, and how it can best serve the needs of the organizations, communities, and environments it affects.

On March 17, 2010, Greenpeace launched one of its most viral campaigns to date against Nestlé for its palm oil sourcing. Moreover, one of Nestlé's palm oil suppliers in Indonesia, Sinar Mas, had been accused of deforesting areas that supported a diminishing orangutan population. Prior to noon on March 17, a "stay tuned" message was posted along with a countdown. When the clock struck 12:00, Greenpeace released a horrific one-minute video. An office worker was depicted opening a Kit Kat package to find a chocolate-covered orangutan finger, which he proceeded to eat as blood poured out. The segment ends by showing an entire orangutan habitat being deforested and then offers a call to action: "Give the orangutan a break. Stop Nestlé buying palm oil from companies that destroy the rainforests."[12] The video became a viral sensation and was supplemented by social media campaigns, which too quickly spread.

Despite a sweeping policy that Nestlé had passed prior to Greenpeace's campaign, the company had failed to inspect all its suppliers properly. Most important, however, was Nestlé's failed response to Greenpeace. Rather than opening up a dialogue to determine how it could ameliorate the situation and improve its impacts, Nestlé requested that Greenpeace's video be removed from YouTube and attempted to eliminate the movement on social media channels. The manager of Nestlé's Facebook page was also combative with the people who posted comments rather than engaging in constructive dialogue. This first response thus led to the campaign going increasingly viral as Greenpeace spread its message through social media channels and in physical spaces. Indeed, activists dressed up in orangutan outfits to protest outside Nestlé's annual meeting on April 15, 2010, and even hid in the ceiling of Nestlé's boardroom to drop down on board members as they convened.

Greenpeace's measures were obviously extreme, but Nestlé's response merely intensified the backlash. It was only when Nestlé agreed to sit down at a table with key stakeholders that real progress was made, and both financial and nonfinancial objectives were achieved. After realizing the futility of trying to control the social media conversation, Nestlé stopped sourcing palm oil from Sinar Mas and actually discussed its supply chain for palm oil with Greenpeace. To help certify its palm oil suppliers and ensure sustainable practices, Nestlé partnered with Tropical Forest Trust and joined the Roundtable for Sustainable Palm Oil to work with other companies and organizations. As of 2013, Nestlé has sourced 100 percent of its palm oil from roundtable-certified suppliers and has engaged directly with 90 percent of its palm oil suppliers.[13]

Action 18: Create a forum for dialogue with stakeholders rather than attempting to silence them.

Building on the notion of empowering stakeholders, giving stakeholders a voice is perhaps one of the most important ways companies can engage with them. While not-for-profit organizations frequently pursue this, organizations themselves are typically the closest to these stakeholders and are ideally positioned to do so, but it is not often in their financial interests. There are some stakeholders, such as the garment workers in Bangladesh, that companies would rather not know about because it is in their financial interests to turn a blind eye.

Shell began exploring for oil reserves in Nigeria in 1937 and exporting oil from the Niger Delta in 1958. The Shell Petroleum Development Company of Nigeria operates the government-owned endeavor, thereby returning a significant amount of profits to the Nigerian government through royalties (95 percent of profits) and taxes.[14] Due to rampant corruption in Nigeria, however, little of this revenue is distributed among the local populations. The Nigerian locals, who reside on the land and are impacted most significantly by the frequent oil spills caused by sabotaged pipelines, started to demand a more equitable value distribution.

The tensions escalated in 1993 when the Movement for the Survival of the Ogoni People (MOSOP) mobilized large protests against Shell and the Nigerian government. Approximately three hundred thousand people, or more than half of the Ogoni population, were involved in peaceful marches that drew international attention. The Nigerian military began occupying the region, leading to various raids and deaths. Many of the MOSOP leadership were imprisoned and sentenced to death, including the prominent Ken Saro-Wiwa.

Unfortunately, this story does not have a happy ending. An international spotlight continues to follow Shell's actions during the crisis, arguing that it ignored or even contributed to the disintegration of MOSOP along with the deaths of its leadership. Problems continue to occur with Shell, which frequently has to decrease or halt its oil production in the region as local groups siphon oil from pipelines or intentionally sabotage them. In addition to the economic losses, the oil that is spilled has severe environmental impacts. Numerous counts of corruption have also been lobbied against Shell. There were a number of stakeholders that Shell had in Nigeria including the Nigeria government, local government of the Niger Delta, local Ongi population, and natural environment, which was affected by Shell's oil operations but lacked a representative to defend its interest. We call this the *silent stakeholder*. The lack of effective dialogue between Shell and local populations continues to leave the region in turmoil. It also hinders Shell's alliances with other key stakeholders. A recent campaign launched by Greenpeace targeted LEGO's partnership with Shell through a viral video that satires *The Lego Movie*.[15] Greenpeace highlights a LEGO-based world that is destroyed by oil, accompanied by a cover of its theme song. LEGO, which had embarked on Shell-branded LEGO Kits, abolished its partnership with Shell.

Action 19: Give silent stakeholders a voice and engage in effective dialogue to determine how all parties can improve their well-being.

One of the biggest impediments to engaging with stakeholders is the underlying prerogative to engage in financially beneficial relationships. Therefore, many stakeholders are ignored and others silenced in this effort. The impetus to engage with stakeholders must be to improve sustainability performance. Giving stakeholders a voice is the first step. Responding is the next. McDonald's has risen to the occasion after significant public relations issues with a variety of stakeholders. In 2001, the US Department of Agriculture approved the limited use of lean, finely textured beef. Coined *pink slime*, lean and finely texture beef is a filler product that helps reduce the overall fat content of lean beef. It is banned in the European Union. Renowned chef Jamie Oliver ran a fantastic feature about lean beef trimmings as a part of his hit series and food education movement, *Food Revolution*.[16] In the episode, Oliver brought in a live stunt cow to demonstrate the choice cuts of meat and then revealed where the contents for lean beef trimmings are located. Thankfully, Oliver leaves Scarlet the cow unharmed, but he does show how fat is separated from these trimmings in large centrifuges, before treating the meat with an ammonia solution to kill off bacteria. The meat is then finely ground—hence the nickname pink slime.

After a news segment by ABC argued that 70 percent of ground beef sold in the United States contains pink slime, many people began looking to McDonald's, which had ammonia-treated meat.[17] The news naturally went viral, prompting various stakeholder groups to begin smear campaigns against McDonald's, which experienced rapidly declining sales to millennials. McDonald's stopped using pink slime in its beef patties and started a dialogue with its stakeholders by launching "Our food. Your questions"—a unique social media campaign that fields questions from its stakeholders and provides answers.

Based on its popularity in the United States, Canada, and Australia, McDonald's has launched a webisode series in which it goes behind the scenes with Grant Imahara, a former host of the hit series *Myth-Busters* on the Discovery Channel, to investigate and discover the answers to many questions. Perhaps one of the most popular questions raised in the campaign was, "Do you use so-called 'pink slime' in your burgers or beef treated with ammonia?" McDonald's response was, "Nope. Our beef patties are made from 100% pure beef. Nothing else is added. No fillers, extenders or so-called 'pink slime.' Some consumers may be familiar with the practice of using lean finely textured beef sometimes treated with ammonia, which is referred to by some as 'pink slime.' We do not use this."[18]

In addition, McDonald's featured a webisode dedicated to this question, revealing the entire assembly line used to make its beef patties.[19] It was a risky move, as the mass production of beef is by no means entirely flattering. The mixed reviews and comments, which have been enabled in an effort to keep stakeholders engaged, underscore this. Nonetheless, Imahara confirms that only choice trimmings are used with no fillers, additives, or preservatives injected into the production line at any point.

Not all companies have to wait for stakeholders to raise pressure before creating dialogues with them. In fact, many companies like to promote what sets their production lines apart to their customers. For instance, Ben & Jerry's, a US-based ice cream company that sources all its milk from local, hormone-free cows, invites the public to tour its manufacturing facility in Vermont. This openness encourages a platform for discussion while ensuring that stakeholders can see the entire process and have their questions answered. Although many companies are unable to invite stakeholders to their shop floors, some can learn from BMW's latest move of providing footage of its actual vehicles being made.[20]

Action 20: Create platforms and processes to show as well as tell stakeholders what they want to know.

A significant theme in this chapter has been the notion of engaging with stakeholders by empowering them—particularly stakeholders that are being negatively impacted by organizations or lack a voice. Sustainable organizations, though, can often hold similar values, beliefs, and agendas as their stakeholders. In these instances, empowering stakeholders can represent something different—for example, organizations can help stakeholders by collaborating with them to achieve a sustainability mission. TOMS shoes and Warby Parker (social enterprises introduced in the previous chapter) are illustrations here. Customers of both companies enjoy seeing the money from their purchases provide shoes and glasses, respectively, to the underprivileged. Panera Bread developed an even tighter collaboration through its not-for-profit initiative Panera Cares.

Introduced in the first case challenge at the end of chapter 4, Ron Shaich, the CEO of Panera Bread, was attempting to launch a nonprofit initiative in 2009 to respond to the problem of food security. Rather than rely on Panera Bread's efforts alone, Shaich was inspired by the SAME Café in Colorado to engage with Panera's existing customers and mobilize them. The SAME Café is an acronym for "So All May Eat" and offers a *pay-what-you-can* business model whereby patrons pay, in the form of a donation, however much they feel is appropriate for their meal. Founded by Brad and Libby Birky, who themselves were inspired by the One World Café in Salt Lake City that had adopted a similar model, the SAME Café espouses its motto of "serving good food for the greater good."[21]

Shaich implemented Panera Cares to engage with customers and make healthy food accessible to all. Beginning with one location in 2010, there are now five community cafés across the United States. All menu items have suggested donation amounts that inform customers of the cost to keep the initiative in place. These amounts incorporate the cost of the meal and amount paid forward to those who cannot afford one. Similar to SAME and One World, guests who are unable to afford a meal can receive a meal voucher by volunteering for an hour at the café.

The five cafés have been tremendous successes, serving one million people every year.[22] Each Panera Cares community café generates enough revenues to pay for its operating costs and meals served. Rather than donating food to the underprivileged, Shaich was able to engage and collaborate with stakeholders through actual platforms (community cafés) to achieve a sustainability mission. Other organizations can borrow this process and discover ways to collaborate with stakeholders in order to achieve common goals.

Action 21: Collaborate with stakeholders to achieve social objectives.

The pay-what-you-can business model highlights an important distinction between the two types of motivation that organizations can use to engage with stakeholders. Moreover, Panera Cares discovered that approximately 60 percent of people donate the suggested amount for each meal, and 15 to 20 percent of patrons leave more than the suggested amount, so that 20 to 25 percent of people do not need to donate.[23] While each of these populations receives a meal, they are driven to support the cause through an intrinsic versus extrinsic motivation. But how effective can intrinsic motivation be when engaging with stakeholders?

The second case in the end of chapter 4 introduced the challenge of rewarding employees based on how they contributed to Triodos Bank's sustainable performance. While financial performance and an employee's contribution toward it were fairly easy to measure (especially in the short term), sustainability performance (as is explored in the next chapter) remains largely elusive. Yet the financial services sector in particular emphasizes annual bonuses tied to an employee's performance in terms of how much money they earn for the firm.

Despite the ambiguity of sustainable performance, many companies are beginning to engage and motivate employees by tying their salaries and bonuses to various sustainability KPIs. This is particularly true for executives; in fact, a joint study in 2013 revealed that 43 percent of Fortune 500 companies base executive pay on sustainable performance.[24] Companies that engage employees around sustainability goals through monetary compensation include Caterpillar, DSM, Intel, and Shell.[25] But is extrinsic motivation the most effective way to engage employees and executives in a company's sustainability agenda? The next chapter demonstrates the difficulty in quantifying sustainability performance. Normalizing it as well as determining how each employee and executive contributed to it is an even more arduous task.

Triodos adopted an alternative approach to engage employees by opting to eliminate bonuses altogether. Taking a step back, Triodos Bank's leadership decided that if sustainability was at the core of its organization, it would hire employees who were dedicated to achieving sustainable best practices in the financial sector. The hiring process thus seeks to identify employees who are committed to and driven by Triodos's mission. Indeed, when interviewing a business school graduate, we discovered that he chose not to apply to Triodos Bank because it was "too sustainable" for him. To ensure competitive wages, Triodos pays higher up-front salaries to its employees and has eliminated bonuses altogether. The bank focuses on intrinsically motivating its employees to engage them around its sustainability agenda. Companies should not underestimate the power of intrinsic motivation, especially for employees who value things other than money and financial returns.[26]

The relationship between stakeholder engagement and a company's mission has been studied over the last eighty-five years. In the 1930s, George Gallup started a worldwide study of human needs and satisfactions, and developed a scientific process to measure people's views. In 1997, the Gallup Organization conducted a meta-analysis to examine the relationship of employee satisfaction and engagement (as measured by twelve key questions, or Q^{12}) to business or work unit profitability, productivity, employee retention, and customer satisfaction/loyalty across 1,135 business units.[27] This meta-analysis also enabled researchers to look at the generalizability of the relationship between engagement and outcomes. Since its final wording and order were completed in 1998, Q^{12} has been administered to more than seven million employees in 112 different countries.[28] The purpose of one question asked of employees was to determine whether the extent to which they are engaged at work is related to the mission or purpose of the company, and if this mission makes them feel that their job is important. In conducting a meta-analysis of 49,928 business units across 192 organizations representing 49 different industries in 34 countries, Gallup scientists discovered that "margin and mission are not at odds with one another at all. In fact, the opposite is true. As employees move beyond the basics of employee engagement and view their contribution to the organization more broadly, they are more likely to stay, take proactive steps to create a safe environment, have higher productivity, and connect with customers to the benefit of the organization."[29]

Action 22: Use the mission of your company to motivate and engage employees as well as achieve higher productivity in your organization.

This chapter introduces a number of key lessens and describes a variety of actions to engage stakeholders, as enumerated in box 5.1 for your convenience. As stressed in this chapter, companies cannot drive sustainability agendas internally; they need to look outward for stakeholder engagement to not only implement sustainable practices but also understand what precisely to implement.

The next step for companies on the sustainability journey is to begin measuring progress. As referenced various times in this chapter, it is difficult to determine how well an organization is meeting stakeholder

Box 5.1
Implementing Sustainability Strategy: Key Lessons and Actions

• As Szekely's interactions with the Mexican ministry demonstrate, prioritizing all stakeholders on the same playing field, including silent or "weak" ones, can help ensure that the needs of all stakeholders are met rather than just the more powerful or weak ones.

Action 15: Identify the interests and needs of all your stakeholders, and pay equal attention to them.

• The first step in stakeholder engagement is to map your primary and secondary stakeholders, and then focus on their needs today and for the future. Gruma is a good example of how an organization can join its stakeholders in its quest for a healthier society.

Action 16: Know thy stakeholders; identify every current, primary, and secondary stakeholder group, and anticipate future stakeholder ones.

• Organizations need to have ongoing dialogues with their stakeholders. The dialogues should focus on discovering the needs, perceptions, and concerns of the stakeholders about the activities of the organization along with its products and services. Conducting these dialogues on a frequent basis reduces the risk of potential conflicts between organizations and stakeholders.

Action 17: Get closer to your stakeholders and listen to what they have to say.

• The case of palm oil and Nestlé shows that it is critical for an organization to engage with its stakeholders, even those who may seem adversarial. While Nestlé felt it was a "small player" in terms of the global consumption of palm oil and looked toward ignoring the implications, it proved to be much more productive to create a meaningful dialogue with stakeholders.

Action 18: Create a forum for dialogue with stakeholders rather than attempting to silence them.

• Not all stakeholders have a voice or can interact with organizations to represent their interest. Such is the case with nature and future generations, which we call silent stakeholders. The organization needs to ask what would these silent stakeholders expect from our actions and how can we satisfy their needs.

Action 19: Give silent stakeholders a voice and engage in effective dialogue to determine how all parties can improve their well-being.

• An effective and vigorous stakeholder engagement can only take place when the attitude of the organization is to share information and be transparent. The Ben & Jerry's and BMW cases clearly make this point. In addition, by asking stakeholders what they want to know, organizations can harness this input to strengthen their sustainability strategies by focusing on what is important and the necessary details of interest to customers.

Action 20: Create platforms and processes to show as well as tell stakeholders what they want to know.

• The Panera Cares case provides an important lesson. There is a benefit organizations derive from engaging with stakeholders who are interested in companies that have a social orientation. By doing so Panera could develop a new business model to make healthy food accessible not only for its customers but also for people who cannot afford to access the organization's products.

Action 21: Collaborate with stakeholders to achieve social objectives.

• One way to achieve internal stakeholder engagement is by having a strong sustainability-oriented mission for the company that will make employees feel like they are working for an organization that is having a positive impact on society.

• Stakeholder alignment takes place when the values of the stakeholders are fully engaged and the organization commits to a strategy that reflects those values. Triodos Bank adopted an alternative approach to promote internal stakeholder engagement by changing its hiring focus from offering only economic incentives to offering work for the values of the organization. Triodos looked for people who were passionate about and committed to achieving sustainable best practices in the financial sector. This case also reiterates the crucial role that a sustainable mission plays in stakeholder engagement. A company's mission defines what a business stands for—its purpose and the reasons for its existence. The mission states what a company seeks to make in the world. A strong sustainability mission—such as in the Triodos case—achieves stakeholder engagement by the people it attracts.

Action 22: Use the mission of your company to motivate and engage employees as well as achieve higher productivity in your organization.

needs and sustainability goals without being able to measure sustainability performance. The following two cases help elucidate the challenges of measuring sustainability performance, which are addressed in the following chapter.

Case 1: Coca-Cola

Coca-Cola reentered India in the 1990s and has faced significant stakeholder pressure since, particularly in the 2000s, surrounding its water use. In March 2004, officials in the Kerala state of India closed a Coke bottling plant after complaints that Coca-Cola's intense water use greatly decreased the amount available to local farmers drawing from the same water table. Local communities also contended that the quality of the water had deteriorated significantly because of Coca-Cola's operations. A court-ordered scientific study a year later confirmed many of these concerns. Other regions in India have complained of the damage that Coca-Cola has caused to groundwater systems, too, with Indian authorities declaring certain water supplies as overexploited.[30] Consequently, Coca-Cola has been forced to close other bottling plants.

To respond to the crisis in India and other areas around the world where Coca-Cola has been negatively impacting important stakeholders, the company has launched a sustainability program to reduce its environmental footprint while improving the health and well-being of one billion people. This is a tremendous undertaking for the beverage giant. Is it enough? If so, which KPIs should it develop and track? If not, what else should Coca-Cola do? Finally, how should Coca-Cola communicate its performance?

Case 2: Nike

In this chapter, we discussed the garment factory tragedy in Bangladesh. Even if the building had not collapsed, what were the working conditions for the garment workers? Oftentimes, employees toil in extremely poor environments that lack air-conditioning and suffer from poor lighting. This issue was brought to the global stage in the 1990s when various not-for-profit and advocacy organizations targeted Nike's overseas production facilities, referring to them as sweatshops.

Nike's initial response was similar to those affiliated with the garment factory in Bangladesh: it does not own the factories and is not responsible for them. Others defended Nike's practices, maintaining that workers were not forced to work and were satisfied with their employment; otherwise, they would not have shown up to work every day. Nonetheless, most organizations argued that the work was exploitative, and workers deserved better conditions and salaries. Consequently, various protests occurred, from colleges to Nike stores, as a greater percentage of the public became aware of Nike's supply chain. In response, Nike launched its SHAPE program, which stands for safety, health, attitude, people, and environment. The initiative has been met with success, as Nike was able to improve working conditions and simultaneously realize greater profitability through the improved workspaces it had established.

Some of Nike's competitors, though, including PUMA and adidas, have long-standing corporate social responsibility programs and are pushing the industry further. If you were Mark Parker, the CEO of Nike, how would you measure Nike's sustainability performance? Would you maintain the SHAPE framework or expand it?

6 Measuring Sustainability Performance: How Do You Measure Nonfinancial Performance?

Business has adopted a simple and pragmatic principle: What gets measured gets done.

Measuring sustainability performance is of paramount importance for organizations that want to assess their progress on their sustainability initiatives. Nevertheless, the task of measuring sustainability is complex, mainly because the firm's actions have diverse impacts; for instance, they impact the economy, ability of ecosystems to absorb change, and well-being of society. Added to this complexity is the fact that the firm's impacts are measured in different units that often cannot be compared or aggregated. For example, measuring the footprint of a firm that pollutes the air—measured in tons of CO_2—and sends toxic waste to the landfill—measured in tons of waste—measures the size of the externality, but it says little about what effect that footprint has on people's health, the productivity of the land, or the quality of the groundwater located near the landfill. Similarly, measuring the impact that the use of asbestos in residential housing has on human health, or that the extinction of a species has on the biodiversity of a geographic area, cannot be easily measured, compared, or aggregated into one single measurement. Due to the complexity of measuring sustainability performance, many organizations have started to measure their yearly success in reducing their footprint, their improvement in resource use efficiency, and their ability to diminish the waste they produce, and then reporting on these improvements. For the past twenty years, sustainability reporting has become synonymous with sustainability performance measurement. Through the GRI and TBL approach, most organizations take sustainability reporting for granted, assuming their sustainability performance can be measured mainly by reporting on different KPIs or by a combination of KPIs such as return on equity.[1] Although this has been a good start for organizations, we argue that it is necessary to improve the sustainability metrics and tools to measure not only the reduction of negative externalities but also the positive impact that the firm has on all of its stakeholders, including the natural environment and future generations that will be touched by the decisions that the firm makes in the present. Firms are not irrational for thinking that reporting performance could be equivalent to measuring because financial reporting can indeed be synonymous with financial performance measurements. Based on an organization's balance sheet, income statement, and cash flows, others can quickly determine its financial performance, more or less.

The same does not hold true in the case of sustainability performance. As described in this chapter, the nuances of nonfinancial performance measurements are not easy to obtain from sustainability reports. While we discuss in this chapter how sustainable organizations should measure their sustainability performance, the next one dives into how they should communicate their performance.

The parallel between financial performance measurement and sustainability performance measurement is, in fact, at the heart of the problem that we face today: organizations with sustainable practices have a difficult time demonstrating their sustainability performance effectively while traditional organizations have been largely successful in *greenwashing* their practices through the current frameworks that exist.[2] Moreover, the TBL approach, which is considered by most organizations as the best practice for sustainability reporting, is grounded in financial accounting theory. That is, the TBL framework builds on the notion of an economic bottom line, and appends environmental and social bottom lines to a company's core objective. Before exploring the important (and limited) implications this has on measuring sustainability performance, we provide a short historical background on the evolution of the TBL.

Despite the strong "social" emphasis of sustainability in the notion of sustainable development, corporate sustainability initiatives have primarily focused on environmental conservation due to the environmental accounting framework on which the TBL framework is based. Robert Gray pioneered the field of environmental accounting and reporting by assessing environmentalism through an accounting lens. In his research, Gray developed three environmental accounting frameworks: the sustainability cost method, natural capital inventory accounting method, and input–output analysis method.[3]

Gray's first framework, the sustainability cost method, was an attempt to measure the cost for returning the earth to its original state before a firm impacts it in a detrimental way. Two critiques immediately emerge, which Gray puts forth: it is difficult to value external costs to the environment, and some costs cannot be recuperated. The *market* approach is therefore extremely difficult to implement, particularly when dealing with infinite costs. For instance, what is the cost associated with destroying whale habitats, or worse, killing the last whale of a species? And who will arbitrate? These questions were raised in 1982, when the International Whaling Commission issued a moratorium (or indefinite ban) on commercial whaling. Thus, taking into consideration Gray's research—which indicates that it is rather difficult to value external costs—a series of guidelines on reporting sustainability initiatives and principles for business have emerged. In 1999, for example, in the United Nations established a clearer set of bounds for businesses to prevent damaging impacts that cannot be recuperated. The nine principles that the United Nations proposed, enumerated below, compose the Global Compact:

Human Rights

Principle 1: Businesses should support and respect the protection of internationally proclaimed human rights.
Principle 2: Make sure that they are not complicit in human rights abuses.

Labor

Principle 3: Businesses should uphold the freedom of association and effective recognition of the right to collective bargaining.
Principle 4: The elimination of all forms of forced and compulsory labor.
Principle 5: The effective abolition of child labor.
Principle 6: The elimination of discrimination in respect to employment and occupation.

Environment

Principle 7: Businesses should support a precautionary approach to environmental challenges.
Principle 8: Undertake initiatives to promote greater environmental responsibility.

Principle 9: Encourage the development and diffusion of
environmentally friendly technologies.
Later, a tenth principle added to deal with anticorruption stated that
"businesses should work against corruption in all its forms, including
extortion and bribery."[4]

The natural capital inventory accounting framework, Gray's second
framework, relaxes the environmental cost scheme and instead focuses
on measuring stocks of natural capital over time to illustrate the declining environment surrounding an organization. The ability to measure
the entire stock of natural capital longitudinally is also a considerable
task, particularly due to the difficulty of placing boundaries on the
"environment surrounding an organization." This approach nonetheless at least avoids the necessity of *pricing the environment* and influ-
ences the third approach.

Gray's final methodology is the input–output analysis, which
assesses the complete set of inputs (materials, energy, natural resources,
etc.) that go into manufacturing a product along with all the outputs
over its complete life cycle (emissions, disposal, etc.). The original
input–output model was actually developed by Wassily Leontief (who
earned a Nobel Prize in Economics for his work) to assess national
and regional economies, but Gray adapted the methodology for a
firm-level analysis to determine the impacts of an organization. It is
this framework—the input–output analysis—that informs the TBL
approach.

John Elkington first coined the TBL phrase in 1999, when he published *Cannibals with Forks*.[5] Expanding on Gray's work, Elkington
used an accounting methodology to extend to the environmental and
social domains, thereby claiming there were three *bottom lines* of a
sustainable company: environmental, social, and economic. At its core,
the TBL approach identifies KPIs in the social, environmental, and
profitability domains (or the three Ps: people, planet, and profit) to
gauge sustainability performance. Through framing sustainability in
terms of traditional, financial constructs, Elkington and other pioneers
were able to encourage early adoption among firms. These initial
contributions allowed many organizations to start looking for
sustainability-relevant data and measure at least some aspects of their
sustainability performance. The main contribution of this approach
was that companies initiated the process of measuring some aspects
of the TBL in quantitative terms. These aspects included, for example,

the amount of firms' externalities such as greenhouse gas emissions, tons of waste generated per unit of production, demand of water and energy resources required per unit of labor, economic saving derived from energy conservation measures, and eventually, cost that some companies had to pay for their externalities or to restore the degradation of some ecosystems. The TBL approach for measuring sustainability performance has been limited, however, because the selected KPIs had different units and could not be aggregated into one measurable indicator. Companies making use of KPIs associated with the TBL approach were in fact measuring the size and nature of externalities, but not the impact of these externalities on the natural, economic, or social environment.

Completely foreign in the early 1990s, sustainability reports became increasingly common as firms, either through reactive or proactive measures, heeded growing pressure to improve nonfinancial performance. As of 2013, 95 percent of the 250 largest companies in the world produced a sustainability report.[6] The pervasive adoption of sustainability reporting can be attributed to increasing demands from shareholders, employees, and members of broader stakeholder groups for more transparency and accountability. The GRI guidelines have become the de facto standard for TBL reporting, employed by 78 percent of reporting companies worldwide.[7] The GRI closely maps its mission, reporting principles, and guidelines to those of financial reporting, thereby facilitating the dialogue to legitimize the GRI.

Action 23: Develop key performance indicators in the social, environmental, and profitability domains through an input–output analysis to understand your firm's direct impacts on stakeholders.

While it is encouraging to note firms' efforts in disclosing nonfinancial KPIs, we challenge the current trend and demonstrate why current frameworks for sustainability reporting fail to effectively measure sustainability performance. The first critique stems from one of the limitations of the input–output analysis that the TBL framework is based on: Are firms actually measuring all their impacts in existing frameworks? Gray expressed the challenges of capturing all the environmental impacts, for which we actually have a rich set of KPIs. What happens when we look at the societal dimension? What are the set of KPIs that capture the impacts an organization has on society, its customers, future generations, and so on? We do not underestimate the difficulty that exists in measuring societal impacts. Yet any thorough measurement of sustainability performance needs to include an evaluation of the impact of the firm on society.

This line of questioning becomes increasingly important in light of the recent subprime mortgage crisis in the United States, which resulted in the global financial crisis of 2007–2008. At the time of this writing, the impacts of the crisis (seven years after the fact) have still not been resolved—especially in Europe. While the causes of the crisis are multifold, as explained below, the central, responsible actors are the banks. Consider that some of the same banks responsible for propagating the subprime mortgage crisis were ranked extremely high on sustainability lists. One example is Goldman Sachs, which appeared on the 2007 and 2009 Global 100 lists. Goldman Sachs not only propagated the subprime mortgage crisis but also benefited from it.[8]

A crucial question thus emerges: How could some of the very companies responsible for causing the global financial meltdown be considered some of the most sustainable ones in the world? It boils down to how we measure sustainability performance. The majority of methodologies in place largely assess sustainability by measuring the ratio of negative impacts that an organization has on the environment to its financial performance. The thought behind this methodology is that it becomes possible to compare differently sized institutions by normalizing for the size of the institution. The size of an institution, though, is not the only thing that differentiates one company from another. As discussed in previous chapters, sustainability needs to begin focusing on the actual goods and services an organization sells along with the impacts that these have on various stakeholder groups.

But these impacts are currently not measured in many sustainability-ranking methodologies and were certainly not measured in the sustainability lists that ranked financial institutions far higher than they should have been ranked. Moreover, under the current system, banks would perform extremely well. It can be argued that if most of their earnings are obtained through various financial deals, banks and other financial institutions make a small impact given the volume of financial transactions. Or do they? As the global financial crisis informed us, financial institutions have a tremendous effect on society, even if their supply chain is minimal. The key is to extend beyond the first-order impacts of an organization, and begin assessing the second- and third-order effects of an organization.

Imagine a drilling company that receives a loan to purchase an oil rig, or a development company that receives a loan to purchase a plot of farmland. While both of these investments as well as the subsequent interest earned appear on a bank's financial statements, the damaging environmental impacts that result from each of these investments is completely absent on any sustainability report. Things get even murkier if the oil rig is involved in an oil spill, or if the development company converts land that was dedicated to making food or serving various ecosystems into luxury homes. None of these third-order impacts makes its way into a sustainability report.

The causes of the subprime crisis highlight the problem by focusing on only the first-order impacts of an organization. Furthermore, the lack of indirect or second-order impacts led to predatory lending practices, whereby homes were sold to homeowners who could not afford them, and the development of derivatives enabled banks to pool risky loans into packaged loan products that they would market to other investors. In each of these instances, banks negatively impacted critical stakeholder groups, leading to a global collapse. Consequently, a study conducted by the Boston Consulting Group found that the largest banks have been fined approximately $180 billion thus far for their actions in the subprime market.

While measuring the tons of CO_2 emitted and gallons of water used is important, it is perhaps the indirect or second- and third-order impacts that we need to spotlight. Through this exercise, we can learn how an organization actually impacts its stakeholder group. If an organization purchases intermediate products from a particular supplier, say, that organization should be responsible for all the impacts their supplier makes. Alternatively, if a company sells a product, it should be responsible for how that product impacts the customer and other members of society. These are just two of countless examples that highlight the need to move beyond simply measuring first-order impacts. Take the case of the pesticide industry. A number of suicide incidents have been reported in some agricultural areas of India by farmers who use pesticides and pesticide containers to poison themselves and end their lives.[9] It is clear that the companies that manufacture the pesticides are not directly responsible for these actions. But do they bear any responsibility?

Action 24: Go beyond the first-order impacts to begin measuring the second- and third-order impacts that your organization has on stakeholder groups.

Failing to account for the indirect actions can lead organizations to unintentionally harm certain stakeholder groups. As introduced by the case in the last chapter, Coca-Cola's bottling plant in India had horrible repercussions on local farmers due to the amount of groundwater it depleted and polluted through its actions. In response, Coca-Cola has initiated a sustainability program and established a suite of KPIs that include the following:[10]

- Improved energy efficiency by 20 percent since 2014.
- Reduced packaging by 8 percent since 2008.
- Replenishment of 68 percent of the water used in "finished" beverages.
- Low- or no-calorie alternatives for nineteen out of twenty brands.

These largely resemble the indicators from most sustainability agendas, although the latter two do include figures that are more specific to the beverage sector. As the case from the previous chapter prompts, is this enough?

There are three areas of improvement that we identify for Coca-Cola's sustainability program. The first is its overwhelming focus on direct impacts. As mentioned in the section above, the direct impacts that a company is responsible for rarely lend themselves to the broader implications of a company on the stakeholder system. One of the largest critiques levied against Coca-Cola has been from farmers in India. How is Coca-Cola actually impacting them? The KPI on replenishing the water used in beverages is a start, but it remains a largely abstract figure and is absent from the actual stakeholder impact that makes KPIs important. The second shortcoming of Coca-Cola's KPIs is that they fail to measure sustainability performance in a meaningful and relevant way. What does the water used in *finished* beverages represent? How much water is used in *unfinished* beverages? In what form is water replenished? Is it filtered and safe for use on crops?

A key theme from the previous chapter was to engage with stake-holders and create forums of dialogue. Developing and measuring KPIs that matter to stakeholders is therefore a concrete outcome of such dialogues. When companies publish various statistics on water usage and CO_2 emissions, what does it actually mean to stakeholders? What does one ton of CO_2 in the air mean in practice? Coca-Cola and other companies should engage with stakeholders and measure KPIs around their specific needs and effects. By doing so, Coca-Cola would be able to communicate how it impacts local water sources and what this means for farmers. It may not be glamorous, but it is meaningful, relevant, and most important, a baseline to improve on. If companies fail to measure impacts in meaningful ways, how can they expect to make meaningful improvements to their stakeholder systems? Nonetheless, almost every company is guilty of this practice.

Action 25: Develop metrics that are meaningful to stakeholders.

The final area for improvement that we identify for Coca-Cola is a shift toward how it positively affects society. Each of the KPIs mentioned concentrates on how Coca-Cola is trying to minimize harm. But what about actually improving its stakeholder system? Rather than reducing the water that Coke takes away from farmers, is there a way it can help them get access to more water or make farming practices more efficient? Coca-Cola has taken some steps in this direction. The company has selected two sustainability targets for the year 2020 to improve the lives of women and communities: "Enable the economic empowerment of 5 million women across our global value chain, and give back at least 1% of the annual operating income of the company to the communities."[11] The question we asked before remains: How can these targets be measured in a meaningful way? Furthermore, what does economic empowerment look like and is it the end goal or the means to a more important goal? It is imperative that companies focus on measuring specific effects in a meaningful way as opposed to developing vague targets that are difficult to measure concretely.

In addition to concentrating on the first-order impacts of an organization and failing to develop meaningful indicators, sustainability reporting is problematic for the type of impacts it focuses on. Consistent with older conceptions of sustainability, current reporting formats primarily revolve around the negative impacts that an organization has, encouraging them to mitigate harm. While minimizing harm is critical, it is only the first step. The larger question is, How can organizations measure the positive impacts they have on society?

Many organizations would need to completely transform their products and services to champion a set of KPIs that focus on their positive impacts on society; hence, that is the reason why companies look to minimize negative externalities instead. According to our positive deviance framework, eliminating harm is the ethical responsibility of all companies. The positive deviance continuum is reproduced in figure 6.1 to show how we distinguish sustainable practices from *do no harm* or socially responsible activities.

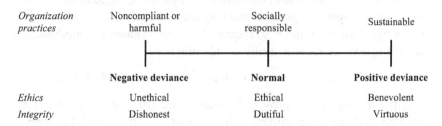

Figure 6.1
Positive deviance continuum
Source: Derived from Arran Caza, Brianna A. Barker, and Kim S. Cameron, "Ethics and Ethos: The Buffering and Amplifying Effects of Ethical Behavior and Virtuousness," *Journal of Business Ethics* 52, no. 2 (2004): 169–178; Gretchen M. Spreitzer and Scott Sonenshein, "Positive Deviance and Extraordinary Organizing," in *Positive Organizational Scholarship*, ed. Kim S. Cameron, Jane E. Dutton, and Robert .E. Quinn (San Francisco: Berret-Kohler Publishers Inc., 2003), 207–224; Gretchen M. Spreitzer and Scott Sonenshein, "Toward the Construct Definition of Positive Deviance," *American Behavioral Scientist* 47, no. 6 (2004): 828–847.

Coca-Cola's focus and the selection of KPIs to measure footprint is not unlike other companies. But how do we shift organizations, like Coca-Cola, to pay attention to the positive impacts they have on society? It begins with the vision and mission of organizations. Coca-Cola's mission is threefold: to refresh the world, inspire moments of optimism and happiness, and create value and make a difference. Can these be measured? If so, how? If not, perhaps the vision needs to be rearticulated. Nestlé and Unilever have both transformed their visions over the past decade. Nestlé, the world's largest consumer goods company, champions itself as the "leading nutrition, health and wellness company," and has launched a campaign called "Creating Shared Value." Similarly, Unilever, the world's third-largest consumer goods company, places the notion of positive impact in its core purpose and principles, aiming to make a positive impact through its brands and relationships.

Although reducing negative environmental impacts is in both Nestlé's and Unilever's sustainability strategies, each has placed an emphasis on improving the lives of stakeholders and thus created KPIs to measure this. Unilever has an ambitious 2020 set of goals across the following three categories:[12]

- Improve the health and well-being of one billion people worldwide (provide safe drinking water and access to sanitation, reduce diseases by encouraging handwashing, lower the sugar and salt content, eliminate trans fat, etc.).
- Halve the environmental footprint.
- Enhance the livelihoods of producers and employees.

It is noteworthy that Unilever's second goal, halving the environmental footprint, centers on reducing harm. It is still extremely important for organizations to ensure that they are not harming any stakeholders in any way. We merely urge organizations to go further. Nestlé, through its shared value creation approach, has also begun to focus on maximizing its positive impacts, as it shifts toward a nutrition company.

Nestlé, Unilever, and countless others still have room for improvement. If an organization has a strong sustainability mission, long-term vision, sustainability strategy that positively impacts all stakeholder groups, and way to engage stakeholders, its ability to develop strong KPIs becomes much simpler. For example, TOMS and Warby Parker both track the number of shoes and eyeglasses, respectively, that they donate through their buy one, give one initiatives. Not all sustainable business models can be captured with one KPI, however. While some KPIs are more specific than others are, the link between a sustainability strategy and positive KPIs is crucial. Critics may argue that positive KPIs are more difficult to benchmark against other organizations, but so are traditional KPIs, as we witnessed in the banking sector.

Action 26: Move beyond measuring how your organization minimizes harm and toward how it positively impacts stakeholder groups; less bad is not good.

While it would be ideal to capture all the impacts of an organization and determine sustainability performance, is it really possible? Current frameworks rely on what is known as a reductionist approach: they take the complex topic of sustainability and attempt to divide it into smaller, measurable parts that account for the whole. This is largely due to the accounting methodology on which the TBL is based. Wayne Norman and Chris MacDonald critique the TBL due to its reductionist approach, contending that the social, environmental, and economic domains cannot be measured objectively, and that the KPIs within each of these domains cannot be aggregated to determine a bottom line.[13]

Moreover, they argue that it is not possible to account for all the impacts that an organization has on the environment or broader society. Doing so would require subjective or value-based judgments, thereby suggesting that quantitative indicators are not sufficient on their own. The pair of authors goes further to demonstrate that even if all the impacts of an organization could be quantified, they cannot be compiled to attain a bottom line of performance. There also is no objective method to combine indicators with different units of measurement such as tons of CO_2, gallons of water, and recycled materials into one comprehensible figure to determine a bottom line of performance. While the previous set of indicators comprises factors in the environmental domain, the task gets even more complicated when attempting to amass social indicators.

Despite the difficulty in achieving an accurate TBL assessment, many have tried. KPMG, for instance, has developed a methodology for organizations to calculate their "true earnings." After calculating financial earnings based on its revenues and costs, an organization determines the net positive economic, social, and environmental earnings. The sum total of all the earnings yields the organization's true earnings. KPMG provides an example for calculating the true earnings of an underwater gold mine in South Africa (the graph is reproduced in figure 6.2).

From looking at the graph, it can be observed that various positive and negative impacts are calculated. As mentioned in the critique above, there is a large amount of subjectivity involved in this—after all, if "health and safety" is a negative social impact, how much is the value of a human life weighted? In addition, how do "low wages" compare to the revenues of an organization? Is it possible to add all these contributing factors together to get a total, "true earnings" figure? This, then, leads to the second critique that Norman and MacDonald make: it is not possible to aggregate various weighted impacts to determine a bottom line. While this is acceptable in financial accounting, it is highly subjective in the realm of sustainability and, most likely, highly inaccurate.

Although many companies do not utilize a true earnings framework such as the KPMG model illustrated in figure 6.2, many organizations implicitly adopt a reductionist approach by attempting to balance negative performance with positive impacts. In 2014, Coca-Cola received criticism from stakeholder groups when it pledged £20 million to launch an antiobesity campaign across the United Kingdom. The

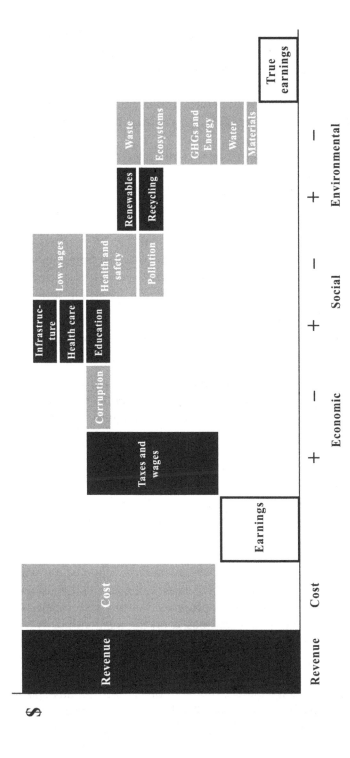

Figure 6.2
KPMG true earnings analysis for South African underwater gold mine
Source: KPMG International, "A New Vision of Value: Connecting Corporate and Societal Value Creation," KPMG, 2014, https://www.kpmg.com/Global/en/topics/climate-change-sustainability-services/Documents/a-new-vision-of-value.pdf (accessed July 17, 2015).

initiative would offer families a variety of free fitness classes, ranging from Zumba to basketball to tennis to archery, at seventy UK parks.[14] Although many stakeholders felt this was a praiseworthy action, health advocacy organizations criticized Coca-Cola for contributing to the obesity epidemic in the United Kingdom, citing this latest initiative as a public relations move that distracts from the true problem at hand.

A survey by Public Health England discovered that soft drinks, along with fruit juices, were the largest sources of sugar for people between the ages of four and eighteen, while another estimated that soft drinks accounted for 30 percent of the sugar intake among eleven- to eighteen-year-olds. Advocates therefore maintain that Coca-Cola, the leading soft drink company in the world with 1.7 billion drinks sold daily, cannot reconcile its core products and services from goodwill efforts such as its antiobesity campaign. Coca-Cola and other companies need to assess their sustainability performance holistically as opposed to aggregating disjointed efforts.

Action 27: Assess performance holistically versus through reductionist approaches; sustainability is not a zero-sum game.

Alternatively, what if stakeholders, rather than the organization itself, became the determinants of sustainability performance? After all, in the current TBL-based frameworks, organizations estimate their positive and negative impacts on various stakeholder groups. But can stakeholder groups themselves not provide this information? If the sustainability of an organization is determined by how positively it impacts all stakeholder groups (the argument we make in this book), we hold that an organization should poll stakeholder groups to determine how they have been affected by the organization's activities.

In 1995, Max Clarkson proposed a new model for analyzing corporate performance, focusing on an organization's relationships with stakeholder groups.[15] Drawing from R. Edward Freeman's 1984 stakeholder model of the firm, Clarkson proposed that the performance of an organization can be determined based on the relationships it has with its primary stakeholders, which include shareholders, managers, employees, customers, suppliers, the government, and communities.[16] Clarkson postulates that a company's success depends on the balanced value creation of its stakeholder groups. In other words, if any stakeholder group is unsatisfied with the wealth and value creation that an organization generates for it, its withdrawal from the organization's ecosystem will drive the firm into serious economic trouble or even bankruptcy. Clarkson suggests that samples of these stakeholders should be polled to determine how satisfied they are with the wealth and value that the company is generating for them.

This is a valuable contribution, and we expand on it to provide a tangible framework that managers can use in their organizations to determine sustainability performance. There are two amendments we would like to make to Clarkson's framework. One is that not all stakeholders have the same amount of power or voice; many are silent stakeholders that still matter and are important. The environment is one example. Society at large and future stakeholders are others. While Clarkson does not consider these stakeholders as "primary," some of the primary stakeholders he does list, such as suppliers, tend to have small voices and so are unable to achieve an appropriate share of the value in the value chain, as explored in chapter 4. In addition, and as described above, it is often the secondary and silent stakeholder groups that feel the ramifications of the second- and third-order impacts of an organization. As an alternative to developing a complex system of KPIs to capture these impacts, organizations can poll a sample of these groups. While not all groups have a voice, most silent stakeholders are still represented by NGOs, which have the ability to represent them. We have seen the effect that Greenpeace has had on organizations in the case of Nestlé and more recently LEGO, while other subsets of civil society were responsible for exposing Nike's sweatshops in the 1990s. Hence, companies can and should reach out to all stakeholder groups— primary and secondary—and ensure that all voices are given significant weight.

This brings us to the second point: the objective of an organization's sustainability performance should not be profitability. Furthermore, Clarkson's model suggests that without the satisfaction of a balanced value distribution among stakeholder groups, a company will not be financially successful. While this is sometimes true, it is frequently not the case. Countless highly profitable organizations in almost every sector harm stakeholder groups, or do not distribute an appropriate amount of value or wealth to them. As mentioned earlier, we do not champion the business case for sustainability because there is not always one. It costs money to pay producers more—an amount that cannot always be recuperated. It also costs money to improve the environment—resources that are not earmarked for any particular

organization. As such, the point of understanding stakeholder satisfaction is to inform an organization how it can become more sustainable—
the motivations for which are often personal or inspired.

We propose that you use the framework diagrammed in figure 6.3
to assist your organization in measuring its sustainability performance. Rather than using the GRI or another TBL-based framework,
you will find this to be a much more enriching process. Adapting
Clarkson's framework to corporate sustainability performance, organizations can sample each stakeholder group and ask respondents to
simply rank how the organization impacts them on a scale of zero
(extremely negative) to ten (extremely positive) in comparison to other
organizations in the same sector. The qualifying statement "in comparison to other organizations in the same sector" is informed by the
positive deviance continuum (see figure 6.1) to create a reference
point, or industry norm, from which stakeholders can compare. Furthermore, according to the positive deviance continuum, the average
firm in an industry, which is compliant and aims to reduce any
harmful impacts it may have on a stakeholder group, is considered

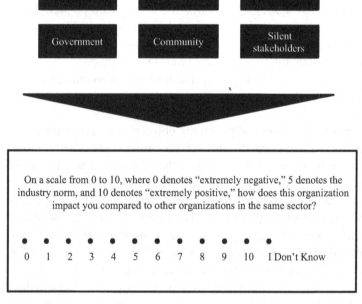

Figure 6.3
Stakeholder-driven methodology for measuring sustainability performance

ethical or socially responsible. Firms that are ranked above this average are considered positively deviant or sustainable, focusing instead on how to improve society. Finally, firms that fail to meet the ethical norm are considered unsustainable.

By auditing members belonging to the various stakeholder groups of an organization, firms can derive average sustainability performance rankings across each stakeholder group. Through this methodology, the firm will fall under one of four cases:

• Sustainable: The firm is ranked highly across all stakeholder groups.
• Socially responsible: The firm receives a mix of high and average rankings across stakeholder groups.
• Unsustainable: The firm receives low rankings from a stakeholder group.
• Unaccountable: The firm receives a high percentage of "I don't know" responses, denoting that it fails to communicate sustainability performance in an effective or meaningful way.

The current KPIs that firms use to measure performance are generally detached from their actual sustainability performance. Consequently, many stakeholders will respond "I don't know" in the framework proposed above, highlighting the lack of accountability that firms currently have to the broader range of stakeholder groups. This is an issue we tackle in the next chapter.

Action 28: Survey stakeholder groups to ensure that your organization is equitably distributing value to all stakeholder groups, even those that do not directly impact financial viability.

Firms can become more proactive in their attempts to positively contribute to society as opposed to being on the defensive end. One important lesson comes from Nike. As presented in the second case challenge from the previous chapter, Nike suffered significant criticism in the early 1990s when advocacy groups shed light on its supply chain. These organizations, which ranged from large NGOs to student groups at various college campuses, pointed to the various sweatshops that Nike sourced its apparel from overseas. While Nike had a history since the 1970s of poor labor practices to ensure the lowest costs, civil society eventually made its voice heard and significantly damaged Nike's reputation.

If Nike followed the framework illustrated in figure 6.3 and routinely surveyed its stakeholders, it would have likely performed reasonably well across stakeholder groups, with the exception of the low scores that it may have obtained from NGOs and its suppliers. After a dialogue, Nike could have embarked on improving its production facilities and begun communicating progress on this goal to its various stakeholders. Such an action would doubtlessly have enabled Nike to avoid the constant turmoil that followed it. Similarly, by appeasing one stakeholder group, Nestlé would have been successful in maintaining its sustainability reputation across all its other stakeholder groups.

Nike's initial stance, however, exacerbated the situation as the company attempted to distance itself from its source factories and claimed minimal responsibility. Nike eventually approached the situation proactively by routinely surveying factory workers under its broader initiative, branded SHAPE. By surveying stakeholders, Nike began to find various pain points in the factories from which it sourced and quickly implemented compliance ratings to improve conditions. Nevertheless, as an MIT study led by Rick Locke highlighted, compliance programs and audits fail to improve labor conditions over the long term.[17]

While investing resources to improve factories and managerial training helped, Nike was able to achieve the most significant gains when it set out to significantly change its relationship with suppliers. By engaging with suppliers and embracing a stakeholder perspective, Nike adopted the collaborative relationships with stakeholders that are necessary to achieve sustainability performance. Yet as Locke warns, firms cannot stop there. They must often transform their business model to assist supply chains by giving greater lead times on production and offering a larger share of the profits.

Action 29: Collaborate with stakeholders to determine sustainable performance.

Measuring sustainability performance is an important exercise for organizations and their stakeholders. In box 6.1, we introduce some key lessons and review the seven actions introduced in this chapter to measure sustainability performance in a meaningful, effective way.

While we encourage companies to collaborate with their constituents, we also stress that companies should ensure that stakeholders have all the information they need. Transparency and accountability

Box 6.1
Measuring Sustainability Performance: Key Lessons and Actions

• The best way to do sustainability accounting is to first identify all the inputs required by an organization and all the outputs that are derived from the firm's actions. Then it is important to develop concrete indicators to assess the social, economic, and ecological impacts that your firm has on all its stakeholders today as well as in the future.

Action 23: Develop key performance indicators in the social, environmental, and profitability domains through an input–output analysis to understand your firm's direct impacts on stakeholders.

• Assessing the size and nature of an organization's externalities—such as the amount of pollution or demand for nonrenewable resources—is a good first step. But it is not enough. It is critical to go beyond measuring externalities in order to determine the impact that those externalities have on the well-being of all the firm's stakeholders.

Action 24: Go beyond the first-order impacts to begin measuring the second- and third-order impacts that your organization has on stakeholder groups.

• An organization can effectively communicate with its stakeholders by providing meaningful sustainability metrics that all stakeholders can easily understand. For example, when informing stakeholders about a percentage of waste recycling or energy conservation, some metaphors could be used to explain the meaning of the sustainability initiative.

Action 25: Develop metrics that are meaningful to stakeholders.

• Unilever's initiative to cut its environmental footprint in half is a positive step. This is not enough since, however, since as we have said, less bad is not good. Other initiatives, such as Nestlé changing its mission to become a "nutrition company," focus organizations on maximizing value.

Action 26: Move beyond measuring how your organization minimizes harm and toward how it positively impacts stakeholder groups; less bad is not good.

• It is useful to place an economic value on some of the firm's externalities, such as assessing the economic cost of ecosystem restoration. Yet the impacts of the externalities generated by the firm cannot be aggregated and added together because they refer to different units. In addition, positive impacts cannot erase negative ones. If a company leads to the extinction of a species or deterioration of a natural resource, no amount of "goodwill" can restore the damage committed.

Action 27: Assess performance holistically versus through reductionist approaches; sustainability is not a zero-sum game.

• The importance of assessing sustainability in a holistic manner from different stakeholder perspectives overcomes the shortcomings of reductionist approaches to measure sustainability. It also offers an effective way for organizations to understand and engage with their stakeholders with regard to corporate sustainability. To use this approach, an efficient process has to be designed and put in place to collect the assessment of various stakeholders on the firm's sustainability performance. The process includes at least four steps: selecting relevant stakeholders (representatives of society that have a stake in the firm's actions); organizing a series of stakeholder consultations (in the form of forums for discussion and dialogue) where the selected stakeholder and representatives of the firm choose a methodology to identify the key issues of interest to stakeholders that will serve to assess the sustainability performance of the firm; identifying an external stakeholder—someone with no stake in the firm—to manage the consultation process and collect the assessment of stakeholders (typically, this is a member of civil society such as a representative from an academic or research institution); and examining the assessment of stakeholders and prioritizing the areas where the firm needs to make improvements to move forward in its journey toward sustainability.

Action 28: Survey stakeholder groups to ensure that your organization is equitably distributing value to all stakeholder groups, even those that do not directly impact financial viability.

• An important lesson from the Nike example is to collaborate with your organization's complete set of stakeholders to measure and define sustainable performance. Instead, the initial attitude was this: "We don't own the factories. We don't control what goes on there." By moving toward a collaborative stakeholder network, Nike and other firms can begin to transform their current business models to focus on the metrics that really matter.Action 29: Collaborate with stakeholders to determine sustainable performance.

are key components of a sustainable enterprise—the topic of the next chapter. Before continuing, we urge you to attempt to respond to the following two case challenges for companies that are trying to go beyond measuring KPIs and move toward informing stakeholders.

Case 1: Honest by

Bruno Pieters is an extremely successful fashion designer who became the creative director for Hugo Boss in 2007. After experiencing the traditional supply chains in the fashion sector, Pieters wanted to establish his own line that would herald the notion of sustainable fashion. So he left Hugo Boss in 2010 and spent an extended period of time in India to better understand the plight of workers in the fashion sector. Inspired and motivated, Pieters launched his own line, Honest by, in 2012. Communicating these changes is often an arduous task. If you were Pieters, how would you make Honest by the most sustainable company in the fashion sector by focusing on the principles of transparency and accountability?

While *sustainable fashion* is a great buzzword, implementing it is much more difficult. Large fashion companies such as PUMA and adidas have gone to great lengths to make their supply chains as sustainable as possible. In the food sector, making sure that your supply chain is fully sustainable is even more challenging. Take a company like Nestlé that operates in 194 countries. Although the Nestlé adopted a supplier code in 2013 that included environmental sustainability as its third principle, it is extremely hard to make sure that over one million suppliers, farmers, packagers, transporters, and others in the supply chain are truly sustainable in a way that can be verified.[18]

Case 2: Lindenhoff Farm

Dirco te Voortwis is the president of Lindenhoff Farm, a family-owned establishment in the Netherlands for four generations. The vision of Lindenhoff Farm is to return authentic flavor to food by raising meat, growing vegetables, and producing dairy products through the organic and natural processes that were prominent before farming became industrialized. From the habitats of animals to the space that they each get, Lindenhoff is a true leader in the sustainable farming sector. The company also employs ex-felons to help rehabilitate them through farmwork.

Yet te Voortwis has expressed the challenge of communicating Lindenhoff's sustainability performance with stakeholders. Like many sustainability pioneers, Lindenhoff's actual sustainability is not properly represented through many metrics. In an effort to be transparent and accountable to stakeholders, Lindenhoff is not content with the current information communicated by sector-specific indicators such as acres of organic farming to truly capture the company's essence. Imagine Lindenhoff hired you to improve its accountability to stakeholders through increased transparency. What would you recommend?

7 Transparency and Accountability: Can You Pass the Newspaper Test?

If stakeholders are the determinants of an organization's sustainability performance, as defined in the previous chapter, how can organizations ensure that their stakeholder constituents have all the information that they need to assess their sustainability performance? Perhaps the most significant barrier to understanding an organization's sustainability performance is the lack of transparency surrounding all its operations and actions. Few organizations are perfect, yet nearly every executive is afraid to reveal information that can place their organization in a bad light. In fact, it was not until *pink slime* rumors went rampant that McDonald's was finally pushed to become more transparent about its practices. Pink slime, as discussed earlier, is a meat-based product used as a food additive in ground beef and beef-based processed meats, as either a filler or to reduce the overall fat content of ground beef. The product is exposed to ammonia gas or citric acid to kill bacteria.[1] The product is regulated in different manners in various regions. In the United States, it is allowed to be used in ground beef, and can be used in other meat products such as beef-based processed meats.[2] The product is banned in Canada due to the presence of ammonia in it, and it is banned for human consumption in the European Union. Through its question-and-answer platform (described in chapter 5), McDonald's became more daring and transparent as it began receiving feedback and praise from its stakeholders.

An important sustainability challenge therefore becomes, What would it take for your organization to become 100 percent transparent? Alternatively stated, would your organization pass the *newspaper test*? If every aspect of your company's practices were placed on the front page of the *New York Times*, would your firm be OK? If not, what should you change? The most sustainable companies are those that can make their operations and impacts completely transparent. Take, for example, the Interface case, which was mentioned earlier. The company has chosen a Mission Zero sustainability objective, although it will take time to achieve this ambitious goal. Interface reported that in the year 2012, only 44 percent of raw materials used were from recycled or bio-based sources.[3] As we demonstrate in the Patagonia and PUMA cases below, not everything your company does has to be positive. But the challenges that your organization is facing along with the negative aspects associated with your products and services are points for improvement that your organization should work toward actively, and they should not be hidden from your stakeholders.

Action 30: Make your operations 100 percent transparent to effectively communicate the sustainability performance of your organization, and if you cannot, then change your operations.

Perhaps the pioneer in *putting it all out there* is Patagonia. Companies have been extremely careful for the most part about sharing their impacts on the environment, erring on the side of caution; instead, they focus on their achievements and positive outcomes. We understand that for public relations executives and legal officers in organizations, it is human nature to want to share only the best aspects and behaviors of your organizations, products, and services. Yet as Jill Dumain, the director of environmental strategy at Patagonia, proclaims, "Anybody in the environmental field knows, if you aren't talking about what's wrong, you're not telling the whole story." Patagonia's founder, Yvon Chouinard, expands on this: "You don't have to be worried about telling everybody about the bad things that you're doing. As long as you say that we're working on these things. But if you try to be dishonest, try to hide it, it is going to come back and bite you in the [expletive]."[4] Patagonia, then, has explicitly stated the negative externalities that are caused by specific articles of clothing, along with the positive aspects that Patagonia has achieved (such as traceable down). Patagonia also reveals where each specific garment comes from, such as the sewing factory and textile mill, along with information about each. It is not perfect, and it is not the most sustainable company, but Patagonia has at least begun to achieve positive stakeholder dialogues through its efforts to become more transparent.

Action 31: Do not be afraid of revealing the negative aspects about your company; instead, create goals around them.

While transparency is an effective strategy to engage better with external stakeholders, it can also be an incredibly valuable practice for driving internal change within a company.

In 2008, PUMA introduced the sustainability concept PUMAVision including the 4Keys—fair, honest, positive, and creative—in order to address its externalities.[5] In 2010, PUMA embarked on a more ambitious journey to not only measure the negative externalities that went into making its shoes and apparel but also estimate the monetary costs associated with these impacts. Although we noted the difficulty in approximating environmental impacts through financial costs in the previous chapter, the purpose of this exercise was to understand and appreciate the environmental costs as a proportion of the company's financial profitability, which does not capture environmental costs. Moreover, PUMA embarked on its environmental profit and loss as a transparency strategy as opposed to a performance measurement strategy. It was one of the first initiatives to put an actual price tag on the *true* cost of doing sales.

The five main categories of environmental effects that PUMA focused on were water use, greenhouse gas emissions, land use conversion (developing production facilities on natural lands rich with biodiversity), other air pollutants (i.e., particulates, sulfur dioxide, ammonia, nitrogen oxide, carbon monoxide, and volatile organic compounds), and waste.[6] PUMA analyzed these impacts throughout its supply chain, dividing it into four segments: operations and manufacturing (tier 1), outsourcing (tier 2), processing (tier 3), and raw materials (tier 4). This breakdown enabled PUMA to understand where the bulk of its negative impacts were amassed.

PUMA revealed that the total cost of its environmental impacts was approximately €145 million. The company had net sales of €2,705 million for the year and net earnings of €202 million, but if it were to account for the cost of its environmental footprint, its net earnings would be reduced to €57 million. Again, this exercise was not about determining performance; rather, by being completely transparent, PUMA revealed the environmental costs for which it (and all other companies) had not accounted.

The analysis shows that the majority of its impacts were in the processing and raw materials stages of the supply chain—accounting for 76 percent of the total environmental cost. These effects were centered in Asia (66 percent), where the crux of PUMA's operations were based, and heavily concentrated in the footwear sector (66 percent). In addition, 66 percent of PUMA's impacts were equally divided between water use and greenhouse gas emissions, while 25 percent were based on land use. The data are reproduced in table 7.1.

Although PUMA produced this report for its external stakeholders, the data have been a significant tool for creating a baseline of the company's performance and developing objectives within the organization. Yet PUMA still needs to address many questions. Will it account for the environmental cost of its operations? If so, will consumers or PUMA

Table 7.1
PUMA's 2010 Environmental Profit and Loss Statement (Total Environmental Cost Is Approximately €145 Million)

	Water use	Greenhouse gases	Land use	Other air pollution	Waste	Total	% of total
	33%	33%	25%	7%	2%	100%	
	Environmental impact (euro million)						
Total	47	47	37	11	3	145	100%
PUMA operations	< 1	7	< 1	1	< 1	8	6%
Tier 1	1	9	< 1	1	2	13	9%
Tier 2	4	7	< 1	2	1	14	9%
Tier 3	17	7	< 1	3	< 1	27	19%
Tier 4	25	17	37	4	< 1	83	57%
Regional analysis							
EMEA	4	8	1	1	< 1	14	10%
Americas	2	10	20	3	< 1	35	24%
Asia/Pacific	41	29	16	7	3	96	66%
Segments							
Footwear	25	28	34	7	2	96	66%
Apparel	18	14	3	3	1	39	27%
Accessories	4	5	< 1	1	< 1	10	7%
Intensity	Environmental impact per hundred euro of sales						
Footwear	1.8	2	2.4	0.5	0.1	6.7	
Apparel	1.9	1.5	0.3	0.3	0.1	4.1	
Accessories	1.2	1.5	0	0.3	0	2.9	

Source: "Environmental Profit and Loss," PUMA, 2011, http://about.puma.com/en/sustainability/environment/environmental-profit-and-loss-account (accessed July 17, 2015).

pay the difference? In 2010, €145 million was approximately 5 percent of the total sales that PUMA generated. If PUMA's customers were to absorb the costs, they would have to pay an additional 5 percent premium. Alternatively, PUMA could absorb the costs and thereby have a stronger incentive to reduce its environmental impacts. Nonetheless, internal stakeholders at PUMA (i.e., managers, employees, and board members) now had an appreciation for the environmental costs of the company's operations, and they began to create concrete goals for reducing them. Through monetizing its impacts, PUMA has been able to create a common language (albeit a flawed one) between its financial and environmental operations.

Over the years, PUMA's ongoing dialogue format with its stakeholders—Talks at Banz—has resulted in valuable and constructive feedback on PUMA's sustainability strategy. According to PUMA,

Over the past eight years PUMA's Talks at Banz has evolved from a small discussion 'round-table' format to an innovative and forward-thinking debate in which representatives from NGOs, industry, suppliers, creative fields, universities, private organizations and PUMA engage. From November 22–24, 2010, PUMA hosted its 8th Talks at Banz at the Banz Monastery in Bad Staffelstein, Germany. The discussion addressed three central issues: "Wages in the Supply Chain," "Business and Biodiversity," and the "Impact of Creative and Peace Initiatives on PUMA's Sustainability Initiatives." Prior to the meeting, we shared the draft agenda with invitees asking for their contributions and comments, and this feedback was factored into the final agenda. Approximately 70 participants joined PUMA's CEO, Jochen Zeitz, and PUMA senior staff at the meeting, including NGO representatives from Greenpeace, WWF, Oxfam, Clean Clothes Campaign, Fair Labor Association, Transfair, and the Asian Floor Wage Campaign.[7]

In the words of Auret van Heerden, president and CEO of the Fair Labor Association, "The 2010 exercise was all the more significant for the fact that the Chair and CEO, Jochen Zeitz, highlighted the issue of living wages in the supply chain and committed the company to work with NGO's to seek practical approaches to this issue. The FLA is now working with PUMA and other FLA-affiliates to develop a pilot project with the Asian Floor Wage to do exactly that."[8]

Action 32: Calculate and share the impacts of your operations on the supply chain to drive internal sustainability agendas forward.

As mentioned at the end of the previous chapter, Bruno Pieters served as the creative director for Hugo Boss, a premier fashion company, from 2007 to 2010. During his tenure there, he began to observe the supply chains employed by fashion companies such as Hugo Boss. The factories that high-end fashion companies source from often pay extremely low wages and offer poor working conditions. Pieters left Hugo Boss in 2010 and relocated to India in order to get a greater understanding of how garments are produced. Passionate about developing a new business model, Pieters launched Honest by in January 2012, claiming it was "the world's first 100% transparent company."[9]

At Honest by, customers and other stakeholders can see exactly what materials go into making each product along with their individual costs. For instance, the cost breakdown overview for a jacket retailing for €1082.69 is detailed in table 7.2. Not all the information is flattering. Honest by, for example, reveals how significant the markup is for each piece of clothing it sells; it determines its wholesale price by marking up each product by 100 percent. The retail price is then obtained through the same process, thereby resulting in a 300 percent markup from the original cost to the company. Although this may appear high, it is in fact an industry norm. Regardless, Honest by is one of the first companies to reveal its pricing publicly.

The information on the website for each product delves even deeper. Each component that is used to make the product is described in detail, including its cost point and the materials used. Additionally, table 7.3 captures the manufacturing details that are published for each product, highlighting the times to cut, knit, assemble, and iron each component. Similar to Patagonia, customers can see where the different parts of the garment were manufactured and produced along with detailed information about each supplier, including the name of the owner, age of the company, number of employees, and company's physical address.

A carbon footprint is included with a meaningful description of the quantitative figure. For instance, the total CO_2 emissions required to produce the jacket described is 2.93 kilograms, which the site says is equivalent to driving a car for 18.31 kilometers or using a classic light-bulb for 112.69 hours. The site also mentions how it would take the average tree approximately 329 days to absorb the CO_2 emitted. While it explains that the calculation only includes the transportation, Honest by states that it is investing in a complete life cycle analysis for each of its products. Such an analysis involves a "cradle-to-grave" approach that assesses all the impacts over the life cycle of a product, beginning with the raw materials and continuing until the product is discarded.

Table 7.2
Honest by Material Breakdown for Men's Organic Cotton and Linen Blend Bomber Jacket

Product part	Material details	Cost (in euros)
Fabrics	Sand twill blend	67.11
Lining	Oekotex-certified cotton lining	N/A
Knit trimmings	100% organic cotton	5.47
Bias tape	Black 100% organic cotton	4.95
Zipper	100% recycled polyester tape and brass (nickel free)	N/A
Sewing thread	100% organic cotton GOTS certified	9.50
Interfacing	White 100% tencel	N/A
Brand label	100% polyester	1.40
Size label	100% polyester	0.04
Care + made in labels	100% cotton	0.74
Security seal	100% polystyrene	0.20
Hang tag	100% FSC recycled	0.29
Cotton thread	100% cotton	0.05
Safety pin	100% nickel free metal	0.03
Total material cost		91.57
Pattern cost		3.81
Manufacturing cost (garment plus knitting production)		106.43
Development cost		3.89
Transportation cost		8.00
Branding cost		10.00
Total cost		223.70
Wholesale markup (x2)		447.39
Honest by retail price (x2) to non-EU customers		**894.79**
Honest by retail price (includes VAT) to EU customers		**1082.69**

Source: "Sand-Colored Organic Cotton and Linen Blend Bomber Jacket," Honest by, http://www.honestby.com/en/product/56/jackets/sand-colored-organic-cotton-and -linen-blend-bomber-jacket.html (accessed June 17, 2014).

Table 7.3
Honest by Manufacturing Details for Men's Organic Cotton and Linen Blend Bomber
Jacket

Manufacturing details

Product code: BPS017F2007C109M
Product description: Organic cotton and linen blend bomber jacket

Pattern
Company: Honest by BVBA
Design time: 24 working hours
Number of fittings: 4

Garment manufacturing
Company: Vanbockryck
Location: Diepenbeek, Belgium
Address: Industrielaan 8–3590 Diepenbeek, Belgium
Owner: Mr. Yvan Vanbockryck
Since: 1985
Number of employees: 24
Cutting time: 19 minutes
Assembly time: 65 minutes
Ironing: 11 minutes
Amount of pieces made (per color): 10 pieces
Amount per size: 2 pieces

Knit trimmings
Company: Pentlja P
Location: Zgornje duplice, Slovenia
Address: Zgornje Duplice 10, 1290 Grosuplje, Slovenia
Owner: Mr. Matija Vene
Since: 1992
Number of employees: 5
Knitting time: 30 minutes
Amount of pieces made: 10 pieces
Amount per size: 2 pieces

This garment is 100% made in Europe for Honest by.

Source: "Sand-Colored Organic Cotton and Linen Blend Bomber Jacket," Honest by,
http://www.honestby.com/en/product/56/jackets/sand-colored-organic-cotton-and
-linen-blend-bomber-jacket.html (accessed May 28, 2016).

The site boasts positive aspects about each piece of clothing, too, noting which clothing items are vegan, organic, skin friendly, produced in Europe, and/or use recycled materials. The company donates 20 percent of all profits to charity.

Through these efforts, customers and other stakeholders know exactly what goes into a product as well as how much it costs, and gain a relative appreciation of the impact it all makes. Few stakeholders will nitpick about the negative impacts of Honest by's suppliers, but those who do can talk about a specific aspect and discuss alternatives with Honest by. Through its transparency, Honest by has been able to achieve significant levels of trust with stakeholders.

Action 33: Make your supply chain completely transparent to build trust with stakeholders.

A strategic aspect for organizations to become completely transparent is to focus on the conversations that really matter with stakeholders by eliminating information asymmetry. Firms will frequently invest large amounts of money to adopt a label or create strong public relations around a brand yet still not obtain the trust of stakeholders for one primary reason: firms have a lot more information that they do not reveal to stakeholders. It is therefore more cost-efficient and productive for firms to become completely transparent. Furthermore, Honest by does not need to invest in achieving any specific ethical label beyond those that are already used to certify materials.

This becomes particularly important in developing contexts. As described earlier, the Fairtrade label requires producer cooperatives to pay high certification costs in order to enter the ethical marketplace. The additional price charged for Fairtrade products is often used to pay for certification procedures; it does not end up in producers' pockets. Furthermore, unethical managers frequently withhold any extra profits that are earned through such ethical labels rather than these profits going to the people they are intended to help. These issues go largely unmentioned, as the Fairtrade label becomes a brand in and of itself. The goal for organizations becomes "How do we get this label?" as opposed to "How do we ensure producers earn more money?" Instead, by making the supply chain transparent and showing exactly how much money is returned to producers, organizations can demonstrate their actual impacts on producers. Such is the case for the Argan Tree, which publishes how much money goes directly to its female producers from each purchase.

Through information transparency, quantitative objectives can be established and real dialogues can begin, not rend. Moreover, many stakeholders are able to see through the greenwashing and various public relations attempts that organizations employ. Transparency, as an alternative to investing in public relations and branding efforts, is largely an unrefined perspective on the actual impacts of an organization. Stakeholders would much prefer being told directly what it is that an organization does versus being given a polished version of it. After all, this is where real dialogues can start and goals can be established. Hence, transparency creates a two-way conversation while eliminating the information asymmetry that commonly exists between firms and their stakeholders.

Three recent events illustrate that it is more cost-effective and productive for a firm—and other social actors—to be completely transparent. On April 21, 2016, Mitsubishi Motors admitted to overstating the fuel efficiency of four types of small cars sold in Japan by 5 to 10 percent, putting at further risk the trust of consumers in the automobile industry, already undermined by the recent Volkswagen (VW) scandal.[10] VW needs to fix at least six hundred thousand cars in the United States, and has set aside €6.7 billion to pay for potential consumer and government penalties. Its sales in Europe have already slowed by 0.5 percent. As it did with VW, where the German company admitted to manipulating emissions test data on its diesel vehicles in the United States and Europe, the falsification of data will certainly have a significant economic impact on Mitsubishi Motors.

In another incident involving misleading consumer information, three government workers in Flint, Michigan, have been charged with covering up evidence of lead contamination in the city's water supply. The workers—a city employee and two state workers assigned to monitor water quality in cities—are the first to face criminal charges in the case in which city residents drank foul and unsafe water for many months.[11]

Why did these car companies exaggerate the sustainability benefits to consumers as well as lie about emissions (in VW's case) and higher fuel performance (in Mitsubishi's case)? And why did government officials cover up vital information and put citizens at risk? Two thoughts come to mind. First, companies recognize now that consumers are more environmentally educated and the market is responding to products with higher sustainability performance. Citizens are likewise demanding to be correctly informed so that they can be sure that governments are meeting their responsibilities to protect their health by keeping vital resources such as water safe. The second thought is that transparency on sustainability has become a key strategic issue for business and governments. This is now of paramount significance to business and governments if they want to earn the trust of consumers and citizens. Long gone are the days of glowing corporate social responsibility reports and politically correct statements in which companies and governments trumpeted their sustainability achievements and commitments, but that members of society could not corroborate. Transparency is today the new word for sustainability.

Action 34: Use transparency as a cost-efficient strategy to eliminate information asymmetry as well as create real dialogues and objectives with stakeholders.

Accountability has become a significant onus for organizations. In a stakeholder view of the firm, managers and firms are responsible for being accountable to their stakeholder constituents. Perhaps one of the most important strategies for actually achieving accountability is complete transparency. Moreover, while KPIs can be important in conveying specific types of information, they can often fall short. Sustainability is a complex topic with information that cannot always be captured through simplification. Instead, complete transparency can be effective in enabling stakeholders to pick the information they need.

Although the examples explored thus far reveal transparency on the supply side of operations, Triodos Bank provides a best practice for the demand side. Many companies will argue that it is impossible to be completely transparent: either they do not have enough information or the information is proprietary. The earlier illustrations show that it is possible to obtain information and publish it in a meaningful way, while the practices at Triodos highlight that a bank's clients (an instance of proprietary information) can indeed be published if organizations truly want to make the sustainability leap.

Introduced in chapter 3, Triodos Bank was founded in the 1970s under the mission to "use money for good." In light of the financial crises at the time, Triodos's founders wanted to develop a new investing strategy whereby they would only invest in sustainable initiatives. Whereas many socially responsible investing funds employ negative screens, such as banning investments in organizations that sell firearms, alcohol, or other *sin* industries, Triodos Bank subscribes to a set of positive screens—choosing to invest only in initiatives that proactively improve society. These can range from museums to organic farms to clean energy initiatives.

Despite its level of sustainability and innovation in the banking sector, the challenge for Triodos was to demonstrate that it actually uses people's money for good. Consequently, Triodos decided to do something quite unthinkable in the banking sector: it shows the destination of all its investments. Through a Google Maps platform, the sustainable bank was able to inform its banking clients exactly where their money was going. Users on the platform can see every investment that Triodos makes, and can click on them to gain further information about the projects and why they meet Triodos's criteria. Users can also sort through investments by sector (environmental, social, and culture) or subsector. The initiative has been a significant success across all stakeholder groups.

Action 35: Embrace transparency to be more accountable to your stakeholders.

Another benefit that Triodos was able to achieve through its innovative platform was demonstrating its sustainability impact and performance. Traditional sustainability frameworks are incapable of grasping the level of performance that Triodos espouses mainly because organizations tend to make only selected information about the activities and externalities of the firm available. By attempting to capture all the sustainability impacts of an organization into a key set of KPIs, many of the actual sustainability practices of an organization would become obscured. While it is easy to show what your company does not do (i.e., negative screens), portraying the positive impacts of an organization is much more difficult. For instance, beyond communicating that all its investments are in sustainable initiatives, Triodos would be unable to capture its practices through KPIs—especially not in a manner that stakeholders would understand.

Many organizations develop KPIs to compare their sustainable practices to others. As mentioned in the previous chapter, however, this is not a simple task. Companies use a variety of different ways to measure impact—largely as a strategy to distinguish themselves from other companies—but in the process make it difficult to develop a standardized comparison. If Triodos attempted to compare itself to another bank, such as Goldman Sachs, say, would it really be able to? Through KPIs, Triodos could demonstrate how many tons of CO_2 it has helped abate through its investments or the acres of organic farming it has financed. But larger banks, which dedicate a much smaller percentage of their portfolio to these activities, could show an even greater impact. Even when ratios are constructed to help normalize and benchmark companies with each other, they still fall short of being meaningful or effective. As mentioned in the previous chapter, most mainstream banks actually appeared more sustainable than Triodos and other sustainable companies when traditional framings are used.

Triodos's platform has enabled it to communicate its practices and performance to stakeholders, and then let them interpret the data how they wished. Rather than summarizing the sustainable impacts from 5 percent of a company's portfolio through metrics (the general practice that encourages greenwashing in many sectors), it would be much more meaningful to understand the remaining 95 percent of a firm's impacts. It is also important to allow stakeholders to deep dive and truly appreciate the quality of sustainability impacts.

As illustrated by Triodos's platform, quantitative metrics are not always sufficient when discussing transparency. Often, qualitative descriptions and measures are necessary to communicate sustainability performance. The second case presented at the conclusion of the previous chapter discusses Lindenhoff Farm. While Lindenhoff would be classified as an organic farm under traditional measures and metrics, its owners argue that it is much more. As a farm in the Netherlands, Lindenhoff's goal is to grow food in the best possible way. While the farm is technically organic, the owners have never pursued organic certification as they contend that it does not say anything about the animals or variety of the food stock. In fact, the only requirements for organic certification are that animals eat all-natural stock (which generally has little variety to minimize costs) and have at least six square meters of space.

Instead, Lindenhoff feeds its cows a variety of crops with the exception of soybeans, due to the displacement of land that often occurs to grow soybeans. Additionally, the cows have ten square meters each inside the barn when they are not roaming freely on the large plot of land available to them. Because the cow's original habitat is the forest, the owners have planted trees inside the barn for shelter and installed sunroofs to let light enter.

Lindenhoff also runs a rehabilitation program, employing former drug addicts, felons, and homeless people. By providing these populations with full-time jobs and responsibilities, Dirco te Voortwis, the president of Lindenhoff Farms, believes he can improve their self-esteem and help them craft new identities.

By focusing on the habitats of animals, their feedstock, and the rehabilitation of farmhands, Lindenhoff adopts a comprehensive view of sustainability that is not effectively captured through quantitative indicators. The company relies on qualitative strategies such as case studies, storytelling, and transparency to demonstrate its sustainability to stakeholders.

Action 36: Employ a balance of qualitative and quantitative measures because numbers alone cannot tell the entire story.

While many executives may fear making their organizations transparent, the cases in this chapter hopefully show that organizations do not need to be perfect. Through honest dialogues with stakeholders, though, organizations can improve their practices. This can only occur when there is no information asymmetry. Therefore, organizations need to practice transparency in order to remain accountable to stakeholders. If you cannot make your operations 100 percent transparent, change them so that you can.

Box 7.1 introduces the key lessons and reviews the seven actions discussed in this chapter.

Up to this point in the book, we have focused on how to transform organizations to become sustainable enterprises. Scaling these sustainable business models is not an easy feat, however. Even companies that are founded as *social enterprises* often sacrifice sustainability performance to achieve scale. We therefore analyze the challenges of scaling sustainable business models in the next chapter. Before moving on, attempt to think through the following two cases to appreciate the challenges of scaling in a sustainable manner.

Case 1: Organic Valley

Organic Valley was originally founded under the name Coulee Region Organic Produce Pool Cooperative in 1988 when family owned farms in Wisconsin began collectively selling vegetables and dairy products. It has since expanded to thirty-two states and three provinces in Canada. Aligning approximately eighteen hundred farmers, it now boasts the largest independent cooperative of family farms in the world. Organic Valley products can be purchased in twenty-eight countries and reached just under $1 billion worth of sales in 2014.

Box 7.1
Transparency and Accountability: Key Lessons and Actions

• The McDonald's case shows that it is far more effective for the organization to be transparent about what it does and how it does it than to have a third party expose the impact on society of the firm's actions, thereby forcing the organization to share information. If an organization is unable to be 100 percent transparent, it needs to change its operations as soon as possible so that it can be transparent.

Action 30: Make your operations 100 percent transparent to effectively communicate the sustainability performance of your organization, and if you cannot, then change your operations.

• Patagonia's attitude toward sharing its environmental challenges demonstrates that far from receiving negative feedback from stakeholders, it earned their trust and loyalty. By being up-front with stakeholders in conveying an issue that your organization is actively tackling, stakeholders adopt a collaborative/supportive stance rather than an antagonistic one.

Action 31: Do not be afraid of revealing the negative aspects about your company; instead, create goals around them.

• PUMA's lesson for business is that to address the social dimension of sustainability, an organization can benefit from informing stakeholders about sensitive issues such as determining what fair wages should be paid to its workers in a quantitative way directly connected with purchases.

Action 32: Calculate and share the impacts of your operations on the supply chain to drive internal sustainability agendas forward.

• By sharing information on every aspect behind a supply chain with its customers and other stakeholders, organizations build trust and earn the right to operate.

Action 33: Make your supply chain completely transparent to build trust with stakeholders.

• A lesson one can learn from Honest by is that the best way to communicate the value of your brand is transparency with your stakeholders and making information publicly available. From VW, Mitsubishi, and the Flint, Michigan, we have learned that hiding information is bad for the short term, long term, and reputation of any organization.

Action 34: Use transparency as a cost-efficient strategy to eliminate information asymmetry as well as create real dialogues and objectives with stakeholders.

• Transparency has two benefits. The first—which was mentioned earlier—is that you earn the trust of customers and stakeholders, and the second is that by being transparent you create expectations from your stakeholders, who will demand that the organization lives up to its promises.

Action 35: Embrace transparency to be more accountable to your stakeholders.

• There are many lessons one can learn from the Triodos and Lindenhoff Farms cases, including what to communicate and with whom to do so. Organizations can use transparency as a cost-efficient strategy to eliminate information asymmetry, create real dialogues and objectives with stakeholders, and earn their trust. This in turn gives organizations the right to operate and the loyalty of their customers. Another lesson from Triodos is how to communicate. Although sustainability requires quantifying economic impacts, costs, and profits, the concept of sustainability is highly emotional because it refers to our very existence as humans along with the future of our species and planet. Thus, using narratives and storytelling to communicate with stakeholders provides the opportunity for organizations to bond with their stakeholders and members of society.

Action 36: Employ a balance of qualitative and quantitative measures because numbers alone cannot tell the entire story.

Despite its success, Organic Valley's scale was not easy to achieve, and often required its leadership to make trade-offs between sustainable performance and financial performance. One of the most significant dilemmas occurred in 2004, when cases of mad cow disease had significantly increased the demand for organic milk. George Simeon, the CEO of Organic Valley at the time, was not able to fulfill all the sudden orders for milk. Some orders had to be shorted by 40 percent, and the cooperative was only able to meet about 80 percent of the overall demand.[12]

Three years earlier, in 2001, Organic Valley sought to enter new markets aggressively through a partnership with Walmart. Walmart and other mass-market accounts represented approximately 55 percent of Organic Valley's total sales—and also its greatest growth potential.[13] Organic Valley was second only to Horizon, owned by Dean Foods, in the organic milk market. While Horizon was not yet in Walmart, it began bidding for Walmart's organic milk contracts in 2004 once it realized Organic Valley was facing a supply shortage.

Simeon faced a tough decision. After realizing that he could not increase the supply of organic milk, he had to strategically decide which customer accounts to maintain, and which he should cut back or eliminate. While the mass-market accounts represented the majority of Organic Valley's customer portfolio and promised greater growth potential, Organic Valley had an initial base of natural grocers, which it had expanded on during its early years. If you were Simeon, which customer accounts would you favor?

Case 2: Mondragon

The Mondragon Corporation, founded in 1956, was the tenth-largest company in Spain with eighty-three thousand employees and nearly €36 billion in consolidated assets. Its strategy for growth was to develop a network of cooperative groups to attain economies of scale as well as create supporting cooperatives to finance growth and provide technical assistance. Its diverse set of cooperatives spanned a significant array of industries, including supermarkets, appliance manufacturers, a polytechnic university, and a cooperative bank.

Yet the Mondragon Corporation was not immune to economic downturns and the difficult trade-offs that take place in the social enterprise space. The financial insolvency of Fagor Electrodomésticos, its oldest cooperative member, presented the most challenging dilemma in Mondragon's long history. Since 2008, the Mondragon Corporation (through its cooperative members) had injected €300 million of debt financing to assist Fagor, but Fagor requested another €180 million.

Txema Gisasola, the president of the Mondragon Corporation, needed to decide whether he should recommend financing Fagor's debt or deny the cooperative's request for assistance. While most Mondragon cooperatives in the past had decided on their own to declare bankruptcy and reallocate workers, it was a tougher scenario for Fagor, which employed fifty-six hundred workers.

Like many social enterprises, not to mention enterprises in general, the Mondragon Corporation was grappling with two competing agendas: its sustainability mission and profitability. Gisasola was searching for answers to the following questions: Could the Mondragon Corporation continue to increase the scale of its operations and remain sustainable? And if so, what viable strategies for growth would enable it to remain a social enterprise? With these questions lingering in the back of his mind, Gisasola wondered if he should recommend financing Fagor's debt.

8   Scaling: Can Sustainability Scale?

In this chapter, we confront a challenging topic: How can sustainability performance be maintained when scaling operations? In other words, can the sustainability strategy of a company succeed if the company shrinks in size, grows, or is absorbed by a bigger organization, and the governance and ownership of the firm changes? Traditional organizations pursue growth in order to achieve greater economies of scale and increase profitability—their primary focus. But organizations pursuing sustainability frequently have two competing agendas: a sustainability mission and profitability. While these two objectives are typically intertwined in the original business model of an organization, they become increasingly disparate over time due to a variety of factors, such as changing economic climates, new revenue streams, competition, employee and shareholder turnover, and so on. There is solid evidence that shows good financial performance and sustainability go hand in hand, though.[1] According to research by Deutsche Bank, which evaluated fifty-six academic studies, companies with high ratings for environmental, social, and governance factors have a lower cost of debt and equity; 89 percent of the studies they reviewed show that companies with high environmental, social, and governance ratings outperform the market in the medium (three to five years) and long term (five to ten years). The Carbon Disclosure Project found something similar. Companies participating in the Carbon Performance Leadership Index, which are included based on disclosure and performance on greenhouse gas emissions, record superior stock market returns. Companies in the Carbon Disclosure Leadership Index substantially outperformed the FTSE Global 500 between 2005 and 2012. Companies in the other index also did better.[2] Despite this evidence, more often than not profitability is prioritized at the expense of the sustainability mission of many organizations. A rising number of cases that support this point lead to the broader question: Can sustainability scale and remain successful when the governance and ownership of the firm changes?

Before continuing, it is important to address a valuable concern: Is growth necessary? As we saw in the case of Patagonia, Yvon Chouinard felt that Patagonia was beginning to fuel the rising problem of consumerism. Furthermore, if the goal was to reduce its footprint, Patagonia would be better served to sell less, not more. As we identify in this chapter, there are a few challenges companies face when scaling with respect to their sustainability agendas. Enterprises usually require financing from individuals or organizations that do not share the same priorities with regard to their sustainability missions. The profit-maximizing attitude impressed on enterprises thus can deteriorate their social impacts. This pressure is further increased during periods of decline, where failure can be attributed to the sustainability mission, which frequently requires time and money to achieve.

Of course, not scaling presents a different set of challenges. Smaller organizations are generally unable to achieve the economies of scale that their larger counterparts benefit from. As such, goods can be costlier to produce and put the company at a disadvantage compared to its competitors. Failing to scale also limits the social impact that an organization can make. Therefore, organizations pursuing sustainability strategies must carefully balance their sustainability missions with financial goals. In this chapter, we propose viable strategies for growth that enable sustainable enterprises to remain sustainable enterprises.

A recent example of the impact scaling has on the sustainability strategy of a company is the Swiss company Syngenta AG, a global agribusiness that produces agrochemicals and seeds. As of 2014, Syngenta was the world's largest crop chemical producer, and strongest in Europe.[3] It ranked third in seeds and biotechnology sales as of 2009. In 2014, Syngenta developed a strong sustainability initiative called the "Good Growth Plan," which has been successfully guiding the company on its journey to sustainability. On February 4, 2016, however, Syngenta was acquired by the conglomerate ChemChina, a state-owned enterprise that resulted from the merger of a number of companies formerly under China's Ministry of Chemical Industry, with a far different attitude toward sustainability than Syngenta's.[4] ChemChina's acquisition of Syngenta will be beneficial for both companies, as it will help improve food security in China while giving the Swiss company the money it needs to meet its own growth targets.[5] But what will happen to Syngenta's Good Growth Plan? Will ChemChina impose its own sustainability agenda on Syngenta, or will Syngenta be able to sell its sustainability strategy to ChemChina? At the time of the acquisition, ChemChina asserted that Syngenta would contribute its experience and know-how in promoting the highest environmental standards and nurturing thriving rural communities. These objectives are reflected in the commitments contained in the Good Growth Plan, which has been explicitly endorsed by ChemChina and will continue to form an integral part of the company's strategy.[6] It will be important to follow the future of Syngenta's sustainability initiative strategy closely to further understand how big a role scaling plays in business strategy.

Another story, Ben & Jerry's, is one of the first cautionary tales for enterprises that have a sustainability strategy. While every company embraces financing to fuel growth, few leaders think about the impacts of investors that are not connected to the sustainability mission of the company. The sustainability mission can become a fair-weather friend to many of these new partners—something that is great to have when a company is succeeding, and may even be the trigger for growth, but is an expensive proposition when a company stops performing.

Childhood friends, Ben Cohen and Jerry Greenfield opened an ice cream parlor at a gas station in Burlington, Vermont, on May 5, 1978. The setting for Ben & Jerry's was not the only thing that set the ice cream company apart. From the outset, Cohen and Greenfield were experimental with their flavors and used large chunks of ingredients in their ice cream concoctions. In 1980, the cofounders rented space in Burlington to begin packaging their famous ice cream in pints. They worked with smaller distributors to get their ice cream pints in small stores across Vermont and neighboring states. Their wholesale business rapidly expanded from sales of $135,000 in 1980 to approximately $1.5 million in 1983 and $10 million in 1985.[7] They also began franchising their stores, with the first one opening in 1981.

To help finance the rapid growth, Cohen and Greenfield were able to obtain small bank loans before receiving a large $2.1 million loan from the Vermont Industrial Development Authority for a state-issued Industrial Revenue Bond. They also raised money by issuing shares that local families could purchase. Almost eighteen hundred families invested, or one out of every hundred Vermont households.[8] By 1985, the restriction of selling stock to residents of Vermont expired. The stocks then went on the *pink sheet* exchange.[9] The stock price tripled, and more shares were subsequently issued. Before long, Ben & Jerry's was listed on the NASDAQ stock exchange.

Although Cohen and Greenfield started their ice cream company to earn a living, they slowly began infusing their values into the company—particularly Cohen. Through a philosophy of *linked prosperity*, Ben & Jerry's aggressively supported local community efforts. Once Ben & Jerry's became a publicly traded company, Cohen established the Ben & Jerry's Foundation to formalize the company's community outreach program and create a vehicle for social change.

In the past, everything had happened informally as all the shareholders were closely affiliated with Ben & Jerry's and understood its mission. This was no longer the case when Ben & Jerry's stock was publicly owned. In addition to giving fifty thousand shares to the foundation from his personal stake in the company, Cohen wanted to dedicate 10 percent of all company profits to fund the foundation. He finally agreed to lower the amount to 7.5 percent on the insistence of various financial advisers, most of whom suggested eliminating the foundation altogether. Cohen also instituted a salary cap ratio of five to one between the highest-paid employee and entry-level staff—an idea borrowed from the Mondragon cooperatives.[10] Ben & Jerry's espoused a values-led sourcing initiative, too, procuring all-natural ingredients that were 100 percent Fairtrade.[11] These practices extended to all the milk that Ben & Jerry's sourced from local, hormone-free cows, and the eggs that all came from cage-free chickens.

In the mid-1990s, however, sales began to dip, and the share price slid from just under $34 in 1993 to $17 in 1999. Ben & Jerry's steady decline enticed larger companies to begin making offers to reprivatize the company under their larger corporate umbrella. Avoiding an offer by Dreyer's Ice Cream to purchase the company in 1998, Cohen and other socially conscious investors, including Anita Roddick (the founder of the Body Shop), formulated a plan to make Ben & Jerry's a private company at $38 per share. Before the team was able to implement their plan, Dreyer's made a counter bid with a higher offer, which was challenged further by Unilever, which offered $43.60 per share.[12]

Many legal scholars and social entrepreneurs have debated the aftermath, but Cohen and Greenfield were eventually forced to sell their company to Unilever. While precedents existed for a shareholder board to accept a lower evaluation (i.e., at the $38 per share offered by Cohen and other investors), it would have been a difficult uphill battle for Cohen and others to pursue, both in the legal system and among the vast majority of shareholders who were looking to maximize their financial return. Instead, Ben & Jerry's board of directors accepted Unilever's bid of $326 million on April 11, 2000, with the enthusiastic approval of shareholders.

The bid was accepted under the condition that certain social practices would be upheld, including allocating 7.5 percent of company profits to the nonprofit umbrella of Ben & Jerry's along with an up-front capital injection. But Unilever did not agree to uphold all social practices. To many, the very sustainability mission that had propelled Ben & Jerry's to achieve early financial success was now weighing the company down. The company's policy of not firing employees was reversed under the new management after the guaranteed waiting period of two years was over. Similarly, the eco-friendly pint containers the company had adopted in the late 1990s were soon replaced to decrease costs.

Unilever's latest push in the sustainability domain has helped some of Ben & Jerry's practices be reinstated. A recent initiative is the "Caring Dairy" program, which helps farmers assess their sustainability according to eleven categories: soil health, soil loss management, nutrients (for high-quality crops), farm financials, social human capital, pest management, biodiversity, animal husbandry/welfare, energy consumption, water usage, and contributions to the local economy.[13]

The story of Ben & Jerry's, from its development of social practices, rapid market growth, and eventual buyout, echo a cautionary tale to social entrepreneurs. While financial numbers are easy to communicate, social practices are often lost on strangers when issuing stock. Ben & Jerry's was able to rapidly expand in the late 1980s and early 1990s by raising money from local banks and families, but its decision to go public disconnected the founders and their mission from the many individuals who now owned the company. It is therefore imperative to ensure that investors are consistently aligned with your sustainability mission—not merely your financial performance. This frequently may come at the expense of scaling too quickly to ensure that shareholders understand and uphold the social as well as financial goals of a company with a sustainability agenda.

What if the opposite had happened? What if Ben & Jerry's had acquired a smaller company under its umbrella? Gruma, the Mexican multinational, which is the world's largest producer of corn and wheat flour, has a sustainability mission to promote a better quality of life with its products. The company has grown at a fast pace by acquiring many corn and wheat flour producers in Latin America, the United States, China, and India. A strategic aspect of its growth is to align the new acquired companies with the sustainability strategy of Gruma. The same can be said of the TATA Group of India, which keeps growing worldwide and makes sure that its commitment to invest in the well-being of the local communities where it operates continues in all its acquired ventures.

Action 37: Ensure that all your investors are committed to your sustainability mission, even if that requires turning down money.

Investors are not the only stakeholder group that needs to be committed to an organization's sustainability mission. Cohen's first fears with the direction of Ben & Jerry's began long before the company was bought by Unilever. When introducing new social practices, he consistently received pushback from people throughout the organization— primarily new leaders and employees who were further removed from the origins of the company than the initial team. This is not a unique phenomenon. Neither is losing ownership of the company you cofounded. In fact, another company founded in Burlington also met a similar fate.

Jeffrey Hollender cofounded Seventh Generation with Alan Newman in 1988, selling resource-saving products through a mail-order catalog service. The name originates from the Iroquois practice of making decisions based on how they would impact the good of the seventh generation.[14] In 1990, the company began its own line of household cleaning products, which were nontoxic (safe for children) and made from recy- · cled materials. After going public in 1993, it rapidly expanded and reported $150 million in annual revenues in 2010.

Hollender, who served as the president and CEO of Seventh Generation for over two decades, was eventually terminated as CEO and a member of the board by the board of directors in 2009. Similar to Cohen, Hollender's aggressive growth strategy led him to have shareholders and employees who were not aligned with his goals for Seventh Generation. In an interview we conducted with Hollender, we asked what he would do differently if he had it to do all over again. In addition to the obvious (not accepting money from the wrong people), Hollender pointed to how he wished he had focused on empowering employees more.

At Seventh Generation, there were regular retreats, high salaries, and other perks to reward employees. While the social goals of Seventh Generation were consistently expressed at retreats and regular meetings, it is difficult to say how well employees absorbed them. In addition, to fuel the rapid growth at Seventh Generation, managers had to constantly hire new employees rather than further develop existing members of the organization who were more connected to the sustainable mission. Hollender therefore stresses the importance of bringing employees along on the sustainability journey. Indeed, he would likely argue that a sustainable enterprise cannot be achieved without a fully committed workforce that embraces the social goals as rigorously as the financial ones. He would look toward cooperative models such as Mondragon (mentioned later in the chapter) to give employees a vested stake in the company, but others exist.

Triodos Bank, which Hollender also points to as a leader in the sustainability space, places a tremendous amount of emphasis on human resources and training to ensure that company values can become institutionalized through the people that exercise them. This is particularly crucial for the sustainable bank, which only invests in projects that proactively improve society. Whenever a controversial decision is made on whether or not to provide a loan, the case is presented to all the loan officers to discuss the rationale behind the decision. In doing so, employees and managers alike are able to consistently evolve on Triodos's sustainability journey.

Action 38: Bring employees along with your organization on the sustainability journey.

Perhaps one of the most difficult aspects of a social agenda is that it provides guidelines but never a set of detailed plans. The significance of leadership often goes unnoticed in organizations that pursue sustainability missions. Social practices are not hard-and-fast rules; they need to be constantly reassessed and integrated into business models— frequently transforming them. Leadership, then, brings *personality* to sustainability missions. Leaders that champion sustainability, such as Cohen and Hollender, are able to proactively identify opportunities to improve the sustainability of their organizations.

Hollender was able to accelerate growth at Seventh Generation when he was able to scale its sustainability mission. By moving beyond developing natural cleaning products toward the broader and more important goal of healthier homes, Hollender helped craft an entirely new sector. In Cohen's case, these included local sourcing, community outreach activities, a wage differential ratio, and all-natural products. These were not all established at the outset; instead, they were introduced over time as opportunities presented themselves.

While many of the above-listed activities can be scaled and replicated, they do not necessarily provide a formula for how to develop new practices. Perhaps the true reason Ben & Jerry's sustainable practices stand out is due to Cohen's ability to inject his personal values into the company. For instance, during the Cold War, he came across the idea that the US Department of Defense should invest a portion of its budget in peace-promoting activities rather than solely war. He thus established 1% for Peace, an organization to lobby Congress for earmarking 1 percent of the defense budget toward initiatives that foster peace versus war. While the agenda item dissolved once the Cold War ended, it ultimately merged into Businesses for Social Responsibility—a conglomerate of many socially responsible businesses.

Cohen also identified an opportunity to align with other nonprofit organizations including the Learning Web to develop "Partnershops." The "Youth Scoops" program that was established helped provide early job experiences for youths. In response to the famous Exxon Valdez oil spill, Cohen later endorsed Ceres, an NGO to sustainability leadership, thereby making Ben & Jerry's the largest company at the signing. Worried about the safety of a nuclear power plant that was being proposed, he launched the campaign "Stop Seabrook, Keep Our Customers Alive and Licking."[15] While the examples are countless, they demonstrate the importance of leaders to mobilize their companies as platforms for social change.

Action 39: Constantly reassess how to integrate social practices into sustainable business models.

In some cases, the sustainability mission directly conflicts with a company's growth plans. The fertilizer industry, for example, was expected to grow an average of 2 percent annually from 2015 to 2019, and was projected to produce two hundred million tons in 2019.[16] But this growth is presently facing a significant sustainability crisis. A major international survey published in September 2009 in *Nature* listed the nitrogen cycle as one of the three "planetary boundaries" that human interventions have disturbed so badly that they threaten the future habitability of the earth.[17] Artificial nitrogen is as ubiquitous in water as synthetic CO_2 is in the air.[18]

Chemical fertilizers are added to soil to improve plant growth and yield. As the world population grows, the chemical fertilizer industry has been successfully growing, too. Today the food production for more than three billion people is dependent on chemical fertilizers.[19] The excessive use of chemical fertilizers, however, has had a harmful effect on the environment. A small amount of the nitrogen contained in the fertilizers that are applied to the soil is actually assimilated into the plants. Much is washed into surrounding bodies of water or filters into the groundwater. This has added significant amounts of nitrates to the water that the public consumes. Agricultural runoff, which contains fertilizers, is a major contributor to the eutrophication of freshwater.[20] In addition, some medical studies have suggested that certain disorders of the urinary and kidney systems are a result of excessive nitrates in drinking water. It is also thought that this is particularly harmful for babies and could even be potentially carcinogenic.[21]

While many social enterprises generally elect to pursue growth with the intention of reestablishing their sustainability missions through future profits, some opt to uphold their sustainability missions at any cost. In the case of Organic Valley, which we introduced in the previous chapter, CEO George Simeon chose to take the path less traveled. One of the most significant challenges Organic Valley faced was how to deal with the surge in demand for organic milk after the outbreak of mad cow disease in 2004. With the ability to fulfill only a fraction of his company's orders, Simeon had to decide whether to supply the natural grocers that had the longest relationship with Organic Valley's cooperative of family-owned farms or Walmart, which accounted for approximately 55 percent of its sales.

To complicate matters further, Organic Valley's largest competitor, Horizon, had begun to bid for Walmart's organic milk contracts. Horizon, owned by Dean Foods, was the only company in the United States to produce more organic milk than Organic Valley. The decision made by Simeon is lauded by most leaders today but was extremely controversial at the time. Rather than fulfill Walmart's contracts and prevent Horizon from entering the rapidly growing retailer, Organic Valley prioritized contracts from the initial base of natural grocers that had contributed to its growth from the outset.

Today, Organic Valley is the largest independent farming cooperative in the world with over eighteen hundred members. Reaching nearly $1 billion in sales in 2014, Organic Valley now has a presence in twenty-eight countries. While its growth has been definitely aggressive since it was founded in 1988, decisions such as the one made in 2004 ensured that this was never at the expense of the company's sustainability mission. Organic Valley has strived to ensure that its present stakeholders are content before scaling its network to new stakeholders.

Action 40: Ensure the satisfaction of your existing stakeholders before scaling to add new ones.

Perhaps no organization provides a better set of best practices in the sustainability sector than the Mondragon cooperatives. It is no coincidence, then, that Cohen, Hollender, and many others have incorporated many strategies introduced by Mondragon. The Mondragon cooperative movement was crafted by Don José María Arizmendiarrieta, or Arizmendi, beginning in the 1940s.

When Arizmendi arrived in Mondragon, the highest level of formalized education was primary schools; no one in the region had ever attended a university. So in 1943, Arizmendi started a technical school, which began as a middle school before evolving into a high school and then technical college. Five of the first eleven graduates of the Escuela Politécnica Profesional were hired at the Unión Cerrajera— Mondragon's sole industrial company. Soon after hiring the new employees, the Unión Cerrajera began selling stock to raise capital. Yet the employees were unable to purchase any of the stock being issued. The group of five therefore took Arizmendi's advice, and sought to create a cooperative based on the social and economic ideals they all valued.

Approximately one year later, on November 12, 1956, Ulgor (formed from the last names of its five founders: Usatorre, Larranaga, Gorronogoitia, Ormaechea, and oRtubay) moved to a building in Mondragon and inaugurated the first cooperative there. Aligning with traditional cooperative bylaws, Ulgor was owned by its employees. As such, all employees had the power to vote, and indeed were required to vote on important leadership and strategic decisions. Based on Ulgor's initial success, a variety of other cooperatives was founded in Mondragon and thus began the Mondragon cooperatives.

By 1976, 57 industrial cooperatives in the Mondragon system were employing 13,537 members. The primary driver behind growth was arguably the financial backbone of the Mondragon group: Caja Laboral Popular (CLP). The CLP was established in 1959 as a cooperative to support the growth and formation of other cooperatives. One crucial statute of the CLP and Mondragon cooperative group was that it required all cooperatives to deposit their working capital and savings into the bank. In return, the CLP was mandated to offer loans with lower interest rates to its members while also providing loans to new cooperatives, which were generally unable to procure financing elsewhere. Through this mutually beneficial partnership, the CLP was able to help grow the Mondragon cooperative network while scaling its operations.

The CLP developed a division to focus on entrepreneurship and supply consulting services to its member cooperatives. This division conducted audits on cooperatives and financed feasibility studies to assist entrepreneurs with the development of new cooperatives. The CLP also founded Lagun Aro, which provided social security and other insurance services to members of the Mondragon cooperatives.

To demonstrate the significance of the CLP, 50 percent of the capital of cooperatives in the Mondragon network was attributed to loans from the CLP at least through the 1970s.[22] Within seven years of its formation, the CLP had 21,653 savings accounts (it also offered banking services to noncooperative members). In 1975, it had 190,000 accounts and employed 1 out of every 25 people in the Mondragon cooperative group.

While the CLP provided financial services to cooperatives and their members, the Escuela Politécnica Profesional supplied highly skilled members to fill their ranks. School enrollments continued to climb, reaching 1,000 students during the 1960s and 2,000 by 1976. In order to better teach and communicate cooperative values, Arizmendi developed a work-study initiative whereby students worked in factories while attending school. In 1966, this initiative was formalized into an independent cooperative from the Escuela Politécnica Profesional and named Alecop. The wages that students earned were extremely competitive—pegged at 90 percent of the hourly rates paid to members. Alecop also included faculty members, who would offer consulting services to cooperatives in the Mondragon group. By 1990, Alecop consisted of 601 students and 33 faculty members, with sales between $9 and $10 million.[23]

Cooperatives in new sectors were established to help further the reach of the Mondragon cooperative network and diversify its assets. One example is Eroski, which has grown to become the largest chain of supermarkets in Spain. Through a strong network of agricultural, industrial, retail, and service cooperatives, Mondragon opted to scale by developing an ecosystem rather than concentrate on scaling a single cooperative.

Action 41: Create and scale a sustainable ecosystem for your organization instead of focusing on a single activity.

Despite the rapid growth that Mondragon experienced throughout much of its history, it was not immune to the various economic shocks that affected it. The oil shocks in the 1970s and resulting global recession had a sharp impact on the Spanish economy. Within five years, Spain had lost nearly one-fifth of its labor force. The Basque Country was hit even harder, particularly heavy industry. In contrast, only 0.6 percent of employees lost their jobs at Mondragon and they were able to receive unemployment benefits.

Perhaps the most important strategy of Mondragon during the recession was transferring employees from distressed cooperatives to those that either needed or could afford to increase their labor force. For instance, Ulgor was forced to downsize from 3,500 members to 2,200 during the recession. Of the 1,300 displaced members, 145 formed a new cooperative, Fagor Clima, 466 left the Mondragon system to be employed elsewhere, and the remaining members were relocated to other cooperatives in the industrial group, Ularco. The few members who were unable to be absorbed by other cooperatives within the network were given 80 percent of their pay for two years to find outside employment with the guarantee that they would be able to rejoin.

As discussed above, Lagun Aro had established a variety of insurance services including unemployment insurance. Beginning in 1980, it also created an unemployment fund that was financed through a 0.5 percent payroll tax on all members in the Mondragon system. This increased to 2.35 percent by 1986 and assisted 26 of 140 member cooperatives during that year alone.[24] The majority of the assistance funds were used to pay for members' relocation fees to other cooperatives and pay unemployed workers while they searched for jobs. Ularco was the main group that suffered due to its industrial focus. Members cut their salaries by 11 percent during the recession to help finance the unemployment fund and lower costs.

The solidarity that Mondragon achieved through its practices enabled it to maintain success even during one of the worst recessions in Spain. As such, Mondragon's social goals were upheld. In contrast, the lack of organizational diversity and assistance programs at Ben &

Jerry's and other companies led many to believe that sustainability missions sometimes have to be abandoned in order for financial progress to be achieved.

Action 42: Develop strategies to improve your organization's resilience so that social goals are not jeopardized.

Despite the various programs in place, Mondragon encountered its toughest challenge in 2009, when the global financial crisis catapulted the market. While many of Mondragon's branches were resilient to the crash, the same cannot be said of Fagor. Founded in 1956, Fagor (formerly Ulgor) was the first Mondragon cooperative and an integral part of Mondragon's transformation into the tenth-largest company in Spain. Fagor specialized in producing household appliances, including cooktops, dishwashers, hoods, ovens, ranges, refrigerators, small appliances, wine coolers, pressure cookers, and specialty cookware.[25]

In 2005, Fagor became the fifth-largest white goods manufacturer in Europe when it acquired 90 percent of Brandt, a privately owned entity that was the leading French white goods manufacturer. Prior to the deal, Fagor employed 6,230 people, controlled 10 production plants globally, and had 14 subsidiaries to market its products in 82 countries. The resulting combined workforce totaled nearly 11,000 people with 16 production plants in Europe, Africa, and Asia, and 100 global retail outlets.[26]

In the years following the crisis, sales were strong, with consolidated current assets valued at an average of €1 billion and a debt-to-equity ratio of approximately five to one. During this period, the European Union was developing approximately 1.4 million apartments per year. Half of these, or 700,000, were in Spain, which represented 30 percent of Fagor's market. After the housing market crashed in 2009, only 50,000 apartments were being developed in Spain, dramatically decreasing the number of appliances sold. In addition, while Fagor maintained its production plants, including the costly ones in Europe, its competitors were shifting their production to low-cost alternatives in Asian countries.[27] By 2012, Fagor's current assets had halved while its debt had doubled, leading to a debt-to-equity ratio of sixteen to one.[28]

In May 2013, the profitable companies within the Mondragon Corporation provided €35 million to Fagor, and an additional €35 million was supplied by all the companies in the Mondragon Corporation regardless of their profitability. This amount was in addition to Mondragon's other injections of capital into Fagor, which totaled approximately €300 million since 2008.[29]

By late 2013, Fagor was €1.1 billion in debt and calculated that it needed an additional €180 million to stabilize the company.[30] Its employees had offered to take a 20 percent decrease in pay. While other cooperatives had decided internally to file bankruptcy in recent years, including Ortza in 2010 (42 members) and Egurko in 2011 (132 members), Fagor's general assembly voted to weather the storm and request another injection of funds from Mondragon. Compared to Fagor's 5,600 workers, it was much easier to relocate Ortza's and Egurko's members to other cooperatives in the Mondragon network.

If the Mondragon Corporation financed Fagor with an extra €180 million, it could potentially save Fagor and reinforce the values championed by its sustainability mission. Other cooperatives were also struggling with the financial crisis, though. The Mondragon Corporation ran the risk of overextending itself, thereby jeopardizing the remaining cooperatives and members by providing Fagor with additional financing. The Mondragon Corporation decided against financing Fagor, which resulted in Fagor filing for bankruptcy on November 13, 2013.

Although the majority of Mondragon cooperatives had instituted various safety measures to insulate themselves from economic shocks, the same was not true for Fagor. Similar to Ben & Jerry's and Seventh Generation, Fagor accelerated its growth when the exciting opportunity to acquire Brandt arrived. While many leaders may argue that each of these three social enterprises faced unique circumstances, the problem is that no organization developed a downsizing plan in case its growth plans failed. If they had done so, they may have been able to scale more cautiously or not at all. The stakes are much higher in the case of a social enterprise because a sustainability mission plus a financial prerogative are at stake. Hence, exercise prudency and ensure that every plan for growth is accompanied by a plan for scaling back.

Action 43: Develop a downsizing plan for every expansion strategy.

As discussed in this chapter, scaling sustainability is an extremely challenging task for social enterprises and can eventually lead to their demise. This does not mean that we recommend a no- or even

Box 8.1
Scaling: Key Lessons and Actions

• The story of Ben & Jerry's shows that sustainability is a value driven proposition. This means that an organization that has a sustainability strategy has implicitly adopted some values and is dedicated to implementing them. Such values include, say, committing to respect the functioning of natural ecosystems, maximizing positive impacts on all stakeholders, paying fair wages, empowering employees, providing healthy products and services, avoiding the use of child labor or any form of discrimination, and establishing specific criteria to select investors. If a large organization buys a smaller one, like Gruma did, or if a smaller company is bought by a larger one, such as in Ben & Jerry's case, it is paramount that the sustainability strategies of both organizations as well as their values and long-term visions are aligned.

Action 37: Ensure that all your investors are committed to your sustainability mission, even if that requires turning down money.

• Organizations can have great sustainability-oriented missions, sustainability strategies, and sustainability commitments. But the key factor for success in the sustainability performance of an organization is to have all its internal stakeholders fully aligned, committed, and inspired to implement the sustainability strategy.

Action 38: Bring employees along with your organization on the sustainability journey.

• Sustainability is a moving target. Environmental, social, and economic conditions change as do the best practices of organizations along with the expectations of various stakeholders in the organizations upholding them. Therefore, organizations need to assess and reassess how effective they are at pursuing sustainability objectives, and need to continuously improve in an iterative manner.

Action 39: Constantly reassess how to integrate social practices into sustainable business models.

• The success of an organization's sustainability strategy is linked to the quality of the relationships the organization has with its stakeholders—especially those stakeholders that have played an important role in the development of the company and its success.

Action 40: Ensure the satisfaction of your existing stakeholders before scaling to add new ones.

• Scaling is a critical topic for sustainability. An organization can successfully address the impacts of scaling on the sustainability strategy of the company by looking beyond the organization and understanding the big picture. This means identifying all the organization's potential stakeholders during the scaling process.

• The Mondragon case and takeover of Syngenta by ChemChina show
that scaling is a crucial factor for the successful implementation of
the sustainability strategy of an organization. For this reason, it is
important that one element of an organization's sustainability strategy
is to prepare for potential scaling up or down.

Action 41: Create and scale a sustainable ecosystem for your
organization instead of focusing on a single activity.

• The social goals of an organization are key components of any
sustainability strategy. Organizations must keep their social goals
intact even when they scale.

Action 42: Develop strategies to improve your organization's resilience
so that social goals are not jeopardized.

• The Fagor case shows how important it is for the sustainability
strategy for an organization to plan and prepare for potential
downsizing, and make sure that the sustainability strategy of the
organization remains.

Action 43: Develop a downsizing plan for every expansion strategy.

slow-growth strategy. Yet if growth is indeed optimal for scaling a
sustainability mission and increasing profitability, the seven actions
developed in this chapter (and summarized in box 8.1 along with some
key lessons) are important to follow to ensure that a social enterprise
remains just that—a social one.

9 Sustainability Innovation: What Makes Sustainability Innovations Unique?

How do you promote sustainability innovation? While a lot of work has been conducted to understand innovation, what do we know about *sustainability innovation*? Is there anything unique about sustainability innovations? For instance, are they motivated in a particular manner or made possible through a distinct set of mechanisms? In this chapter, we explore sustainability innovations and propose a framework to help understand: how sustainability innovations are triggered, the types of actors that promote sustainability innovations, and how innovations are achieved.

To help clarify what we mean by a sustainability innovation, we propose merging a commonly accepted definition of innovation with the definition of sustainability we offer in chapter 4. That is, a sustainability innovation can be defined as "the generation, acceptance, and implementation of new ideas, processes, products, or services" that positively impact all stakeholder groups in the short and long term.[1] Through the various cases that we examine, we argue that sustainability innovations are achieved by networks of *positive ethical* actors in response to a social need. By positive ethical, we refer to the positive deviance continuum discussed in earlier chapters. The primary differentiators for sustainability innovations are as follows: they are triggered in direct response to a social need, and are mobilized by actors driven to create positive change.

As shown on the continuum, positive ethical refers to people who can be characterized as being virtuous. There is a rich body of literature that supports the claim that virtuousness fosters *prosocial* behavior, or individual behavior that is directed toward benefiting other people, not due to reciprocity but out of self-motivation.[2] This is an important part of the sustainability innovation framework we propose, where we demonstrate that positive ethical actors mobilize in response to a social need. In particular, the social needs that tend to motivate these actors into action are those that affect the sustainability of society. This is precisely what makes sustainability innovations unique: they aim to solve social, economic, and environmental problems.

To highlight how sustainability innovations are triggered and realized, we reference various cases, ranging from companies such as Tesla and Patagonia to new sectors including microfinance and socially responsible investing. Through these cases, we show that sustainability innovations are triggered in response to a social need (economic, social, or environmental) and facilitated through the creation of networks by positive ethical actors driven by the opportunity to improve society. Organizations can utilize the framework we develop to inform their future business models—ensuring that they are addressing social problems and building strategic partnerships to foster sustainability innovations. As you read the chapter, think about the following questions: What is a current, impending, or evolving social need to which your organization can respond, and who are the strategic partners necessary to foster a solution?

Many of the pioneers in the sustainability movement explored in this book thus far have emerged as a result of effectively responding to a social need. After all, the first element in our business model for sustainability is having a sustainability mission. To eliminate waste, Interface became one of the first companies to embrace the circular economy. Tesla emerged in an attempt to develop a cleaner fleet of vehicles to mitigate against greenhouse gas emissions and global warming. In an effort to curb consumerism and bring attention to the problem, Patagonia decided to launch its "sell less campaign." And to increase accountability in the financial sector, Triodos Bank makes its investments completely transparent. Vincenzo Muccioli saw the plight of young, unemployed individuals who were developing drug addictions and decided to start San Patrignano to give them a new lifestyle. To ensure producers earned a fair share of the final markup of their goods, the Max Havelaar and Fairtrade labels emerged while cooperative models expanded. This book is thus ripe with examples of sustainable initiatives that occurred in direct response to a societal problem.

Action 44: Determine how your organization can address a current social need through innovation.

A common descriptor for a sustainability innovation is *transformational*. In fact, we would argue that most sustainability innovations are transformational, and vice versa. We distinguish transformational innovation from other forms through a hierarchical approach in which we identify four major types of innovation: incremental, radical, game changing, and transformational. These four different levels of innovation can most easily be differentiated through the framework depicted in figure 9.1. The two axes in the framework provide structure to a sustainability innovation, which can be either a low-risk innovation that uses existing technologies in current markets (incremental innovation), or a high-risk one that either utilizes new technologies (radical innovation), opens new markets (game-changing innovation), or both (transformational innovation). It is the latter form of innovation that we urge organizations to pursue.

To help clarify the different forms of innovation, we look at sustainability innovations in the plastic materials sector. Society consumes about 415 billion pounds of plastic materials annually.[3] Aquafina was an early innovator in the sector, realizing that it could decrease costs if it were to reduce the amount of plastic in its water bottles. Aquafina's decision to decrease the amount of plastic in its water bottles by 50 percent is an example of incremental innovation. It is now a common practice throughout the beverage company and other sectors that use

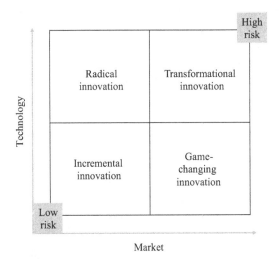

Figure 9.1
The four types of sustainability innovation

plastic to transport their products. While it did not open new markets or use new technologies, the innovation saved Aquafina a significant amount of money in material and transportation costs while reducing its footprint on the world. Most incremental innovations can be described as "low-hanging fruit"—saving organizations money even as it reduces their negative externalities.

Another interesting example of incremental innovation is from method—a company that primarily focuses on cleaning products. What distinguishes the company from others is the fact that it uses ocean waste in its bottles. There are "100 million tons of garbage floating in the Pacific Ocean alone."[4] Of this debris, 80 percent is estimated to be plastic, with approximately 46,000 pieces of plastic floating on every square mile of ocean. UNEP estimates that 8 million tons of plastic enter the oceans every year, and there are 250 million tons of plastic waste in the oceans around the world. This waste has led to the deaths of over 1 million species of marine life.[5] Method thus works with beach cleanup groups to convert plastic waste into bottles. On average, roughly 25 percent of each bottle is from recycled ocean plastic while the remainder comes from mainstream recycled plastic.[6]

Although it can be argued that method utilizes a new technology to transform ocean plastic into a material that can be used in recycled bottles, it is largely similar to the current process for recycling materials. Ambercycle, however, promises to change that with a new technology, thereby demonstrating radical innovation in the sector. Polyethylene terephthalate, or PET, is currently the most widely circulated plastic. While PET can be recycled, only 6 percent is actually recycled in the way most people conceptualize it, while 10 percent is burned, and the remaining 84 percent is returned to the environment. To increase the efficiency and decrease the cost of the recycling process, the team at Ambercycle is developing unique enzymes that can degrade PET into the two chemicals that make up the plastic: terephthalic acid and ethylene glycol.[7]

As Akshay Sethi admits, Ambercycle does not alter the current industry but rather fits into existing value chains. So what does a game-changing innovation look like, or one that actually creates a new market? In 2001, first-year college student Tom Szaky started producing organic fertilizer from worm poop, which he packaged in used soda bottles. Pursuing a vision to eliminate the concept of waste, Szaky dropped out of Princeton University and founded Terracycle. As described above, only a small portion of recyclable goods actually gets recycled. Szaky therefore decided to scale his operation by continuing to use discarded bottles versus purchasing them. Terracycle soon began setting up collection bins at schools, companies, and various facilities. In many instances, the company pays organizations for the bottles it collects. As such, Terracycle has created a new value chain for plastic bottles by simply cleaning and reusing them as opposed to breaking them down.

But what if there were a new, more sustainable way to produce plastic in the first place? After all, plastics are presently made from petroleum products. This amounted to 2.7 percent of the petroleum consumption in the United States and approximately 4 percent in Europe in 2010.[8] A model for transformational innovation, Newlight Technologies has invented a carbon-capture technology capable of developing plastics from greenhouse gases. Methane, or CH_4, is the second most prevalent greenhouse gas, and has an effect on climate change twenty times more potent than CO_2 over a hundred-year time frame.[9] In fact, methane leakage, in addition to other negative externalities, is the source of most criticism directed at the fracking industry. Newlight Technologies is able to capture methane from the atmosphere and combine it with oxygen to develop what it coins "AirCarbon," a carbon-negative plastic that can replace the traditional ones we use every day.

As described, sustainability innovation can range from decreasing materials to developing new technologies, creating new sectors, or combining all the above. It is the lattermost category that defines transformational innovation, and the one that we urge all organizations to pursue. It is important to note that organizations do not need to go through each stage of an innovation. Instead, they can leapfrog stages by focusing on transformational innovations, as Newlight demonstrated. While it may be a higher risk to pursue, transformational innovation promises to disrupt existing technologies and industries as well as create the largest, positive impact.

Action 45: Focus on transformational innovation.

While the previous conversation revolves around product-centric approaches, sustainability innovations can also be realized through transformative business models and value chains. As mentioned earlier, the social needs that motivate actors into promoting sustainability innovations are those oriented with the social, economic, and environmental aspects of sustainability. The first two categories of social needs, namely social and economic, suggest that sustainability innovations can occur by empowering stakeholders through the creation of new value chains, or development of new business models and modes of thinking. While environmental crises, such as the one confronting the plastics sector explored above, are more traditional problems, it is the social and economic challenges that are perhaps the most devastating to society.

Figure 9.2 presents a new way of differentiating between the four types of innovation we have identified. Instead of concentrating on technology and markets, innovations can be categorized based on business models and value chains. Are they entrenched in current systems or developing new ones? These forms of innovation should not be undervalued, as defended above. There is a limit to the benefits reaped from technological innovation. We need to change our mental models and the way we distribute value. After all, in the realm of sustainability, profitability is a means, not an end.

Sustainability innovations in two different sectors—garment production and finance—help us distinguish between the four different stages of innovation. The Nike sweatshop case we looked at in chapter 6 highlighted the problems of global supply chains on the world stage, causing consumers in the 1990s to start questioning the sources of their goods. The much more recent Rana Plaza factory collapse in Bangladesh demonstrated that we still have not fixed many of the problems.

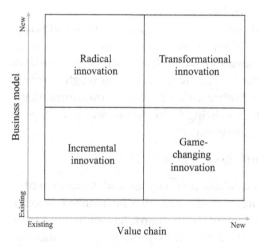

Figure 9.2
Rethinking the differentiators of innovation

Nonetheless, the development of labor standards in response to these crises is an example of incremental innovation—innovations that use existing business models and value chains but still begin to address a social need. Fairtrade and the development of other labels have been radical innovations in the space. While the value chains have remained largely the same, a new business model emerges: How can we ensure producers earn a fair wage for their work? As noted in chapter 7, these innovations have not been flawless. Yet they present a new mode of thinking.

The supply chain innovations introduced by Patagonia and Honest by are instances of game-changing innovation. Rather than focusing on innovating on the business model, these companies have radically altered value chains by eliminating middlepersons and developing relationships directly with the factories in which goods are produced. They have also made the process completely transparent, which informs stakeholders of how their value chains work.

The cooperative form of enterprise is perhaps the best illustration of transformational innovation here. As opposed to earning fair wages, producers have been able to earn equity and distribute profits. As shown by the Argan Tree in chapter 7 and Mondragon Corporation in chapter 8, cooperatives have the capacity to transform value chains and introduce new business models to address a dire social need— empowering marginalized producers of the world's goods.

The long history of the sustainable finance movement also evidences the impacts of sustainability innovations. One of the first innovations was a fair interest rate on loans. At the time, the lower classes in many societies lacked access to alternative sources of capital, and the upper classes prospered greatly from the lower classes by charging exorbitant interest rates, or usury. Because this interest rate innovation did not create a new business model or value chain, it can be considered an incremental innovation in the space.

An example of radical innovation is socially responsible investing, which emerged from various religious jurisprudences including Judaism and Islam, but began more formally in the mid-1700s with the Quakers and Methodists. The rise of the slave trade in the 1700s led Quakers and Methodists to develop the first negative-screening criteria in investments, refusing to invest in slave-trade-enabled products and war-related activities.[10] The modern socially responsible investing movement has been traced to the political crises of the 1960s, including the anti–Vietnam War protests and civil rights movement—particularly the race riots that ensued after the assassination of Martin Luther King Jr.[11] This movement was further shaped and formalized in the late 1980s by an innovative financial response by churches, universities, and community groups to the Apartheid movement in South Africa.[12] We consider the socially responsible investing movement a radical innovation. Despite not significantly altering value chains, it represented a new way of thinking about money and consequently a change in current business models.

Although traditional lending is based largely on a borrower's collateral (if the borrower defaults on a loan), microfinance enables the world's poorest to obtain financing—a population that was considered too *high risk* (with respect to defaulting on loans). The formation of formalized microcredit institutions started in Europe during the eighteenth century to address economic crises afflicting lower social classes. For instance, the microcredit funds of Ireland emerged in the 1720s in response to extreme poverty and the lack of banking services for the poor, who often needed loans to offset a bad harvest or illness.[13] Additionally, Raiffeisenbanken and Volksbanken in Germany originated as savings and credit cooperatives to serve the poor in rural and urban areas after the hunger years of 1846–1847.[14] Of course, many are already familiar with the modern-day microfinance boom, which has reached approximately 130 million of the world's poor.[15]

One of the most popular microfinance institutions is Grameen Bank, which was founded by Muhammad Yunus in 1977. In 1976, while serving as a professor at Chittagong University in Bangladesh, Yunus decided to loan forty-two women in a neighboring village $27 each to help them create small businesses that could sustain them.[16] After the success of this venture, Yunus secured a credit line to replicate his model on a larger scale, founding Grameen Bank in 1977. To help ensure repayment, borrowers accepted loans in groups of five people, thereby using social ties as collateral. Grameen Bank had approximately $1.7 billion in assets as of 2010, and by 2011, had over eight million borrowers across 97 percent of the villages in Bangladesh. Yunus and the Grameen Bank received a Nobel Prize in 2006 for their sustainability innovation.

We consider microfinance a game-changing innovation. While the business model is the same (banks loan money to lenders), the value chain has been completely altered by the inclusion of a new segment of the population. Triodos Bank's activities, on the other hand, would be an example of transformational innovation. By only using money for good, Triodos is one of the first financial institutions that actually perceives financial gain as a means, not an end. Beyond developing negative screens, Triodos Bank has a set of positive screens, which allows only companies that positively impact stakeholders to receive funding. Organic farms that aren't innovative enough or companies that are but do not address a social need (such as a paintball company that uses biodegradable paint) are common illustrations of initiatives that Triodos refuses to fund. In addition to developing a new way of thinking about money (and therefore, a new form of business model), Triodos makes funding accessible to groups (such as those seeking microfinance) and initiatives (one of the first wind farms in Europe) that otherwise would not receive funding.

These impactful innovations are not constrained to products but instead to the way money works and how it is distributed. Furthermore, or as a substitute for product-centric processes, organizations can develop new business models and create alternative value chains to address a wider variety of societal needs.

Action 46: Identify new ways of thinking and connect them to new value chains to determine how your organization can lead transformational innovation beyond product-centric approaches.

More often than not, sustainability innovation cannot be realized alone. Instead, it requires a strong network of positive ethical actors working in collaboration with each other. The rise of the wind energy sector is a testament to this. In 1986, the worst nuclear power plant disaster in history occurred at Chernobyl in the Ukraine. Highly radioactive fallout escaped into the atmosphere over an extensive geographic area. The strength of the explosion was four hundred times greater than that of the atomic bomb that exploded over Hiroshima.

The Chernobyl disaster sparked a discussion about alternative sources of energy in Europe. Moreover, due to the risks associated with developing nuclear power and the various nuclear weapons treaties emerging, companies, NGOs, consumers, and legislators began supporting the development of alternative energy sources that did not pollute in the way that fossil fuels did. In 1986, however, wind energy technology was in the early stages of its technological development. It was expensive, inefficient, and entirely unfunded.

Three important actors came together to develop the first wind farm in Europe. The first was a small engineering company in the Netherlands that conducted a feasibility study for a potential wind farm project in Denmark. Although the feasibility study demonstrated that the potential wind farm in Denmark was promising, no bank in Europe offered any investment products in *clean* energy. If any bank were to support such a risky investment, it would be motivated by nonfinancial objectives. Thus, Triodos Bank became the second crucial partner for making the wind farm possible. Yet Triodos was much smaller at the time and did not have the capital necessary to invest. What it did have, though, was a strong contingent of passionate depositors—the third partner in the network.

In order to move Dutch society toward renewable energy, Triodos realized it needed a much larger depositor base to be invested. It developed a unique financial vehicle to make that possible. Rather than have depositors put money into traditional checking and savings accounts, what if they could *invest* their deposits into a targeted investment fund—the Wind Fund? To help frame its *ask* and gather deposits/ investments, Triodos Bank calculated and communicated that every Dutch family would need to invest 1 guilder per kilowatt-hour a year in green energy in order offset their personal energy footprint, or an average of 3,000 guilders per year (about US$1,700). CEO Peter Blom recalls how inspired Triodos's depositors were to make exact calculations of how much they would need to invest in order to clean up their personal energy record.

The collaboration enabled the development of one of the earliest large-scale wind farms in Europe. The engineering company developed the technology and oversaw the project management of the wind farm, while Triodos financed the project through the investment vehicle it developed for its customers' deposits. But the network did not stop there, and neither did the impacts achieved through the initial innovation.

To further expand the Wind Fund, which eventually grew into the Green Fund, Triodos recognized the need to provide people with financial incentives. So it made the strategic decision to invite key policy makers to a workshop on green investments. Two of the participants went on to develop a policy proposal, later ratified by Parliament, which created tax incentives for private investors in green funds. Consequently, green funds became a popular financial product offered by the majority of banks in the Netherlands.

This case demonstrates the evolution of a positive ethical network (PEN), as the original PEN coordinated by Triodos Bank was expanded beyond the initial set of actors on multiple occasions to increase the impact of clean energy funds. A PEN benefits from a mechanism that scholars refer to as the amplifying effect, or the phenomenon that positive ethical behaviors and actions are reciprocated by those who witness them, thereby creating a positive, upward spiral. As such, a PEN becomes greater than the sum of its parts, enabling a sustainability innovation to succeed and scale.

Action 47: Develop a network among positive ethical actors who are motivated to address a similar societal problem.

We have identified three primary stages for making a sustainability innovation successful. The first is to address a social need directly; this social need is generally external to an organization, and affects the social, economic, and/or environmental fabric of society. The next step is to develop an innovation, either through a product or new business model. Finally, broad-sweeping innovations require PENs to realize the innovation. This process is outlined in the framework illustrated in figure 9.3.

Box 9.1 lists the actions in this chapter and introduces some key lessons.

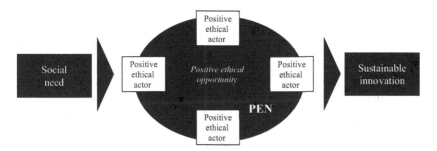

Figure 9.3
Sustainability innovation framework
Source: Zahir Dossa and Katrin Kaeufer, "Understanding Sustainability Innovations through Positive Ethical Networks," *Journal of Business Ethics* 119, no. 4 (2014): 543–559.

Box 9.1
Sustainability Innovation: Key Lessons and Actions

• Innovation is an important trigger for business success. The innovative new business models by Tesla and Triodos Bank highlight how companies can address societal needs as well as create long-term, lasting impacts on society and future generations (stage 4: the sustainable enterprise).

Action 44: Determine how your organization can address a current social need through innovation.

• Most "innovations" that occur in organizations are incremental, despite being branded as otherwise. Transformational innovations are extremely unique and special; they are what distinguish organizations as stage 4 sustainable companies. The Aquafina, method, and Terracycle cases show different levels of innovation, before the Newlight Technologies case helps illustrate what sets a transformational innovation apart. This is what defines the sustainable enterprise.

Action 45: Focus on transformational innovation.

• As we shift to service-oriented solutions in the sustainability space, we explore the different levels of innovation in the retail and finance space. The traditional innovation model, which relies on technology and markets, can be evolved to instead focus on business models and value chains. Transformational innovations are those that push the boundaries on both—creating new business models and new value chains.

Action 46: Identify new ways of thinking and connect them to new value chains to determine how your organization can lead transformational innovation beyond product-centric approaches.

• A positive ethical network has enormous potential. This is mainly because the members of the network share values and can together formulate a shared future for a sustainable society. Organizations need to become members of ethical networks and coordinate/collaborate with them to develop innovation initiatives—particularly transformational ones.

Action 47: Develop a network among positive ethical actors who are motivated to address a similar societal problem.

10 Making It Happen

Sustainability is a new paradigm for business. When companies and business executives attempt to develop sustainable organizations, however, the challenges they confront are significant. Embracing the sustainable business model necessitates more than the *cosmetic* organizational changes that we commonly encounter in industry. As we emphasize in this book, business leaders require a different way of thinking and need to adopt a new business model. Albert Einstein once said, "Problems cannot be solved at the same level of awareness that created them."[1] In order to go on the sustainability journey, business leaders and organizations must change the existing mental models that they have been following for many years. They must question the status quo of the present economic model in which business operates today in order to find more effective ways to achieve profitability in a sustainable manner.

Discussing the relationship between business and a healthy environment did not seem urgent sixty years ago. At that time, we thought that natural resources were mainly unlimited and technology would be the answer to any ecological imbalance. We know today that a healthy and sustainable business can only succeed in a healthy and sustainable society. The contrary is also true. The efforts of many organizations to reduce their environmental footprint are a good first step in the right direction. Nevertheless, they are not enough given the seriousness and urgency of contemporary global and local sustainability challenges. Recycling waste as well as becoming more energy efficient and less polluting is not enough to stop the degradation of ecosystems. Governments have done their share by establishing some policies and laws. Now it is time for business leaders and business organizations to act. We cannot continue borrowing from the wealth of future generations to support the present wasteful society. Business

Table 10.1
New Mental Models

Mental model	Old way	New way
Mission	This is who we are and what we do	Connect mission to a sustainability need
Stakeholders	We should minimize our negative impacts	Less harm does not mean good; focus on producing positive outcomes
Externalities	Minimize harm from first-order impacts	Second- and third-order impacts also need to be accounted for
Natural resources	Infinite and cheap to access	Finite, and need to be protected and conserved
Economics of sustainability	We can pay for negative impacts such as buying carbon offsets	Not everything can be monetized, particularly the impacts on silent stakeholders
Sustainable practices	Zero-sum game: negative impacts can be overcome with positive onew	Companies need to positively impact all stakeholders
Value chain	Create value in the supply chain	Equitably distribute value across actors in the supply chain
Profitability	Focus on short-term costs and revenues	Adopt a twenty-five-year long-term vision

leaders need to adopt new mental models, which are highlighted in table 10.1.

There have been many leaders in all realms of life—government, business, science, and others—who have expressed their commitment and acknowledged the significance of developing sustainable organizations. Yet only a few have led the way by breaking from old mental models and challenging how we do business. Through our research, we have identified some of these sustainability leaders, or *sustainability heroes*, and have examined how they think, act, and relate to others when dealing with risk, uncertainty, and adversity. Most important, we assess how they made it happen. They represent *role models* who can serve as both inspiration and benchmarks for leaders who want to transform their organizations into sustainable enterprises.

These sustainability leaders come from different parts of society. Examples of leaders who have pushed the frontier of knowledge as well as response of business to environmental and social challenges include writers, scientists, NGO activists, academic leaders, political leaders, and business leaders, as described below.

Writers: Rachel Carson, a US marine biologist and conservationist. Her 1962 book, *Silent Spring*, and other writings touched deep emotions in the general public, and are credited with advancing the global environmental movement.

Scientists: Mario Molina, a Mexican chemist and the most prominent precursor to the discovery of the Antarctic ozone hole. He was highly criticized by business when, as a graduate student, he published the results of his research indicating that a synthetic product (chlorofluorocarbons) was thinning the *ozone layer*—a life-supporting system. Molina was later a corecipient (along with Paul J. Crutzen and F. Sherwood Rowland) of the 1995 Nobel Prize in Chemistry for his role in elucidating the threat chlorofluorocarbons pose to the earth's ozone layer.

NGO activists: Wangari Muta Maathai, a Kenyan environmental and political activist. In the 1970s, Maathai founded the Green Belt Movement, an environmental NGO focused on the planting of trees, environmental conservation, and women's rights. In 1986, she was awarded the Right Livelihood Award, and in 2004, became the first African woman to receive the Nobel Peace Prize for "her contribution to sustainable development, democracy and peace."[2]

Academic leaders: Barry Commoner, a longtime university professor at Washington University in St. Louis, founder of modern ecology, and one of its most provocative thinkers and mobilizers in making environmentalism a people's political cause. Commoner was a leader among a generation of activist scientists who recognized the toxic consequences of the post–World War II technology boom in the United States, and one of the first to stir the national debate over the public's right to comprehend the risks and make decisions about them. Richard Freeman, another important academic, was critical in defending the stake that stakeholders had in organizations; he argued that it was the responsibility of companies to appease stakeholders. Freeman therefore expanded an organization's scope of social responsibilities far beyond the fiduciary ones it had to its shareholders.

Political leaders: Indira Gandhi, the prime minister of India from 1966 to 1977, and from 1980 until 1984 (when she was assassinated). She made an emphatic statement at the UN Stockholm Conference in 1972 that "one cannot be truly human and civilized unless one looks upon not only all fellow-men but all creation with the eyes of a friend." Gandhi declared that the very spirit that created the United Nations

was "concern for the present and future welfare of humanity."[3] Gro
Harlem Brundtland, the former prime minister of Norway, was
critical in following through with the charge, and established the term
sustainable development for mainstream use after forming and chairing
the WCED. In the famous publication she helped author, *Our Common
Future*, Brundtland and others defined the concept as "development
that meets the needs of the present without compromising the ability
of future generations to meet their own needs"—the definition that is
still widely circulated today.[4]

Business leaders: Finally, we have business leaders. James Burke from
J&J fought to restore the influence of the credo of his organization and
apply it in a time of crisis when he found out that J&J's most profitable
product—Tylenol—was contaminated with cyanide. In addition, Ray
Anderson of Interface decided his company should aim to not only
reduce waste but also adopt a *zero-waste* goal and manufacturing
philosophy. And Jeffrey Hollender, founder of Seventh Generation,
recognized that reducing the negative impacts of products does not
make them sustainable. As he said clearly, "Less bad does not equal
good."[5]

Yvon Chouinard, Patagonia's founder. During his lifetime of rock
climbing, which began in 1953 at the age of fourteen, Chouinard learned
the importance of protecting and conserving natural resources. Following his passion for climbing, he later developed his company in order
to produce climbing hardware. By 1970, Patagonia had become the
largest supplier of climbing hardware in the United States. But then
Chouinard realized that his equipment—which was selling well—was
not good for the environment because it was damaging rock permanently. He decided to phase out of the piton business. Chouinard found
an alternative—aluminum chocks that could be wedged by hand rather
than hammered in and out of cracks—and Patagonia was the first to
announce the chocks for sale in its catalog. When Patagonia switched
to selling sports clothes, it was one of the first garment companies to
adopt organic cotton.

More recently, Elon Musk has been leading the automobile industry
in a new direction. He is the CEO and CTO of SpaceX, the CEO and
product architect of Tesla Motors, and chair of SolarCity. Musk is
also the founder of SpaceX and a cofounder of PayPal. He has launched
a subcompact Model 3 for less than $35,000, and is also building
and selling electric vehicle power train components so that other

automakers can produce electric vehicles at affordable prices without having to develop the products in-house. Several mainstream publications have compared him to Henry Ford for his work on advanced vehicle power trains.

What do all these people—our sustainability heroes—have in common? We identify seven key competencies from our analysis:

Pioneering/agent of change: Each of the leaders had the ability to embrace change. They were not satisfied with the way their own organizations were responding to the sustainability call. They acknowledged that they had to do something more fundamental than just reducing their footprints and any potential harm they were causing society. Thus, they adopted new mental models to guide their organizations in maximizing their positive impacts on all stakeholders.

Inspirational: They were able to motivate people intrinsically. Because sustainability is an issue closely related to the values of the individual—and society—leaders who know how to touch people's hearts will achieve more engagement in implementing the sustainability strategy of their companies.

Visionary: Each of them had the capacity to develop a long-term vision around a values-based mission. They were motivated by a societal problem, and were determined to proactively act on it by forming a values-driven or sustainability mission. They then created a vision for their organizations around this calling. These values were expected to provide their organizations with the shining light on the path to implementing a new and sustainable business model.

Systems thinker: They had the ability to focus on the entire system, not only their organizations or products. They defined business success with a metric that was broader than just profits.

Risk taker: These leaders re-created the way we think about business success. Their stated main organizational purpose (or raison d'être) was not to maximize profits but instead to develop a solution to a social need in a profitable manner.

Resilient: Our heroes had a great capacity to confront pressures and face many hurdles while steering their organizations in a direction quite different from their competitors in the same industry. They undertook the risk to be different and create something that others had not tried before, even if it took time, effort, and many failures before they succeeded.

Ethical: Each of our sustainability leaders was virtuous—or positively ethical—always wanting to improve the world around them.

These leaders developed a new way of thinking that *challenged the status quo* but was *the right thing to do*. They were not trying to please shareholders with short-term profits, or appease the criticisms of environmental and consumer organizations. They developed new business models based on a new definition of sustainability, which attempted to maximize its positive impact on all stakeholders.

It might seem that a single person cannot undertake the enormous task of changing the present economic model, which is mostly linear and unsustainable. Our book begs to differ, and is ripe with countless examples. The US anthropologist Margaret Mead once said, "Never doubt that a small group of thoughtful, committed citizens can change the world; indeed, it's the only thing that ever has."[6]

So, How Can You Become a Sustainability Leader and Make It Happen? Take Action

In this book, we have outlined eight steps and forty-seven actions for taking the sustainability journey. We briefly summarize the different actions necessary and highlight the dilemmas of actually taking them in an organization. There is a forty-eighth and final action, though, that we have not discussed yet.

Action 48: Return to action 1 and repeat.

Sustainability is a journey—a continuous one. There is no end point where an organization can proclaim it has done everything possible to exemplify the sustainable enterprise. As contexts change, new crises and societal problems occur. These need new, innovative solutions that we argue organizations are ideally positioned to develop and implement. This, after all, has been a book that caters to leaders in enterprise. While there is a place for civil society, NGOs, the government, and other sectors of society to address the sustainability challenge, we contend that organizations can tackle them best—and using the sustainable business model framework we have developed in this book.

·It is also important for businesses to acknowledge and remedy the problems they have helped create.

The greatest variable when pursuing sustainability is you. While this book is a tool, it is up to you whether or not you use it. Can you make it happen?

In the opening chapter, we attempted to distinguish what we refer to as *sustainable* by describing four stages of sustainability: survival, environmentalism, social responsibility, and sustainability. A considerable obstacle for sustainability is that it is often reduced to survival, environmentalism, or social responsibility. Instead, we assert that sustainability is positively impacting all stakeholders of an organization. This means moving beyond doing *less harm* and toward *maximizing good*. While there is sometimes a business case for sustainability, sustainable practices may not always be profitable. Rather, we propose a business model for sustainability, which is reproduced in figure 10.1. By transforming the traditional business model, it is possible to achieve the sustainable enterprise—one that is not only profitable but more important also directly addresses a societal problem.

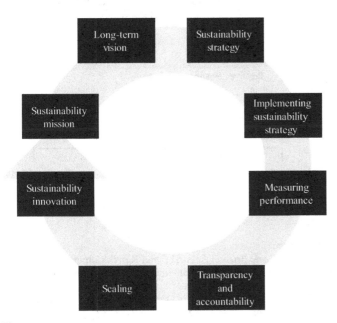

Figure 10.1
Sustainability business model

Chapter 2: Sustainability Mission

In the second chapter, we explored the notion of a sustainability mission. A sustainability mission extends beyond the traditional corporate mission in that it forces an organization to define what its purpose for being is: How is it contributing to society? The positive deviance continuum, reproduced in figure 10.2, is a framework that can help distinguish sustainable actions as positively deviant from the norm.

The sustainability journey begins by transforming a corporate mission into a sustainability mission: What problem in society are you attempting to alleviate? The evolution of Seventh Generation's mission into a sustainability-oriented one helps identify precisely what this process looks like.

Action 1: Establish your sustainability mission by explicitly indicating how the raison d'être of your company answers a sustainability need.

One strategy for ensuring that your organization remains vigilant in pursuing its mission is to develop and track indicators. This strategy enabled Interface to become one of the first companies to pursue a circular, zero-waste business model.

Positive deviance continuum

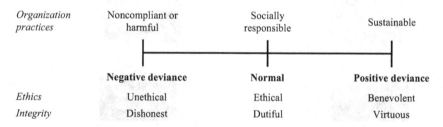

Organization practices	Noncompliant or harmful	Socially responsible	Sustainable
	Negative deviance	**Normal**	**Positive deviance**
Ethics	Unethical	Ethical	Benevolent
Integrity	Dishonest	Dutiful	Virtuous

Figure 10.2
Positive deviance continuum
Source: Derived from Arran Caza, Brianna A. Barker, and Kim S. Cameron, "Ethics and Ethos: The Buffering and Amplifying Effects of Ethical Behavior and Virtuousness," *Journal of Business Ethics* 52, no. 2 (2004): 169–178; Gretchen M. Spreitzer and Scott Sonenshein, "Positive Deviance and Extraordinary Organizing," in *Positive Organizational Scholarship*, ed. Kim S. Cameron, Jane E. Dutton, and Robert E. Quinn (San Francisco: Berret-Kohler Publishers Inc.), 207–224; Gretchen M. Spreitzer and Scott Sonenshein, "Toward the Construct Definition of Positive Deviance," *American Behavioral Scientist* 47, no. 6 (2004): 828–847.

Action 2: Translate your sustainability mission into concrete indicators and measure them to determine success.

While developing a sustainability mission is important, following it is a much greater challenge. J&J's fast reaction in recalling Tylenol during the "Chicago Tylenol murders" in the early 1980s is a testament to how a leader should uphold and embrace a sustainable mission. In contrast to J&J's rapid recall, many companies are not willing to part with short-term profitability. The failure of Toyota to quickly respond to automobile defects serves as a cautionary tale to organizations that prioritize short-term performance over adhering to a sustainability mission.

Action 3: Use your core values to uphold your mission even if there are short-term costs involved in addressing crisis situations.

Chapter 3: Long-Term Vision

When asked what their organizations will look like in twenty-five years, many executives admit that they will barely resemble the organizations in existence today, expressing the idea that the organizations of the future will address various sustainability challenges. Yet few executives focus on the long term when making current decisions. One exception is Jeff Bezos, who envisioned his company, Amazon, decades before it was realized.

Action 4: Focus on the long term.

When adopting a long-term vision, a systems perspective is required to achieve transformational as opposed to incremental change. The development of San Patrignano is an example of how a leader, Vincenzo Muccioli, transformed how rehabilitation works by developing an entirely new system.

Action 5: Adopt a systems perspective to pursue transformational as opposed to incremental changes.

An easy strategy for ensuring that your organization will lead the sector is to make sure you are always ten years ahead of the competition. Because of its foresight, Tesla Motors has become the clear leader in the electric vehicle sector.

Action 6: Make sure you are always ten years ahead of the competition.

The evolution and success of Tesla is a direct result of GM's dissolution of the electric vehicle program, which was well ahead of its time, but the program was a costly investment that was not deemed worthy.

Action 7: Prioritize long-term goals over short-term profit maximization.

It is never too late to become a sustainability pioneer. We explore how even a company such as PMI could transform its products and sector if it invested its full capacity to move away from traditional tobacco products toward sustainable agriculture or biofuels.

Action 8: Use your organization's full capacity to pursue long-term, sustainable objectives.

Chapter 4: Sustainability Strategy

We define sustainable organizations as those that positively impact all stakeholder groups in the short and long term. While not perfect, the buy one, give one model that companies such as TOMS shoes and Warby Parker employ illustrates how societal contribution can be directly incorporated into an organization's core strategy.

Action 9: Incorporate societal contribution into the core business strategy as opposed to treating it as an afterthought.

Producers are one of the most critical stakeholder groups yet are often marginalized. The fair trade movement has been an important achievement for increasing wages, but the cooperative movement and other models demonstrate how producers can be empowered by eliminating middlepersons and engaging in profit-sharing strategies.

Action 10: Eliminate unnecessary middlepersons to ensure value is appropriately distributed in value chains while empowering important actors.

It is also crucial to view customers as a stakeholder group that your organization should positively impact; the types of products and their impacts are important to consider. Patagonia has made significant strides in addressing consumerism and providing what customers need rather than what they want.

Action 11: Reimagine your business strategy by selling customers what they need versus what they want, and promote awareness to help customers distinguish between the two.

There is not always a business case for sustainability. Nevertheless, Triodos Bank demonstrated the positive linkages that can occur when pursuing sustainable initiatives that positively impact stakeholders.

Action 12: Pursue sustainability strategies even if there is not an obvious business case for them.

When a business case for sustainability does not exist, it is possible to lobby legislators to make one. While the opposite of this generally happens, Triodos Bank's proposition for green tax credits in the Netherlands exhibits how sustainability agendas can be made more feasible and profitable with legislation.

Action 13: If there is not a business case for sustainability, promote legislation to make one.

Organizations are frequently reactive versus proactive in terms of their sustainability agendas, focusing more on doing less harm rather than doing good. We explore the successes and challenges that McDonald's has faced in its journey to become more sustainable.

Action 14: Adopt a holistic sustainability strategy that positively impacts all stakeholder groups rather than minimizing harm or only targeting specific groups.

Chapter 5: Implementing Sustainability Strategy

Organizations currently do not prioritize the interests of stakeholders equally; instead, they largely give more weight to stakeholders who have economic ties to an organization such as investors, employees, and customers. Stakeholder theory, however, is based on the premise that it is not solely a financial interest that gives a group a *stake* in an organization but rather the sum of various impacts between the two. To become a sustainable organization that effectively engages with stakeholders, each stakeholder group's interests need to be equally weighted.

Action 15: Identify the interests and needs of all your stakeholders, and pay equal attention to them.

Oftentimes, leaders do not have a clear understanding of all the stakeholder groups that are impacted by or are impacting the organization. Before engaging with stakeholders, it is first important to know exactly who your organization's stakeholders are.

Action 16: Know thy stakeholders; identify every current, primary, and secondary stakeholder group, and anticipate future stakeholder ones.

As organizations scale, so too do their stakeholder networks. It is essential to constantly stay *close* to your stakeholders and understand their needs. Failure to do so results in tragedies such as the Rana Plaza factory collapse in Bangladesh.

Action 17: Get closer to your stakeholders and listen to what they have to say.

When differences arise with a stakeholder group, it is crucial to create a forum to work toward a solution versus ignoring the problems raised, as demonstrated by Nestlé's experience with Greenpeace.

Action 18: Create a forum for dialogue with stakeholders rather than attempting to silence them.

Not all stakeholder groups have a voice, but that does not mean companies should ignore or harm them. From the environment to marginalized populations, including the case with Shell in Nigeria, organizations consistently harm silent stakeholders rather than focus on how they can improve their status.

Action 19: Give silent stakeholders a voice and engage in effective dialogue to determine how all parties can improve their well-being.

In an effort to engage with stakeholders after various issues including pink slime, McDonald's launched an extensive online campaign to field various stakeholder questions and concentrate on the real issues concerning stakeholders.

Action 20: Create platforms and processes to show as well as tell stakeholders what they want to know.

Sustainable organizations can often hold similar values, beliefs, and agendas as their stakeholders. In these instances, organizations can engage with stakeholders by collaborating with them, such as the way Panera Bread did when it partnered with its customers to form Panera Cares in order to help feed people who cannot afford healthy meals.

Action 21: Collaborate with stakeholders to achieve social objectives.

Employees, the rudder and engine of any organization, are also an important stakeholder group to engage. While many companies engage employees through monetary compensation and bonuses, other organizations such as Triodos Bank mobilize employees around sustainability goals through intrinsic motivation.

Action 22: Use the mission of your company to motivate and engage employees as well as achieve higher productivity in your organization

Chapter 6: Measuring Sustainability Performance

Assess all the inputs and outputs in your organization's value chain to understand the impacts your firm has on various stakeholder groups. Develop KPIs around these data to help guide sustainability goals.

Action 23: Develop key performance indicators in the social, environmental, and profitability domains through an input–output analysis to understand your firm's direct impacts on stakeholders.

While organizations have improved tracking their first-order impacts through frameworks based on the TBL, most firms fail to track the indirect impacts they have on stakeholder groups. The role of financial institutions in the subprime financial crisis demonstrates the significance of measuring beyond the direct effects of a firm.

Action 24: Go beyond the first-order impacts to begin measuring the second- and third-order impacts that your organization has on stakeholder groups.

Rather than getting bogged down with a multitude of abstract metrics, focus on those that are meaningful and relevant to stakeholders.

Action 25: Develop metrics that are meaningful to stakeholders.

While it is important to eliminate the negative effects your organization has on stakeholder groups, sustainable organizations are those that positively impact all stakeholders.

Action 26: Move beyond measuring how your organization minimizes harm and toward how it positively impacts stakeholder groups; less bad is not good.

There are two problems with the TBL: the three domains (social, environmental, and economic) cannot be measured objectively, and the KPIs within each of these domains cannot be aggregated to determine a bottom line.

Action 27: Assess performance holistically versus through reductionist approaches; sustainability is not a zero-sum game.

What if stakeholders, rather than the organization itself, became the determinants of sustainability performance? If the sustainability of an organization is determined by how positively it impacts all stakeholder groups, an organization can poll stakeholder groups to determine how they have been touched by the organization's activities.

Action 28: Survey stakeholder groups to ensure that your organization is equitably distributing value to all stakeholder groups, even those that do not directly impact financial viability.

A critical lesson derived from Nike's engagement with its sweatshops is the importance of working with stakeholders to develop and measure key performance indicators for sustainability.

Action 29: Collaborate with stakeholders to determine sustainable performance.

Chapter 7: Transparency and Accountability

Perhaps the most significant barrier to understanding an organization's sustainability performance is the lack of transparency surrounding all its operations and actions. Few organizations are perfect, yet nearly every executive is afraid to reveal information that can show their organization in a bad light. An important test is the following: If every aspect about your company were placed on the front page of the *New York Times*, would your firm be OK? If not, what should you change?

Action 30: Make your operations 100 percent transparent to effectively communicate the sustainability performance of your organization, and if you cannot, then change your operations.

Companies have been extremely careful for the most part about sharing their impacts on the environment; instead, they focus on their achievements and positive outcomes. Patagonia, on the other hand, has not been afraid to show its weaknesses through transparency, and it actively works to improve itself.

Action 31: Do not be afraid of revealing the negative aspects about your company; instead, create goals around them.

In 2010, PUMA embarked on an ambitious journey to not only measure the negative externalities that went into making its shoes and apparel but also estimate the monetary costs associated with these impacts. Through monetizing its impacts, PUMA has been able to create a common language (albeit a flawed one) between its financial and environmental operations.

Action 32: Calculate and share the impacts of your operations on the supply chain to drive internal sustainability agendas forward.

At Honest by, customers and other stakeholders can see the cost point and sourcing for every component of each of the company's articles of clothing.

Action 33: Make your supply chain completely transparent to build trust with stakeholders.

Firms will frequently invest large amounts of money to adopt a label or create strong public relations around a brand but still not obtain the trust of stakeholders for one primary reason: firms have a lot of information that they do not reveal to stakeholders. Alternatives to the Fairtrade model reveal that it is more productive for firms to become completely transparent in their operations and revenue distribution.

Action 34: Use transparency as a cost-efficient strategy to eliminate information asymmetry as well as create real dialogues and objectives with stakeholders.

To respond to the lack of transparency and accountability in the financial sector, Triodos Bank decided to do something quite unthinkable: it showed where all its investments are located. Therefore, organizations can employ transparency to become more accountable to their stakeholder constituents.

Action 35: Embrace transparency to be more accountable to your stakeholders.

By attempting to grasp all the sustainability impacts of an organization through KPIs, many of the actual sustainability practices of an organization can become obscured. Capturing the positive impacts of an organization often requires qualitative descriptions and measures.

Action 36: Employ a balance of qualitative and quantitative measures because numbers alone cannot tell the entire story.

Chapter 8: Scaling

Traditional organizations pursue growth in order to achieve greater economies of scale and increase profitability—their primary focus. Organizations pursuing sustainability often have two competing agendas, however: a sustainability mission and profitability. As many social enterprises scale, including Ben & Jerry's, they lose ownership to investors who do not necessarily share a strong commitment to the sustainability mission.

Action 37: Ensure that all your investors are committed to your sustainability mission, even if that requires turning down money.

Rapid growth can also lead to another problem: an ever-growing workforce that is not as invested in the sustainability mission of an organization. Through its rigorous growth strategy, Seventh Generation was forced to hire new experts rather than train existing employees, which ultimately jeopardized the sustainability mission.

Action 38: Bring employees along with your organization on the sustainability journey.

Perhaps one of the most difficult aspects about a social agenda is that it provides guidelines but never a set of detailed plans. The importance of leadership frequently goes unnoticed in organizations that pursue sustainability missions. Leaders that champion sustainability, such as Ben Cohen (Ben & Jerry's) and Hollender (Seventh Generation), are able to proactively identify opportunities to improve the sustainability of their organizations.

Action 39: Constantly reassess how to integrate social practices into sustainable business models.

In some cases, the sustainability mission directly conflicts with a company's growth plans. While many social enterprises generally elect to pursue growth with the intention of reestablishing their sustainability missions through future profits, some opt to uphold their sustainability missions at any cost. If Organic Valley is any indication, preserving relationships with current stakeholder networks always benefits organizations in the long term.

Action 40: Ensure the satisfaction of your existing stakeholders before scaling to add new ones.

The Mondragon cooperative movement began in the 1940s under the guidance of Don José María Arizmendiarrieta. Through a strong network of agricultural, industrial, retail, and service cooperatives, Mondragon opted to scale by developing an ecosystem rather than scaling a single cooperative. As of 2014, it is the tenth-largest company in Spain.

Action 41: Create and scale a sustainable ecosystem for your organization instead of focusing on a single activity.

Despite the rapid growth that Mondragon experienced throughout much of its history, it was not immune to the various economic shocks that affected it. Through an employee-transfer program and unemployment fund financed by its cooperative members, though, the Mondragon cooperative network has been largely successful during recessions.

Action 42: Develop strategies to improve your organization's resilience so that social goals are not jeopardized.

The stakes are much higher in the case of a social enterprise because a sustainability mission in addition to a financial prerogative is at stake. Hence, sustainable organizations should exercise prudency and ensure that every plan for growth is accompanied by a plan for scaling back.

Action 43: Develop a downsizing plan for every expansion strategy.

Chapter 9: Sustainability Innovation

We define a sustainability innovation as "the generation, acceptance, and implementation of new ideas, processes, products, or services" positively impacting all stakeholder groups in the short and long term.[7] Sustainability innovations, then, are those that occur in direct response to a societal problem.

Action 44: Determine how your organization can address a current social need through innovation.

We identify four major types of innovation: incremental, radical, game-changing, and transformational. An incremental innovation is generally low risk, and relies on existing technologies and markets. Radical and game-changing innovations are higher risk, and are based on developing new technologies or new markets, respectively. Transformational innovation achieves both and is the highest risk, but it is the innovation that most directly addresses a social need. We assess examples in the plastic materials sector, including Aquafina, method, Ambercycle, Terracycle, and Newlight Technologies, in order to distinguish among the different forms of innovation.

Action 45: Focus on transformational innovation.

Sustainability innovations can also be in the form of developing new value chains or business models rather than a specific product. We explore innovations that took place in the garment production (labor standards, fair trade, transparency, and cooperatives) and finance sector (fair interest rates, socially responsible investing, microfinance, and sustainable banking) to demonstrate the range of innovations that respond primarily to social and economic crises.

Action 46: Identify new ways of thinking and connect them to new value chains to determine how your organization can lead transformational innovation beyond product-centric approaches.

More often than not, sustainability innovation cannot be realized alone. Instead, it requires a strong network of positive ethical actors working in collaboration with each other. One of the earliest wind farms in Europe and the larger green movement, for instance, was initiated through the collaboration between Triodos Bank, an engineering firm, socially conscious depositors, and legislation.

Action 47: Develop a network among positive ethical actors who are motivated to address a similar societal problem.

As discussed above, our business model is a circular one that does not terminate. Enterprises need to constantly iterate to maintain sustainability performance.

Action 48. Return to action 1 and repeat.

For your convenience, all the actions have been listed below. Remember, this process (let us call it step 0) starts with you. Are you ready to make it happen? Then here is what you should do:

1. Establish your sustainability mission by explicitly indicating how the raison d'être of your company answers a sustainability need.
2. Translate your sustainability mission into concrete indicators and measure them to determine success.
3. Use your core values to uphold your mission even if there are short-term costs involved in addressing crisis situations.
4. Focus on the long term.
5. Adopt a systems perspective to pursue transformational as opposed to incremental changes.
6. Make sure you are always ten years ahead of the competition.
7. Prioritize long-term goals over short-term profit maximization.
8. Use your organization's full capacity to pursue long-term, sustainable objectives.
9. Incorporate societal contribution into the core business strategy as opposed to treating it as an afterthought.
10. Eliminate unnecessary middlepersons to ensure value is appropriately distributed in value chains while empowering important actors.
11. Reimagine your business strategy by selling customers what they need versus what they want, and promote awareness to help customers distinguish between the two.
12. Pursue sustainability strategies even if there is not an obvious business case for them.
13. If there is not a business case for sustainability, promote legislation to make one.
14. Adopt a holistic sustainability strategy that positively impacts all stakeholder groups rather than minimizing harm or only targeting specific groups.
15. Identify the interests and needs of all your stakeholders, and pay equal attention to them.
16. Know thy stakeholders; identify every current, primary, and secondary stakeholder group, and anticipate future stakeholder ones.
17. Get closer to your stakeholders and listen to what they have to say.
18. Create a forum for dialogue with stakeholders rather than attempting to silence them.

19. Give silent stakeholders a voice and engage in effective dialogue to determine how all parties can improve their well-being.

20. Create platforms and processes to show as well as tell stakeholders what they want to know.

21. Collaborate with stakeholders to achieve social objectives.

22. Use the mission of your company to motivate and engage employees as well as achieve higher productivity in your organization.

23. Develop key performance indicators in the social, environmental, and profitability domains through an input–output analysis to understand your firm's direct impacts on stakeholders.

24. Go beyond the first-order impacts to begin measuring the second- and third-order impacts that your organization has on stakeholder groups.

25. Develop metrics that are meaningful to stakeholders.

26. Move beyond measuring how your organization minimizes harm and toward how it positively impacts stakeholder groups; less bad is not good.

27. Assess performance holistically versus through reductionist approaches; sustainability is not a zero-sum game.

28. Survey stakeholder groups to ensure that your organization is equitably distributing value to all stakeholder groups, even those that do not directly impact financial viability.

29. Collaborate with stakeholders to determine sustainable performance.

30. Make your operations 100 percent transparent to effectively communicate the sustainability performance of your organization, and if you cannot, then change your operations.

31. Do not be afraid of revealing the negative aspects about your company. Instead, create goals around them.

32. Calculate and share the impacts of your operations on the supply chain to drive internal sustainability agendas forward.

33. Make your supply chain completely transparent to build trust with stakeholders.

34. Use transparency as a cost-efficient strategy to eliminate information asymmetry as well as create real dialogues and objectives with stakeholders.

35. Embrace transparency to be more accountable to your stakeholders.

36. Employ a balance of qualitative and quantitative measures because numbers alone cannot tell the entire story.

37. Ensure that all your investors are committed to your sustainability mission, even if that requires turning down money.

38. Bring employees along with your organization on the sustainability journey.

39. Constantly reassess how to integrate social practices into sustainable business models.

40. Ensure the satisfaction of your existing stakeholders before scaling to add new ones.

41. Create and scale a sustainable ecosystem for your organization instead of focusing on a single activity.

42. Develop strategies to improve your organization's resilience so that social goals are not jeopardized.

43. Develop a downsizing plan for every expansion strategy.

44. Determine how your organization can address a current social need through innovation.

45. Focus on transformational innovation.

46. Identify new ways of thinking and connect them to new value chains to determine how your organization can lead transformational innovation beyond product-centric approaches.

47. Develop a network among positive ethical actors who are motivated to address a similar societal problem.

48. Return to action 1 and repeat.

Notes

Preface

1. "Less Bad Does Not Equal Good: Seventh Generation CEO Jeffrey Hollender," uploaded September 16, 2010, https://www.youtube.com/watch?v=hgbCGBRVGqw, (accessed September 13, 2016).

Chapter 1

1. "World Footprint: Do We Fit on the Planet?" Global Footprint Network: Advancing the Science of Sustainability, http://www.footprintnetwork.org/en/index.php/GFN/page/world_footprint/ (accessed April 18, 2016).

2. "The United Nations World Water Development Report 3: Water in a Changing World," UNESCO http://www.unesco.org/new/fileadmin/MULTIMEDIA/HQ/SC/pdf/WWDR3_Facts_and_Figures.pdf (accessed April 18, 2016).

3. "Fifth Assessment Report (AR5)," Intergovernmental Panel on Climate Change, Bali, October 2009, https://www.ipcc.ch/report/ar5/ (accessed April 18, 2016).

4. Chris Laszlo and Nadya Zhexembayeva, *Embedded Sustainability: The Next Big Competitive Advantage* (Stanford, CA: Greenleaf Publishing, 2011); Adam Werbach, *Strategy for Sustainability: A Business Manifesto* (Boston: Harvard Business Press, 2009); Daniel C. Esty and Andrew S. Winston, *Green to Gold: How Smart Companies Use Environmental Strategy to Innovate, Create Value, and Build Competitive Advantage* (Hoboken, NJ: John Wiley and Sons, 2009).

5. Aquafina is a bottled water brand manufactured by PepsiCo. Its latest lightweight half-liter bottle—called Eco-Fina—uses 50 percent less plastic. The new bottle will save an estimated seventy-five million pounds of plastic annually. Tray Granger, "New Aquafina Bottles Reduce Plastic Use by 50 Percent," *Earth 911*, March 30, 2009 http://earth911.com/food/new-aquafina-bottles-reduce-plastic-use-by-50-percent/ (accessed May 7, 2016).

6. The West African black rhinoceros (*Diceros bicornis longipes*) was declared extinct in 2011, although it could have been extinct as early as 2006. The cause of extinction has been attributed to poaching and the illegal market for rhinoceros horns.

7. Marc J. Epstein, *Making Sustainability Work: Best Practices in Managing and Measuring Corporate Social, Environmental, and Economic Impacts* (Sheffield, UK: Greenleaf Publishing, 2008).

8. Simon Bell and Stephen Morse, *Sustainability Indicators: Measuring the Immeasurable?* 2nd ed. (Milton Park, UK: Earthscan, 2008).

9. "EU-Wide Ban on Phosphates in Household Detergents Adopted," www.ewa-online.eu/issue-26-may-2012.html?file=tl_files/_media/content/documents_pdf/Publications/Newsletter/2012/Newsletter_26_2012/2_EWA-Newsletter_26-2012_EU -wide-ban-on-phosphates.pdf (accessed September 13, 2016).

10. Roger S. Gottlieb, *This Sacred Earth: Religion, Nature, Environment* (New York: Routledge, 1996).

11. Michael Kioni Dudley, "Traditional Native Hawaiian Environmental Philosophy," in *This Sacred Earth: Religion, Nature, Environment*, ed. Roger S. Gottlieb (New York: Routledge, 1996), 111–115; Peter Matthiessen, *Indian Country* (New York: Penguin Books, 1984); John S. Mbiti, "African Views of the Universe," in *This Sacred Earth: Religion, Nature, Environment*, ed. Roger S. Gottlieb (New York: Routledge, 1996), 174–180; Desta Mebratu, "Sustainability and Sustainable Development: Historical and Conceptual Review," *Environmental Impact Assessment Review* 18, no. 6 (1998): 493–520.

12. Robert Riddell, *Ecodevelopment: Economics, Ecology, and Development: An Alternative to Growth Imperative Models* (London: Gower, 1981).

13. Paul R. Ehrlich, *The Population Bomb* (New York: Ballantine, 1968).

14. Thomas Robert .Malthus, *An Essay on the Principle of Population* (anonymously published, 1798), 91–92.

15. The model was developed independently by Solow and his colleague Trevor Swan in 1956. Robert M. Solow, "A Contribution to the Theory of Economic Growth," *Quarterly Journal of Economics* 70 (1956): 65–94.

16. Jay W. Forrester, *World Dynamics* (Cambridge, MA: Wright-Allen Press, 1971).

17. Donella H. Meadows, Dennis L. Meadows, Jørgen Randers, and William W. Behrens III, *The Limits to Growth* (New York: Universe Books, 1972).

18. Barry Commoner, *The Closing Circle: Nature, Man, and Technology* (New York: Knopf, 1971).

19. Rachel Carson, Lois Darling, and Louis Darling, *Silent Spring* (Boston: Houghton Mifflin, 1962).

20. "Persistent Organic Pollutants: A Global Issue, a Global Response," https://www.epa.gov/international-cooperation/persistent-organic-pollutants-global-issue -global-response (accessed April 19, 2016).

21. Rachel Carson and Katherine L. Howe, *The Sea around Us* (New York: Oxford University Press, 1951); Rachel Carson and Bob Hines, *The Edge of the Sea* (Boston: Houghton Mifflin, 1955).

22. H. Patricia Hynes, *The Recurring Silent Spring* (New York: Pergamon Press, 1989), 3.

23. "The Costs of Air Pollution: Health Impacts of Road Transport," May 21, 2014, http://www.oecd.org/env/the-cost-of-air-pollution-9789264210448-en.htm (accessed April 19, 2016).

24. Wassily Leontief, *Input–Output Economics* (New York: Oxford University Press, 1966).

25. Commoner, *The Closing Circle*.

26. Stephan Schmidheiny, *Changing Course: A Global Business Perspective on Development and the Environment* (Cambridge, MA: MIT Press, 1992).

27. William McDonough and Michael Braungart, *Cradle to Cradle: Remaking the Way We Make Things* (New York: North Point Press, 2002).

28. As defined by Ellen MacArthur, the circular economy is restorative and regenerative by design, and aims to keep products, components, and materials at their highest utility and value at all times. The principles of a circular economy are: preserve and enhance natural capital: initial resources that are selected should be renewable and perform their utility at a high level; optimize resource yield to keep circulating resources within the technical or biological cycles; and foster system effectiveness by designing out externalities. "The Circular Economy Overview," Ellen MacArthur Foundation, http://www.ellenmacarthurfoundation.org/circular-economy/overview (accessed May 7, 2016).

29. "The New Plastics Economy: Rethinking the Future of Plastics," Ellen MacArthur Foundation, 2016, https://www.ellenmacarthurfoundation.org/publications/the-new -plastics-economy-rethinking-the-future-of-plastics (accessed June 29, 2016).

30. Marcus Eriksen, Laurent C. M. Lebreton, Henry S. Carson, Martin Thiel, Charles J. Moore, Jose C. Borerro, Francois Galgani, Peter G. Ryan, and Julia Reisser, "Plastic Pollution in the World's Oceans: More than 5 Trillion Plastic Pieces Weighing over 250,000 Tons Afloat," *PLOS ONE*, December 10, 2104, http://journals.plos.org/plosone/ article?id=10.1371/journal.pone.0111913 (accessed May 8, 2016).

31. "Ocean Plastics Pollution: A Global Tragedy for Our Oceans and Sea Life," Center for Biological Diversity, http://www.biologicaldiversity.org/campaigns/ocean _plastics/ (accessed May 8, 2016).

32. Robert Gray, "Accounting and Environmentalism: An Exploration of the Challenge of Gently Accounting for Accountability, Transparency, and Sustainability," *Accounting, Organizations, and Society* 17, no. 5 (1966): 399–425; Robert Gray, "Corporate Reporting for Sustainable Development: Accounting for Sustainability in 2000 AD," *Environmental Values* 3, no. 1 (1994): 17–45; Robert Gray and Jan Bebbington, *Accounting for the Environment* (Thousand Oaks, CA: SAGE Publications Limited, 2001).

33. Gro Harlem Brundtland, *Our Common Future* (Oxford: Oxford University Press, 1991).

34. R. Edward Freeman, *Strategic Management: A Stakeholder Approach* (Boston: Pitman, 1984).

35. John Elkington, *Cannibals with Forks: The Triple Bottom Line of 21st Century Business* (Oxford, UK: Capstone, 1999).

36. Gale Boyd and Gang Zhang, "Measuring Improvement in the Energy Performance of the U.S. Cement Industry," https://www.energystar.gov/sites/default/files/ buildings/tools/Duke%20Report%20on%20Cement%20EPI%20Update.pdf (accessed April 19, 2016).

37. Milton Friedman, "The Social Responsibility of Business Is to Increase Its Profits," *New York Times Magazine* 13 (1970): 32–33.

38. John R. Ehrenfeld, *Sustainability by Design: A Subversive Strategy for Transforming Our Consumer Culture* (New Haven, CT: Yale University Press, 2008).

39. Laszlo and Zhexembayeva, *Embedded Sustainability*; Esty and Winston, *Green to Gold*.

40. "The Good, the Bad, and the Ugly: Sustainability at Nespresso," http://www .theguardian.com/sustainable-business/2015/may/27/nespresso-sustainability -transparency-recycling-coffee-pods-values-aluminum (accessed April 19, 2016).

41. Ibid.

42. Alexander Osterwalder and Yves Pigneur, *Business Model Generation: A Handbook for Visionaries, Game Changers, and Challengers* (Hoboken, NJ: Wiley, 2013).

43. Noah Whalley and Bradley Whitehead, "It Is Not Easy to Be Green," *Harvard Business Review*, May–June 1994, 46–51; McKinsey Sustainability Practice Workshop, Puerto Vallarta, Mexico, 1995.

44. "Sustainability, Walmart, http://corporate.walmart.com/global-responsibility/ sustainability/ (accessed April 19, 2016).

Chapter 2

1. Milton Friedman, "The Social Responsibility of Business Is to Increase Its Profits," *New York Times Magazine*, September 13, 1970; Isabel Rimanoczy, "What Is the Purpose of Business?" *Huffington Post*, April 21, 2015, http://www.huffingtonpost.com/isabel -rimanoczy-edd-/what-is-the-purpose-of-bu_b_7100126.html (accessed April 19, 2016).

2. Quoted in Steve Dening, "The Dumbest Idea in the World: Maximizing Shareholder Value," *Forbes*, November 2011, http://www.forbes.com/sites/stevedenning/2011/11/ 28/maximizing-shareholder-value-the-dumbest-idea-in-the-world/#4e555f622224 (accessed July 1, 2016).

3. Quoted in Bruce Jones, "The Difference between Purpose and Mission," *Harvard Business Review*, February 2, 2016, https://hbr.org/sponsored/2016/02/the-difference -between-purpose-and-mission (accessed May 8, 2016).

4. Jeffrey Hollender (former CEO and founder of Seventh Generation), e-mail message to authors, September 21, 2014.

5. Ibid.

6. Ibid.

7. Paul Hawken, *The Ecology of Commerce: A Declaration of Sustainability* (New York: Harper Business, 1993).

8. Paul Hawken. *The Ecology of Commerce: A Declaration of Sustainability* (New York, NY: HarperBusiness, 1993).

9. "Interface's Values Are Our Guiding Principles," Interface, http://www.interfaceglobal .com/Company/Mission-Vision.aspx (accessed May 30, 2015).

10. Ibid.

11. Ramon Arratia, "The 7 Fronts of 'Mount Sustainability,'" Interface, September 30, 2014, http://www.interfacecutthefluff.com/7-fronts-mount-sustainability/ (accessed July 1, 2016).

12. David W. Pearce and R. Kerry Turner, *Economics of Natural Resources and the Environment* (Baltimore: Johns Hopkins University Press, 1989).

13. "Manifesto for Resource-Efficient Europe," http://europa.eu/rapid/press-release_MEMO-12-989_en.htm (accessed April 19, 2012).

14. Key elements of the revised waste proposal include a common EU target for recycling 65 percent of municipal waste by 2030, a common EU target for recycling 75 percent of packaging waste by 2030, and a binding target to reduce landfill to a maximum of 10 percent of all waste by 2030.

15. "HBS Awards for Alumni Achievement 2003—James E. Burke HBS MBA 1949," Harvard Business School Archive, October 27, 2003, http://hbswk.hbs.edu/archive/3755.html (accessed May 30, 2015).

16. "Our Credo," Johnson & Johnson, https://www.jnj.com/sites/default/files/pdf/jnj_ourcredo_english_us_8.5x11_cmyk.pdf (accessed September 13, 2016).

17. "Our Vision," Toyota, http://www.toyota.com.au/toyota/company/vision-and-philosophy (accessed May 30, 2015).

18. "Remarks as Prepared for Delivery by Attorney General Eric Holder at the Press Conference Announcing Criminal Charge and Deferred Prosecution Agreement with Toyota Motor Corporation," US Department of Justice, http://www.justice.gov/opa/speech/remarks-prepared-delivery-attorney-general-eric-holder-press-conference-announcing (accessed, July 17, 2015).

19. Jeffrey K. Liker, *The Toyota Way: 14 Management Principles from the World's Greatest Manufacturer* (New York: McGraw-Hill, 2004).

20. "Nestlé's Corporate Business Principles," Nestlé, http://www.nestle.com/aboutus/businessprinciples(accessed September 22, 2014).

21. Ibid.

22. Ibid.

23. Zero emissions refers to the amount of tailpipe pollutants emitted by vehicles, and therefore has no implication on the emissions used to manufacture the vehicle. This became a contentious issue later on.

24. "Annual Report," Philip Morris International, http://investors.pmi.com/phoenix.zhtml?c=146476&p=irol-reportsannual (accessed June 11, 2015).

25. "Company Overview," Philip Morris International, http://www.pmi.com/eng/about_us/company_overview/pages/company_overview.aspx (accessed May 30, 2015).

26. "2013 Annual Report," Philip Morris International, http://media.corporate-ir.net/media_files/IROL/14/146476/PMI-ANNUAL-2013-FINAL/index.html (accessed July 17, 2015).

Chapter 3

1. Quoted in Morten T. Hansen, Herminia Ibarra, and Urs Peyer, "The Best-Performing CEOs in the World," *Harvard Business Review*, January–February 2013.

2. Eric Jackson, "6 Things Jeff Bezos Knew Back in 1977 That Made Amazon a Gorilla," *Forbes*, November 16, 2011, http://www.forbes.com/sites/ericjackson/2011/11/16/

6-things-jeff-bezos-knew-back-in-1997-that-made-amazon-a-gorilla/ (accessed May 30 2015).

3. "Amazon Prime Air," Amazon, December 1, 2013, https://www.youtube.com/watch?v=98BIu9dpwHU (accessed May 30, 2015).

4. Quoted in Patrick Hull, "Be Visionary. Think Big," *Forbes*, Decebmer 19, 2012, http://www.forbes.com/sites/patrickhull/2012/12/19/be-visionary-think-big/#3b22889f22f7 (accessed September 13, 2016).

5. Dominic Barton and Mark Wiseman, "Perspectives on the Long Term," *McKinsey Quarterly*, March 2015, http://www.mckinsey.com/global-themes/leadership/perspectives-on-the-long-term (accessed July 2, 2016).

6. Paul Pollman, "Business, Society, and the Future of Capitalism," *McKinsey Quarterly*, May 2014, http://www.mckinsey.com/business-functions/sustainability-and-resource-productivity/our-insights/business-society-and-the-future-of-capitalism (accessed July 2, 2016).

7. Challenges and Opportunities for the Sustainable Energy Enterprise workshop, held by Francisco Szekely, October 2014.

8. Richard Anderson, "Sustainability the Key to Long-Term Corporate Health," BBC News, April 6, 2016, http://www.bbc.com/news/business-35430228 (accessed July 2, 2016).

9. Nate Abrams, "Let NASA Explore the Stars, but Let SpaceX Build the Rockets That Get Us There," Policy.Mic, August 10, 2012, http://mic.com/articles/12573/let-nasa-explore-the-stars-but-let-spacex-build-the-rockets-that-get-us-there (accessed May 30, 2015).

10. Lorraine Chow, "Elon Musk Unveils Tesla Model 3: Accelerating Sustainable Transport Is 'Important for the Future of the World,'" *EcoWatch*, April 1, 2016, http://ecowatch.com/2016/04/01/elon-musk-unveils-model-3/ (accessed July 2, 2016).

11. Tesla Team, "The Week That Electric Vehicles Went Mainstream," Tesla Blog, April 7, 2016, https://www.teslamotors.com/blog/the-week-electric-vehicles-went-mainstream (accessed April 19, 2016).

12. Quoted in Tad Friend, "Plugged In: Can Elon Musk Lead the Way to an Electric-Car Future?" *New Yorker*, August 24, 2009, http://www.newyorker.com/magazine/2009/08/24/plugged-in (accessed July 17, 2015).

13. *Who Killed the Electric Car*, directed by Chris Paine (Rosamond, CA, 2006), documentary.

14. Bill Moore, "Do 10 Million Californians Want EVs? An Interview with Michael Coates," *EV World*, 2000.

15. Quoted in Keith Naughton, "Why Toyota Is Becoming the World's Top Carmaker," *Newsweek*, March 11, 2007, http://www.newsweek.com/why-toyota-becoming-worlds-top-carmaker-95469 (accessed July 17, 2015).

16. At the height of the tobacco epidemic in the early 1960s, the per capita consumption in the United States was 4,166 cigarettes per year. More recently in 2011, per capita cigarette consumption is 1,232 annually in the United States. Centers for Disease Control and Prevention and US Department of Agriculture, 2012.

Chapter 4

1. "The Business Case for Sustainability," International Finance Corporation, http:// www.ifc.org/wps/wcm/connect/9519a5004c1bc60eb534bd79803d5464/Business+Case +for+Sustainability.pdf?MOD=AJPERES (accessed April 19, 2016).

2. Ibid.

3. "Catastrophe in the Gulf of Mexico: Devastation Persists," Center for Biological Diversity, http://www.biologicaldiversity.org/programs/public_lands/energy/dirty_energy _development/oil_and_gas/gulf_oil_spill/index.html (accessed April 19, 2016).

4. "Performance with Purpose: Sustainability Report 2014," PepsiCo, http://www .pepsico.com/docs/album/sustainability-reporting/pep_csr14_sus_overview.pdf (accessed April 19, 2016).

5. Department of Nutrition at Harvard School of Public Health, "Fact Sheet: Sugary Drink Supersizing and the Obesity Epidemic," June 2012, https://cdn1.sph.harvard.edu/ wp-content/uploads/sites/30/2012/10/sugary-drinks-and-obesity-fact-sheet-june -2012-the-nutrition-source.pdf (accessed April 19, 2016).

6. Ibid.

7. "One for One," TOMS, http://www.toms.ca/improving-lives (accessed April 19, 2016).

8. Blake Mycoskie, "How I Did It: The TOMS Story," *Entrepreneur*, September 20, 2011, https://www.entrepreneur.com/article/220350 (accessed July 3, 2016).

9. C. W., "The Economics of TOMS Shoes: Putting the Boot in Development," *Economist*, October 27, 2014, http://www.economist.com/blogs/freeexchange/2014/10/economics -toms-shoes (accessed May 8, 2016).

10. Bruce Wydick, Elizabeth Katz, and Brendan Janet, "Do In-Kind Transfers Damage Local Markets? The Case of TOMS Shoe Donations in El Salvador" (paper, University of San Francisco, March 12, 2014).

11. Warby Parker, "Year in Review 2014," https://www.warbyparker.com/year-in -review-2014 (accessed July 3, 2016).

12. "Buy a Pair, Give a Pair," Warby Parker, https://www.warbyparker.com/buy-a-pair -give-a-pair (accessed June 2, 2015).

13. "FAQs: Frequently Asked Questions," Fairtrade International, http://www.fairtrade .net/about-fairtrade/faqs.html (accessed July 3, 2016).

14. Joni Valkila and Anja Nygren, "Impacts of Fair Trade Certification on Coffee Farmers, Cooperatives, and Laborers in Nicaragua," *Agriculture and Human Values* 27, no. 3 (September 2010): 321–333; Ellen Pay, "The Market for Organic and Fair-Trade Coffee," Food and Agriculture Organization of the United Nations, 2009, http://www.fao.org/ fileadmin/templates/organicexports/docs/Market_Organic_FT_Coffee.pdf (accessed June 2, 2015).

15. See, for example, Gavin Fridell, "Fair-Trade Coffee and Commodity Fetishism: The Limits of Market-Driven Social Justice," *Historical Materialism* 15, no. 4 (2007): 79–104; Sarah Lyon, "We Want to Be Equal to Them: Fair-Trade Coffee Certification and Gender

Equity within Organizations," *Human Organization* 67, no. 3 (2008): 258–68; Deborah Sick, "Coffee, Farming Families, and Fair Trade in Costa Rica: New Markets, Same Old Problems?" *Latin American Research Review* 43, no. 3 (2008): 193–208.

16. Joni Valkila, Pertii Haaparanta, and Niina Niemi, "Empowering Coffee Traders? The Coffee Value Chain from Nicaraguan Fair Trade Farmers to Finnish Consumers," *Journal of Business Ethics* 97, no. 2 (December 2010): 257–270.

17. René Mendoza and Johan Bastiaensen, "Fair Trade and the Coffee Crisis in the Nicaraguan Segovias," *Small Enterprise Development* 14, no. 2 (2003): 36–46.

18. Michael E. Porter, *Competitive Advantage: Creating and Sustaining Superior Performance* (New York: Free Press, 2004).

19. Zoubida Charrouf and Dom Guillaume, "Sustainable Development in Northern Africa: The Argan Forest Case," *Sustainability* 1, no. 4 (2009): 1012–1022.

20. "Biosphere Reserves—Learning Sites for Sustainable Development," UNESCO, http://www.unesco.org/new/en/natural-sciences/environment/ecological-sciences/biosphere-reserves/ (accessed June 2, 2015).

21. Tashelhit is spoken in the geographically remote southwest of Morocco. Tashelhit speakers are the most isolated of all the Berber communities.

22. Zahir Dossa, one of the authors of this book, is the founder of the Argan Tree.

23. Andrew Soergel, "Everything You Always Wanted to Know about Thanksgiving with Leftovers," *US News and World Report*, November 27, 2014, http://www.usnews.com/news/blogs/data-mine/2014/11/27/everything-you-ever-wanted-to-know-about-thanksgiving-with-leftovers (accessed June 2, 2015).

24. Agriculture is one of the largest sources of pollution. Cotton is planted on 2.4 percent of the world's cropland, and yet it accounts for 24 and 11 percent, respectively, of the global sales of insecticide and pesticides. The unsafe use of agricultural chemicals severely impacts the health of workers in the field and ecosystems that receive excess doses of runoff from farms. Additionally, it takes more than twenty thousand liters of water to produce one kilogram of cotton, the equivalent of a single T-shirt and pair of jeans. Seventy-three percent of the global cotton harvest comes from irrigated land. "The Impact of Cotton on Fresh Water Resources and Ecosystems," WWF, http://d2ouvy59p0dg6k.cloudfront.net/downloads/impact_long.pdf (accessed April 19, 2016); "Cotton Farming. Cotton: A Water Wasting Crop," WWF, http://wwf.panda.org/about_our_earth/about_freshwater/freshwater_problems/thirsty_crops/cotton/ (accessed April 19, 2016).

25. The Zero Emission Vehicle Program enacted in 1990 by the California Air Resources Board required auto companies to produce 2 percent of zero-emission vehicles, such as hydrogen fuel cell and electric battery, for sale in California in 1998, and 10 percent of vehicles for sale in California in 2003. In 1996, due to pressure from auto companies and concerns about the state of technology, the board eliminated the intermediate 1998 requirement, but kept the 2003 target of 10 percent zero-emission vehicles in place. Significant changes to the program begin in 2018. The volumes effectively triple in 2018, and then rapidly ramp up through 2025, when about one out of every seven cars sold must be a zero-emission vehicle. By 2025, the mandate requires that 3.3 million zero-emission vehicles be sold, or about 15 percent of new vehicles sales. "History of California's Zero Emission Vehicles (ZEV) Program," Union of Concerned Scientists,

http://www.ucsusa.org/clean_vehicles/smart-transportation-solutions/advanced
-vehicle-technologies/electric-cars/californias-zero-emission-1.html#.Vw1pk_krKUk
(accessed April 19, 2016).

26. "Understanding Cholesterol Numbers," *WebMD*, http://www.webmd.com/
cholesterol-management/guide/understanding-numbers (accessed June 2, 2015).

27. "World Famous Fries: Nutrition and Ingredients," McDonald's, http://www
.mcdonalds.com/us/en/food/product_nutrition.snackssides.6050.small-french-fries
.html (accessed June 2, 2015).

28. "Fries: Ingredient and Allergen Information," McDonald's, http://www.mcdonalds
.co.uk/ukhome/product_nutrition.sides.44.french-fries-medium.html (accessed June 2,
2015).

29. Fabiola Czubaj, "Se acerca el fin de las grasas trans para los alimentos argentinos, "
La Nacion, December 2, 2014, http://www.lanacion.com.ar/1748702-se-acerca-el-fin-de
-las-grasas-trans-para-los-alimentos-argentinos (accessed June 2, 2015).

30. Suresh Gupta, "The Specialty Eateries Sector Tastes Good," *Seeking Alpha*, January
23, 2013, http://seekingalpha.com/article/1127071-the-specialty-eateries-sector-tastes
-good (accessed June 2, 2015).

31. Krystina Gustafson, "Panera Is First National Chain to Post Calorie Counts," CNBC,
March 10, 2010, http://www.cnbc.com/id/35801022(accessed September 13, 2016).

32. Ben Steverman and David Bogoslaw, "The Financial Crisis Blame Game," *Business
Week* 10 (2008).

33. Ibid.

Chapter 5

1. Richard E. Freeman, *Strategic Management: A Stakeholder Approach* (Boston: Pitman,
1984).

2. "Mission Baked Tostadas 22ct," http://www.missionmenus.com/en/products/
view/mission-baked-tostadas-22ct (accessed May 8, 2016).

3. "9 Stellar Examples of the Unintended Use of Products," Printwand, http://
www.printwand.com/blog/9-stellar-examples-of-the-unintended-use-of-products
(accessed June 12, 2015).

4. *Federal Register* 59, no. 46 (March 9, 1994).

5. SAIC Motor Corporation, "Annual Report 2014," Beijing, April 2014.

6. "Passenger and Commercial Vehicle Sales in China from 2008 to 2016," Statista,
http://www.statista.com/statistics/233743/vehicle-sales-in-china/ (accessed April 19,
2016).

7. VDA German Association of the Automobile Industry (VDA), *Automotive News*, 2014.

8. Sarah Butler, "Bangladeshi Factory Deaths Spark Action among High-Street Clothing
Chains," *Guardian*, June 23, 2013, http://www.theguardian.com/world/2013/jun/23/
rana-plaza-factory-disaster-bangladesh-primark (accessed June 12, 2015).

9. "Bangladesh Factory Collapse Kills More Than 70, Injures Hundreds," *Huffington Post*, June 24, 2013, http://www.huffingtonpost.com/2013/04/24/bangladesh-factory -collapse_n_3144613.html (accessed May 8, 2016).

10. Arun Devnath and Mehul Srivastava, "'Suddenly the Floor Wasn't There,' Factory Survivor Says," *Bloomerg*, April 25, 2013, http://www.bloomberg.com/news/2013-04 -25/-suddenly-the-floor-wasn-t-there-factory-survivor-says.html (accessed June 12, 2015).

11. Butler, "Bangladeshi Factory Deaths Spark Action."

12. Viewer discretion advised: "Have a Break," Greenpeace UK, March 17, 2010, https:// www.youtube.com/watch?v=VaJjPRwExO8 (accessed June 12, 2015).

13. "Nestlé Committed to Traceable Sustainable Palm Oil to Ensure No-Deforestation," Nestlé, October 30, 2012, http://www.nestle.com/media/Statements/Update-on -deforestation-and-palm-oil (accessed June 12, 2015).

14. "Shell at a Glance," Shell, http://www.shell.com.ng/aboutshell/at-a-glance.html (accessed June 12, 2015).

15. "LEGO: Everything Is NOT Awesome," Greenpeace, July 8, 2015, https:// www.youtube.com/watch?v=qhbliUq0_r4 (accessed June 12, 2015).

16. "Pink Slime—Jamie Oliver—Food Revolution," http://www.dailymotion.com/ video/xphjdl_pink-slime-jamie-oliver-food-revolution_lifestyle(September 13, 2016).

17. Jim Avila, "70 Percent of Ground Beef at Supermarkets Contains 'Pink Slime,'" ABC News, March 7, 2012, http://abcnews.go.com/blogs/headlines/2012/03/70-percent-of -ground-beef-at-supermarkets-contains-pink-slime/ (accessed June 12, 2015).

18. "Do You Use So-called 'Pink Slime' in Your Burgers or Beef Treated with Ammonia?" McDonald's, http://www.mcdonalds.com/us/en/your_questions/our_food/do-you -use-so-called-pink-slime-in-your-burgers.html (accessed June 12, 2015).

19. "McDonald's—Our Food, Your Questions—Beef," McDonald's, February 16, 2015, https://youtu.be/Q6IMQaiYKeg(accessed September 13, 2016).

20. "Wife's 2013 BMW x3 Being Built," BMW, August 5, 2012, https://www.youtube.com/ watch?v=kN4Tc-grhrw (accessed on June 12, 2015).

21. "About," SAME Café, http://www.soallmayeat.org/about/ (accessed June 12, 2015).

22. "What We Do: FAQs," Panera Cares, http://paneracares.org/what-we-do/ (accessed June 12, 2015).

23. Ibid.

24. Walter Wang, "Sustainable Companies Give Green for Going Green," Cleantechies, May 9, 2013, http://cleantechies.com/2013/05/09/sustainable-companies-give-green -for-going-green/ (accessed June 12, 2015).

25. Keith Patterson, "Top Companies Tie Compensation to Sustainability," CSRHub, May 9, 2013, http://www.csrhub.com/blog/2013/05/top-companies-tie-compensation -to-sustainability.html (accessed June 12, 2015); Hugh Welsh, "An Insider's View: Why More Companies Should Tie Bonuses to Sustainability," *Guardian*, August 11, 2014, http://www.theguardian.com/sustainable-business/2014/aug/11/executive

-compensation-bonuses-sustainability-goals-energy-water-carbon-dsm (accessed June 12, 2015).

26. Michael C. Mankins, "Three Ways to Actually Engage Employees," Harvard Business School, June 16, 2014, https://hbr.org/2014/06/three-ways-to-actually-engage -employees/ (accessed June 12, 2015).

27. James K. Harter and A. Creglow, *A Meta-Analysis and Utility Analysis of the Relationship between Core GWA Employee Perceptions and Business Outcomes* (Lincoln, NE: Gallup Organization, 1997).

28. James K. Harter, Frank L. Schmidt, Emily A. Killham, and James W. Asplund, "Q^{12}® Meta-Analysis," Gallup Consulting, 2006, https://strengths.gallup.com/private/ resources/q12meta-analysis_flyer_gen_08%2008_bp.pdf (accessed May 8, 2016).

29. Chris Groscurth, "Why Your Company Must Be Mission-Driven," Gallup, March 6, 2014, http://www.gallup.com/businessjournal/167633/why-company-mission-driven .aspx (accessed May 8, 2016).

30. "Water Conditions Worsen around Coca-Cola Plant, Declared 'Over-Exploited,'" November 18, 2014, http://www.indiaresource.org/news/2014/1031.html (accessed April 19, 2016).

Chapter 6

1. John Hagel III, John Seely Brown, and Lang Davison, "The Best Way to Measure Company Performance," *Harvard Business Review*, March 4, 2010, https://hbr.org/2010/03/ the-best-way-to-measure-compan.html (accessed July 5, 2016).

2. Greenwashing refers to the technique of disguising business-as-usual practices as sustainable.

3. Robert Gray, "Accounting and Environmentalism: An Exploration of the Challenge of Gently Accounting for Accountability, Transparency, and Sustainability," *Accounting, Organizations, and Society* 17, no. 5 (1992): 399–425; Robert Gray, "Corporate Reporting for Sustainable Development: Accounting for Sustainability in 2000 AD," *Environmental Values* 3, no. 1 (1994): 17–45; Robert Gray and Jan Bebbington, *Accounting for the Environment* (Thousand Oaks, CA: SAGE Publications Limited, 2001).

4. "The Ten Principles," United Nations Global Compact, https://www.unglobalcompact .org/AboutTheGC/TheTenPrinciples/index.html (accessed June 12, 2015).

5. John Elkington, *Cannibals with Forks: The Triple Bottom Line of 21st Century Business* (Oxford: Capstone, 1999).

6. Ernst Ligteringen, "Executive Perspective: Global Reporting Initiative's Chief Executive Ernst Ligteringen," Thomson Reuters, April 11, 2013, http://sustainability .thomsonreuters.com/2013/04/11/executive-perspective-global-reporting-initiatives -chief-executive-ernst-ligteringen/ (accessed July 6, 2016).

7. Dror Etzion and Fabrizio Ferraro, "The Role of Analogy in the Institutionalization of Sustainability Reporting," *Organization Science* 21, no. 5 (2010): 1092–1107; KPMG, *KPMG International Survey of Corporate Responsibility Reporting 2013* (London: KPMG, 2013).

8. Kate Kelly, "How Goldman Won Big on Mortgage Meltdown," *Wall Street Journal*, December 14, 2007, http://www.wsj.com/articles/SB119759714037228585 (accessed July 6, 2016); James Quinn, "Goldman Sachs' Sub-Prime Bet Pays Off," *Telegraph*, December 18, 2007, http://www.telegraph.co.uk/finance/newsbysector/banksandfinance/4666432/Goldman-Sachs-sub-prime-bet-pays-off.html (accessed July 6, 2016); Allan Sloan, "Junk Mortgages under the Microscope," *Fortune Magazine*, October 16, 2007, http://archive.fortune.com/2007/10/15/markets/junk_mortgages.fortune/index.htm (accessed July 6, 2016).

9. David Gunnell and Michael Eddleston, "Suicide by Intentional Ingestion of Pesticides: A Continuing Tragedy in Developing Countries," *International Journal of Epidemiology* 32, no. 6 (2003): 902–909.

10. "2014/2015 Sustainability Report," Coca-Cola, http://www.coca-colacompany.com/content/dam/journey/us/en/private/fileassets/pdf/2015/07/2014-2015-sustainability-report.15_080415.pdf (accessed April 19, 2016).

11. Ibid.

12. Unilever, "Introducing Our Plan: The Unilever Sustainable Living Plan," https://www.unilever.com/sustainable-living/the-sustainable-living-plan/ (accessed September 13, 2016).

13. Wayne Norman and Chris MacDonald, "Getting to the Bottom of 'Triple Bottom Line,'" *Business Ethics Quarterly* 14, no. 2 (April 2004): 243–262.

14. Laura Donnelly, "Coca Cola in Controversy over £20m 'Anti-Obesity' Drive," *Telegraph*, May 25, 2014, http://www.telegraph.co.uk/news/health/news/10855425/Coca-Cola-in-controversy-over-20m-anti-obesity-drive.html (accessed June 12, 2015).

15. Max E. Clarkson, "A Stakeholder Framework for Analyzing and Evaluating Corporate Social Performance," *Academy of Management Review* 20, no. 1 (1995): 92–117.

16. R. Edward Freeman, *Strategic Management: A Stakeholder Approach* (Boston: Pitman, 1984).

17. Richard M. Locke, *The Promise and Limits of Private Power: Promoting Labor Standards in a Global Economy* (New York: Cambridge University Press, 2013).

18. "The Nestlé Supplier Code," Nestlé, December 2013, https://www.nestle.com/asset-library/documents/library/documents/suppliers/supplier-code-english.pdf (accessed April 19, 2013).

Chapter 7

1. Lorna Barrett, "Consumer Concerns about What's in Ground Beef," NewsNet5.com, March 8, 2012.

2. Philip E. Galasso, "Pink Slime Is Banned in Europe, It Should Be Banned in the U.S.," *Citizens' Voice*, April 30, 2012, http://citizensvoice.com/opinion/letters/pink-slime-is-banned-in-europe-it-should-be-banned-in-the-u-s-1.1307028 (accessed April 20, 2016).

3. "Interface Carpet Guides Sustainability with Five Critical Questions," Sustainable Plant, August 8, 2012, http://www.sustainableplant.com/2012/08/interface-carpet-guides-sustainability-with-five-critical-questions/(accessed May 8, 2016).

4. "Why Patagonia Tells Customers Its Coats Are Toxic," *Bloomberg*, September 25, 2013, http://www.bloomberg.com/news/videos/b/ebadd27f-a944-400a-904b-12ddc572d9d4 (accessed June 13, 2015).

5. "Talks at Banz," PUMA Annual Report 2010, http://about.puma.com/damfiles/default/investor-relations/financial-reports/en/2010/AR-2010-14db11370ece92c7ae49dc5cc15f5604.pdf (accessed July 6, 2016), 18–19.

6. "Environmental Profit and Loss Account," PUMA, 2011, http://about.puma.com/en/sustainability/environment/environmental-profit-and-loss-account (accessed June 12, 2015).

7. "Talks at Banz," 18.

8. Ibid.

9. "100% Transparent," honest by, http://www.honestby.com/en/news/147/100-transparent.html (accessed September 13, 2016).

10. Kana Inagaki and Peter Campbell, "Mitsubishi Admits Falsifying Car Fuel Performance Data," *Financial Times*, April 21, 2016, https://next.ft.com/content/b0ede3a6-06c5-11e6-a70d-4e39ac32c284 (article requires subscription; accessed September 13, 2016).

11. Monica Davey and Richard Pérez-Peña, "Flint Water Crisis Yields First Criminal Charges," *New York Times*, April 20, 2016, http://www.nytimes.com/2016/04/21/us/first-criminal-charges-are-filed-in-flint-water-crisis.html (accessed May 8, 2016).

12. Kermit Pattison, "Case Study: Could Organic Valley Thrive without Wal-Mart?" *Inc.*, July 1, 2007, http://www.inc.com/magazine/20070701/casestudy.html (accessed June 13, 2015).

13. Ibid.

Chapter 8

1. Sheila Bonini and Steven Swartz, "Profits with Purpose: How Organizing for Sustainability Can Benefit the Bottom Line," McKinsey&Company, 2014, http://www.mckinsey.com/business-functions/sustainability-and-resource-productivity/our-insights/profits-with-purpose-how-organizing-for-sustainability-can-benefit-the-bottom-line (accessed July 10, 2016).

2. Mark Fulton, Bruce M. Kahn, and Camilla Sharples, "Sustainable Investing: Establishing Long-Term Value and Performance," DB Climate Change Advisors, Deutsche Bank Group, 2012.

3. "Annual Review 2015," Syngenta, http://annualreport.syngenta.com/assets/pdf/Syngenta-annual-review-2015.pdf (accessed April 20, 2016).

4. Tony Dreibus, "ChemChina's Purchase of Syngenta Won't Be the Last in the Chemical Sector," *U.S. News*, February 9, 2016, http://money.usnews.com/investing/articles/2016-02-09/chemchinas-purchase-of-syngenta-wont-be-the-last-in-the-chemical-sector (accessed July 10, 2016).

5. "ChemChina Cash Offer to Acquire Syngenta at a Value of over US$ 43 Billion," February 3, 2016, PR Newswire, http://www.prnewswire.com/news-releases/chemchina

-cash-offer-to-acquire-syngenta-at-a-value-of-over-us-43-billion-300214306.html (accessed July 10, 2016).

6. Ibid.

7. Fred Lager, *Ben & Jerry's: The Inside Scoop: How Two Real Guys Built a Business with a Social Conscience and a Sense of Humor* (New York: Crown Publishers, 1994).

8. Ibid.

9. A pink sheet or over-the-counter exchange is a publication by the National Quotation Bureau for companies that are generally not filed with the Securities and Exchange Commission.

10. Lager, *Ben & Jerry's*.

11. "Fairtrade," Ben & Jerry's, http://www.benjerry.com/values/issues-we-care-about/fairtrade (accessed June 13, 2015).

12. Anthony Page and Robert A. Katz, "The Truth about Ben and Jerry's," *Stanford Social Innovation Review*, Fall 2012, http://www.ssireview.org/articles/entry/the_truth_about_ben_and_jerrys (accessed June 13, 2015).

13. "Caring Dairy," Ben & Jerry's, http://www.benjerry.com/caringdairy#12timeline (accessed June 13, 2015).

14. The Iroquois, or Haudenosaunee, are a Native American confederacy that consists of six nations: Mohawk, Onondaga, Oneida, Cayuga, Seneca, and Tuscarora.

15. Lager, *Ben & Jerry's*.

16. Patrick Heffer and Michel Prud'homme, "Fertilizer Outlook 2015–2019," International Fertilizer Industry Association, 2015, http://www.fertilizer.org/imis20/images/Library_Downloads/2013_chicago_ifa_summary.pdf?WebsiteKey=411e9724-4bda-422f-abfc-8152ed74f30 (accessed July 10, 2016).

17. "Earth's Boundaries? An Attempt to Quantify the Limits of Humanity's Load on Our Planet Opens an Important Debate," *Nature* 461 (September 24, 2009): 447–448, http://www.nature.com/nature/journal/v461/n7263/full/461447b.html (accessed July 11, 2016).

18. Fred Pearce, "The Nitrogen Fix: Breaking a Costly Addiction," *Yale Environment 360*, November 5, 2009, http://e360.yale.edu/feature/the_nitrogen_fix_breaking_a_costly_addiction/2207/ (accessed July 11, 2016).

19. Ibid.

20. H.J.M. van Grinsven, H.F.M. ten Berge, T. Dalgaard, B. Fraters, P. Durand, A. Hart, G. Hofman, B. H. Jacobsen, S.T.J. Lalor, J. P. Lesschen, B. Osterburg, K. G. Richards, A.-K. Techen, F. Vertès, J. Webb, and W. J. Willems. "Management, Regulation, and Environmental Impacts of Nitrogen Fertilization in Northwestern Europe under the Nitrates Directive," *Biogeosciences* 9 (2012): 5143–5160, http://www.biogeosciences.net/9/5143/2012/ (accessed May 9, 2016).

21. "Fertilizers: How Products Are Made, 1988, http://www.encyclopedia.com/topic/fertilizer.aspx (accessed April 20, 2016).

22. David Morris, "The Mondragon System: Cooperation at Work," Institute for Local Self-Reliance, November 5, 1992, https://ilsr.org/mondragon-system-cooperation-work/ (accessed July 11, 2016).

23. Ibid.

24. Ibid.

25. For Fagor's online site for US customers, see www.fagoramerica.com (accessed July 11, 2016).

26. "Fagor Now Controls ElcoBrandt After Agreement with Elco (4/19)," *Appliance Design*, April 19, 2005, www.appliancedesign.com/articles/88332-fagor-now-controls -elcobrandt-after-agreement-with-elco-4-19 (accessed June 13, 2015).

27. Christopher Bjork, "Recession Frays Ties at Spain's Co-ops: Home Appliance Maker Fagor Shuts Factories after Failing to Get Lifeline," *Wall Street Journal*, December 26, 2013, http://online.wsj.com/news/articles/SB10001424052702303290904579276551484127412 (accessed June 13, 2015).

28. "Auditorías de Entidades: Fagor," CNMV, emisorashttp://cnmv.es/Portal/ Consultas/IFA/ListadoIFA.aspx?id=0&nif=F-20020517 (accessed June 13, 2015).

29. Bjork, "Recession Frays Ties at Spain's Co-ops."

30. "Spanish White Goods Company Fagor Seeks Protection from Creditors," Reuters, October 16, 2013, www.reuters.com/article/2013/10/16/spain-fagor -idUSL6N0I61WA20131016 (accessed June 13, 2015); "Bankruptcy of Mondragon Company Demonstrates Limits of Cooperation under Capitalism," *Systemic Disorder*, November 13, 2013, http://systemicdisorder.wordpress.com/2013/11/13/capitalism -limits-cooperation/ (accessed June 13, 2015).

Chapter 9

1. Victor A. Thompson, "Bureaucracy and Innovation," *Administrative Science Quarterly* 10, no. 1 (1965): 1–20.

2. C. Daniel Batson, *The Altruism Question: Toward a Social-Psychological Answer* (Hillsdale, NJ: Lawrence Erlbaum, 1991); Leonard Berkowitz, "Social Norms, Feelings, and Other Factors Affecting Helping and Altruism," in *Advances in Experimental Social Psychology*, ed. Leonard Berkowitz (New York: Academic Press, 1972), 63–108; Kim S. Cameron, "Organizational Virtuousness and Performance," in *Positive Organizational Scholarship*, ed. Kim S. Cameron, Jane E. Dutton, and Robert E. Quinn (San Francisco: Berret-Kohler Publishers Inc., 2003), 48–65.

3. "Innovators," Launch, http://www.launch.org/innovators/akshay-sethi;https:// vimeo.com/76075098 (accessed June 13, 2015).

4. "It's the World's First Bottle Made with Ocean Plastic," method, http:// methodhome.com/beyond-the-bottle/ocean-plastic/ (accessed June 13, 2015).

5. "Trash-Free Waters," US Environmental Protection Agency, http://epa.gov/region9/ marine-debris/faq.html (accessed June 13, 2015); "A Sea of Plastic: More Plastic Than Plankton in Our Ocean," Think Outside the Bin, http://thinkoutsidethebin.com/2011/ 06/02/a-sea-of-plastic-more-plastic-than-plankton-in-our-ocean/ (accessed June 13, 2015).

6. "Turning Ocean Plastic Pollution into Bottles," method, September 19, 2011, http://methodhome.com/blog/ocean-plastic-into-bottles/ (accessed June 13, 2015).

7. "Ambercycle Inc.: Akshay Sethi," Launch, https://vimeo.com/76075098(accessed June 13, 2015).

8. "How Much Oil Is Used to Make Plastic?" US Energy Information Administration, http://www.eia.gov/tools/faqs/faq.cfm?id=34&t=6 (accessed June 13, 2015); "Making Plastic: Extracting Raw Material," Paprec Group, http://www.paprec.com/en/understanding-recycling/recycling-plastic/making-plastic-extracting-raw-material (accessed June 15, 2015).

9. "Overview of Greenhouse Gases," US Environmental Protection Agency, http://epa.gov/climatechange/ghgemissions/gases/ch4.html (accessed June 13, 2013).

10. R. Bruce Hutton, Louis D'Antonio, and Tommi Johnsen, "Socially Responsible Investing: Growing Issues and New Opportunities," *Business and Society* 37, no. 3 (1998): 281–305; Peter D. Kinder, Steven D. Lydenberg, and Amy L. Domini, *Investing for Good: Making Money While Being Socially Responsible* (New York: Harper Business, 1993); Steve Schueth, "Socially Responsible Investing in the United States," *Journal of Business Ethics* 43, no. 3 (2003): 189–194.

11. Hutton, D'Antonio, and Johnsen, "Socially Responsible Investing"; Schueth, "Socially Responsible Investing in the United States."

12. Terrence Guay, Jonathan Doh, and Graham Sinclair, "Non-Governmental Organizations, Shareholder Activism, and Socially Responsible Investments: Ethical, Strategic, and Governance Implications," *Journal of Business Ethics* 52, no. 1 (2004): 125–139.

13. Aidan Hollis and Arthur Sweetman, "Microcredit in Pre-Famine Ireland," *Explorations in Economic History* 35, no. 4 (1998): 347–380; Hans Dieter Seibel, "History Matters in Microfinance," *Small Enterprise Development* 14, no. 2 (2003): 10–12.

14. Friedrich W. Raiffeisen, *The Credit Unions*, 7th ed. (Neuwied, Ger.: Verlag der Raiffeisendruckerei, 1866); Seibel, "History Matters in Microfinance."

15. "Microfinance," International Finance Corporation, http://www.ifc.org/wps/wcm/connect/Industry_EXT_Content/IFC_External_Corporate_Site/Industries/Financial+Markets/MSME+Finance/Microfinance/ (accessed June 13, 2015).

16. Muhammad Yunus and Alan Jolis, *Banker to the Poor: Micro-Lending and the Battle against World Poverty* (New York: Public Affairs, 1999).

Chapter 10

1. "Albert Einstein Quotes," last updated January 8, 2012, http://www.alberteinsteinsite.com/quotes/einsteinquotes.html (accessed September 13, 2016).

2. "The Nobel Peace Prize 2004," http://www.nobelprize.org/nobel_prizes/peace/laureates/2004/ (accessed September 13, 2016).

3. Indira Gandhi, "Plenary Session" (talk presented at the UN Conference on Human Environment, Stockholm, June 14, 1972).

4. Gro Harlem Brundtland, *Our Common Future* (Oxford: Oxford University Press, 1991).

5. "Less Bad Does Not Equal Good: Seventh Generation CEO Jeffrey Hollender," uploaded September 16, 2010, https://www.youtube.com/watch?v=hgbCGBRVGqw, (accessed September 13, 2016).

6. Attributed in Frank G. Sommers and Tana Dineen, *Curing Nuclear Madness: A New-Age Prescription for Personal Action* (Toronto: Methuen, 1984), 158.

7. Victor A. Thompson, "Bureaucracy and Innovation," *Administrative Science Quarterly* 10, no. 1 (1965): 1–20.

Index

Printed in the United States
by Baker & Taylor Publisher Services